MW00720735

THIN BRUISED LINE

THIN BRUISED LINE

THE IMMINENT THREAT TO POLICE AND PUBLIC SAFETY

DOUG CLARK

KEY PORTER BOOKS

Library and Archives Canada Cataloguing in Publication

Clark, Doug, 1952-
Thin bruised line : the imminent threat to police and public safety / Doug Clark.

ISBN 978-1-55470-194-0

1. Police--Canada. 2. Public safety--Canada. 3. Police--Recruiting--Canada. I. Title.

HV8157.C533 2010   363.20971   C2009-903791-2

ONTARIO ARTS COUNCIL
CONSEIL DES ARTS DE L'ONTARIO

The publisher gratefully acknowledges the support of the Canada Council for the Arts and the Ontario Arts Council for its publishing program. We acknowledge the support of the Government of Ontario through the Ontario Media Development Corporation's Ontario Book Initiative.

We acknowledge the financial support of the Government of Canada through the Book Publishing Industry Development Program (BPIDP) for our publishing activities.

Key Porter Books Limited
Six Adelaide Street East, Tenth Floor
Toronto, Ontario
Canada M5C 1H6

www.keyporter.com

Text design and electronic formatting: Alison Carr

Printed and bound in Canada

10 11 12 13 14 5 4 3 2 1

To the men and women standing fast in the Thin Bruised Line
and to William Connor and the next generation

CONTENTS

IDENTITY THEFT

The seed for this book was sown in 2006 when, six months apart, the commissioners for two of Canada's largest police forces abruptly resigned their posts. While they left for vastly different reasons, few front-line officers mourned the departure of Giuliano Zaccardelli, of the Royal Canadian Mounted Police (RCMP), or Gwen Boniface, of the Ontario Provincial Police (OPP). In both cases, the political overseers went outside those departments to find replacements. That wasn't without precedent. In this era of corporate headhunters, it's fairly common for large agencies to commission broad searches to locate the best candidates, and the police are no exception. Still, the appointment of former Toronto Police chief Julian Fantino surprised many within and outside the OPP while Deputy Commissioner Jay Hope, who seemed poised to cap a twenty-seven-year policing career by becoming the first black officer to head a major force in Canada, replaced Fantino as Ontario's commissioner of Emergency Management. The OPP had once had a civilian commissioner when lawyer Eric Silk was appointed in 1963 to clean up a force plagued by mismanagement, low officer morale, and mass resignations. There are still veteran officers from that era who insist Silk was one of the best leaders they ever had, stark contrast to the outcry from the Mounties and the public when Prime Minister Stephen Harper broke with all tradition of promoting from within at the national level by naming career bureaucrat William Elliott as the first civilian RCMP commissioner since the Force was created as the North West Mounted Police in 1873.

But questions remained. Had the federal and provincial politicians who oversee the police seen no talent in those departments worthy of assuming the top job? Were they handpicking their new top cops to tighten the leash and shorten the historic arm's-length distance between politics and policing? Was oversight becoming intrusion? Or did they simply want new perspectives and a gust of fresh air to revive those departments?

I found no answers in the mainstream media who showed up en masse a year later when lawyer David Brown, former head of the Ontario Securities Commission (OSC), issued his 2007 report *Governance and Cultural Change in the Royal Canadian Mounted Police*, which identified a host of problems within the legendary national police force. And the media were back when Brown returned to suggest solutions to those problems in his 2008 follow-up report, *Rebuilding the Trust*. The media frenzy stopped short of asking if what ailed the Mounties also afflicted policing elsewhere in Canada.

Quite simply, what is the state of policing in Canada? How did we get here and where do we go from here? Is there a widespread disconnect between senior officers and the rank and file? Between those who make the laws and those who enforce them? If so, what does this disconnect mean to the rest of us who rely on the police to keep us safe?

Answering those questions is the focus of this book. It was impossible to canvass those on the front lines across Canada or to interview every chief, commissioner, or police association president to gauge their feelings and priorities. And so this book has relied heavily on the public record. Using a library card and online search engines, email, and a smattering of phone calls, I searched for policing issues that had been identified by the police, their political overseers, pundits and academics, and the media. I let the public record speak for itself.

With so many issues facing the police at so many levels—federal, provincial, and municipal—the trick was to find their common issues. I opted to examine leadership, political oversight, the courts, recruitment, media impact, and public support, all drawn primarily from the public record. Policing may be the most scrutinized profession in Canada. Hundreds of books, studies, reviews and inquiries, news items, and feature stories totalling millions of words have been written by auditors, academics, jurists, psychologists, politicians, public servants, management consultants, and journalists. I acknowledge my debt to them all. But they are police outsiders. As am I.

I have never been a cop, but I did work shoulder to shoulder with front-line municipal, provincial, and even federal police in sometimes critical situations as a young ambulance driver many years ago. I was also a licensed private investigator long enough to learn that surveillance can be very boring. My insight to reporting on visible-minority issues is guided by personal experience. As a journalist, I was the only Caucasian outside of the investigators to work closely in the Chinese community with Asian reporters and police officers to try to understand the horrific murder of a young woman from Shanghai from their cultural perspective. In my youth, I worked with Detroit paramedics in that inner city; the sole white face at any scene wherever we responded to a call for assistance.

I do not presume to speak for the police; neither am I their apologist. I freely accept that there are bad apples, dirty cops who should never have been issued a sidearm … just as there are doctors who should never touch a scalpel, journalists who should never tap a keyboard, teachers who should be denied access to young minds, and lawyers who never found a bar they couldn't lower. We agree to arm our police and justifiably hold them to a higher standard, but bad cops, no matter how newsworthy, are incredibly rare and routinely rooted out by the good cops who have investigated them. Who else is qualified to do that?

Much has changed in policing because much has changed in Canadian society, and the police are expected to reflect our diversity and our values—particularly the impact of the *Canadian Charter of Rights and Freedoms* on a country founded on "Peace, Order and Good Government" and the rise of human rights tribunals where the accused seem to be presumed guilty until proven innocent. The "enlightened" response to rename police forces as "services" does little to demonstrate progress or enlightenment and nothing to enhance officer and public safety. In an era of mission statements, slick slogans, and organizational values, the police role risks falling from the mandate of catching bad guys to the doomed bid to be all things to all people.

The reality for police today is that any problem—criminal, social, financial, political, and even some health issues—left unresolved by the agencies created and funded to address them, will be dumped in the police's lap and they will be told: "Fix this." Yet when they do—as they almost always do if only to slap a Band-Aid on the symptom of a larger problem not of their creation (for example, the police can get a person to a shelter; they can't cure homelessness)—there is scant praise or recognition for a job well done. The police must simply suck it up and resume their frantic call-to-call duties patrolling our city streets and rural roads. But if the police seem to be struggling to redefine their identity, was it stolen or crippled in a self-inflicted wound? And what does the answer to that question mean to the men and women on the front lines?

The thin blue line has become a thin bruised line ... grayed, frayed, and stretched to the breaking point. That's bad for the authorities and possibly worse for us; if they falter, who will serve and protect us from threats, perceived or real? With too few doing too much with too little support from the political level, the press, the public, or even their own superior officers, this thin bruised line can likely feel its vaunted Blue Wall crumbling beneath its boots. It is all part of what the Police Sector Council, an Ottawa-based think tank, warns is a "perfect storm" of shifting demographics, changing laws, and unrealistic expectations. The police are digging in behind their fragile Blue Wall as recruiters scramble to attract the best and brightest—sometimes settling for the least dangerous—candidates to fill the ranks depleted by the thousands of retiring veteran officers over the next few years. Too few are stepping up to fill the ranks. Policing, it appears, is not a preferred career, despite the consistently high rating of public support confirmed by pollsters. For those who choose it, policing is a calling, not a job.

Yet many veteran officers, who admit they loved their time in uniform, sound unsure if they would do it today when every move can be recorded on a cellphone camera and played out of context as "proof" to substantiate any complaint, no matter how thin or vexatious.

What little we know, or think we know, about policing is likely skewed, based as our perception is on novels we've read or police dramas we've watched on American television or in Hollywood movies. Admittedly, these portrayals have a core of fact in them, but they patently bear little resemblance to the reality of being a peace officer in Canada in the twenty-first century.

I have done my best to dispel those myths, and to uncover core issues, and to impart useful and truthful information about policing in Canada. I have done my best to get it right and apologize now if I did not. My hope is that this effort generates discussion and helps to initiate change even as policing once more transforms itself to keep up with the changing times and, most important, will help enhance officer and public safety.

Doug Clark
November 2009

DÉJÀ VU ALL OVER AGAIN

We have truly handcuffed our police—not, as some say, by court decisions on civil liberties or by reform strengthening civilian control, but by starvation budgets, antiquated police training, non-operating procedures, political manipulation and public hypocrisy.

—John Vliet Lindsay

That sentiment, which could have been torn from today's headlines or the pages of recent police reviews and inquiries, was written by John Vliet Lindsay in the foreword to *Police in Trouble: Our Frightening Crisis in Law Enforcement*, written by James Ahern, the former police chief of New Haven, Connecticut. That was in 1972.

Clearly, policing issues and discontent are not new.

John Lindsay, the long-serving congressman and two-term mayor of New York City, was the cover story for *Time* magazine on November 12, 1965, as he explained why anyone from such a privileged family background as his would stoop to the push and shove of municipal politics: "I'm running for mayor," he said, "because the city is in crisis. The streets are filthy. We'll rip down the cruddy slums in this town. There is crime. And 125,000 teen-agers roam the streets with no jobs, no schooling. New York is the heroin capital of the world. And people are afraid."

Lindsay's sentiments found voice in Ahern's book, which argued that fighting crime involved fixing the police and changing "the system" to protect them from the corrupting and undermining influence of outside political pressures. Policing in America has always differed from the Canadian experience. Ahern's book lamented that virtually every stage in a police officer's career was determined, or impacted, by political patronage from recruitment to promotion right up the ranks to chief or commissioner. He notes that when New York City decided to hire police officers from outside centres to avoid corruption, most of those who expressed interest only wanted to come to the Big Apple to cash in on the extra money they could get through extortion.

Canadian police were historically less corrupt; abuse of power was less prevalent. There were, to be sure, times when the thin blue line of provincial and municipal peace officers were tarnished and the Red Wall of the Royal Canadian Mounted Police cracked under pressure; incidents and individuals that shamed the police uniform. But they were rare and usually isolated, a far cry from the American experience and the excesses of the police in the streets of Chicago in 1968 or the Rampart Scandal in Los Angeles linking cops to street gangs and drug dealers in the late 1990s. In contrast to the police in the southern United States who turned a blind eye to the beatings, murders, and lynchings of black Americans or used dogs and water cannons on civil rights marchers in the 1950s and 1960s, the entire Winnipeg Police Force was fired for refusing to strong-arm demonstrators in that city's General Strike in 1919. Outsiders were brought in and showed no compunction in mowing down the strikers.

The police in Canada are not saints. Some turn to the dark side. But they are so few that given the intoxicating availability of money, drugs, and sex to so many of them on a daily basis, particularly in large cities, it is not surprising that some succumb, but rather a miracle that so many do not. Ahern's police response to a Black Panther protest in New Haven over the May Day weekend in

1970, a demonstration which had a high potential for violence giv-
en the extreme racial tensions between black and white Americans
at that time, was similarly a stark reminder of just how well the
police in the United States could perform under severe duress giv-
en strong leadership, clear instructions, and proper training. More
on that later.

Police in Trouble was the first book of its kind, a plain-language
alarm free of legalese and political jargon, a direct appeal to the
public, warning that all was not well in the world of policing.
Government and think-tank studies certainly existed—all of which
were presumably "public," if you knew where to find them and how
to cut through the jargon and acronyms to decipher them.
Preserving the status quo had seemed the best option to many
politicians and police chiefs before Ahern broke ranks and blew the
whistle, insisting that any national overview of policing is meaningless without understanding that the entire system rests upon
what he called the "individual integrity and capability" of police
officers. Writing two years before women were recruited into the
Royal Canadian Mounted Police and Ontario Provincial Police in
significant numbers, his insight to the realities of policing in 1972
still resonates today.

"In recent years, platitudes about the policeman's role have
changed," Ahern wrote. "He used to be a cops-and-robbers carica-
ture. Now he is a psychologist, a social worker, a doctor, a lawyer,
and a part-time judo expert who occasionally arrests criminals as a
sideline. It is true that in failing to provide people with so many
basic services, our society has forced the policeman to perform
many of them by default. But to maintain seriously that they are
valid police functions is to approve of the removal of more and
more of society's responsibilities onto the shoulders of a group that
cannot meet even the special challenges of its own profession. It is
to say that there is no law-enforcement function and that social
workers should be sent to (combat) syndicated crime."

Conceding that the police officer is, by necessity, a generalist
who "must briefly and superficially play a number of roles," Ahern
argued that unless he is trained and educated to respond as a

generalist "diagnostician," a police officer "may attempt to be a number of things he is not; and he will be frustrated." He stressed that their frustration had less to do with being unable to perform tasks they should never have been assigned than with being denied a legitimate chance to do the job they had actually signed on for. "The policeman today is not a frustrated psychologist or lawyer. He is a frustrated policeman," Ahern concluded. "It is only because he has no support in his role as a policeman that he is sometimes tempted to try to solve problems that should not be his. The fact that he may be so tempted (or forced) does not mean that he has any power to act meaningfully on the social and personal problems that confront him, any more than he is free to discharge the primary obligations of his profession."[1]

In 2007, lawyer David Brown's report, *Governance and Cultural Change*, on the Royal Canadian Mounted Police, and his report a year later, *Rebuilding the Trust*, suggest that little has changed in policing. Certainly it is more professional, officers are better trained and better paid than in 1972, and corruption has always been less of a problem in Canada than in the United States where political connections can often prove vital to career advancement, from recruitment to retirement. This kind of corruption is a partial holdover from the Wild West days that were in marked contrast to Canada's more professional approach to policing, including the creation of the North West Mounted Police in 1873 to help settle western Canada without resorting to the genocidal Indian Wars waged against Native tribes by the U.S. army to clear the American West and pave the way for white settlement. But all was not well with our cherished Mounties, as Brown confirmed in his 2008 report, saying that "trust in the management of the RCMP has been shaken" in recent years, adding: "This has had a stunning impact on the members and employees of the RCMP and on the Canadians they serve. Trust in the management of the RCMP needs to be rebuilt."

Like Ahern, Brown and his colleagues discounted any quick fix to the "scope and depth" of the issues. Addressing them would require challenging "traditional concepts and practices" to identify "innovative and lasting solutions." Beyond health-and-safety issues, they heard, "with remarkable consistency," complaints about the disciplinary system, recruitment, performance evaluation, promotion, and personal development—while simultaneously witnessing "the dedication and consuming pride" expressed by all uniformed members and civilian staff in their Force.

The Brown reports—*Governance and Cultural Change* (2007) and *Rebuilding the Trust* (2008)—were just the latest evidence to suggest that keeping the peace and enforcing the law were not going to be easy in the twenty-first century. Organized crime flourished and international terrorism had returned with a vengeance unknown since Ahern's era when federal sky marshalls were first seated at the rear of jetliners to prevent the hijackings that began in 1961 during the John F. Kennedy presidency. By 1970, the U.S. Customs Service had expanded that program to 1,784 federal air marshalls at the height of the seventy-five skyjackings of U.S. airliners, almost all of them to Cuba. Their role lapsed over time as air travel became safer, but was revived after two hijacked aircraft were transformed into guided missiles that struck and toppled the twin towers in New York City on the morning of September 11, 2001. Killing thousands of people in front of millions of witnesses was one of the terrorists' goals. Their "success" resulted in draconian responses from Washington and Ottawa, which courts later ruled trampled the constitutional rights of citizens and prompted Canadian lawyer Rocco Galati to lament, "Nineteen terrorists in six weeks have been able to command 300 million North Americans to do away with the entirety of their civil liberties that took 700 years to advance...."

If the more immediate threat in Canada seemed to be the alarming rise of gun use and the prevalence of gangs on our city streets, the murder of four Mounties in March 2005, at a farm in northern Alberta, near Mayerthorpe, reminded us that while Canadian troops are at grave risk fighting the war in Afghanistan, our front-line police also face mortal danger on the home front. That tragedy marked the greatest single loss in the Force's history since the four North West Mounted Police officers who became known as the Lost Patrol strayed off course with their dogsleds and froze or starved to death in the Arctic Barrens in 1910. In the same year that the four Mounties were gunned down in Mayerthorpe, fifty-two of the seventy-eight homicides in Toronto were listed as gang related, prompting the media to proclaim it the "Year of the Gun," culminating with the tragic murder of fifteen-year-old Jane Creba, who was killed in the crossfire between rival gangs while shopping on Yonge Street on Boxing Day. In September 2006, a lone gunman sporting a Mohawk haircut and black clothing opened fire inside Montreal's Dawson College, murdering one woman and wounding nineteen before shooting himself. By 2009, Vancouver streets became free-fire zones, with the *Vancouver Sun* reporting on March 6 a total of thirty shooting incidents, causing twelve deaths and inflicting sixteen injuries by early March. Almost exactly one year earlier, the *Sun* had headlined a 2008 Statistics Canada study that identified metropolitan Vancouver (including police in Richmond, Delta, New Westminster, West Vancouver, and Port Moody) as having the highest gun-related death rate of any major centre in Canada, edging out Toronto by 45.3 versus 40.4 violent offences involving guns per 100,000 population—alarmingly higher than the national average of 27.5. Using data provided by the police in 2006, the study listed Vancouver third, with 455 victims of "violent firearm-related crime," behind Toronto, with 1,993 victims and Montreal with 1,291.

All eyes turned to the police as the politicians, the press, and the public feared they had lost control of the streets. Public safety dominated the debate as the federal government vowed to get tough on crime by responding in its traditional manner: throw money at the problem. However, the promised funding to hire more front-line officers rings hollow as there aren't enough recruits lining up to fill the spaces. That was confirmed by another Statistics Canada study, *Police Resources in Canada 2008*, which showed that while police numbers were up, reported crimes were down, and more were being solved than before, police ranks still lagged 5 per cent behind the 1975 peak. The otherwise cheerful report card made no mention that those peak numbers were exactly the ones now set to retire en masse, but did concede that despite the increased number of uniformed officers, civilian employee ranks were growing at a faster rate and that 13,234 "authorized" positions remained unstaffed.

This study provides possibly the best and most recent official snapshot of policing in Canada today and bears examination in detail.

POLICE PERSONNEL AND EXPENDITURES

Following a period of decline throughout the 1990s, police strength in Canada has increased over the past decade. At 196 officers per 100,000 population, the 2008 rate was 8 per cent higher than in 1998, although 5 per cent lower than its peak in 1975.

While police officer strength has been increasing, Canada's police-reported crime rate has been decreasing. The 2007 crime rate was at its lowest point in more than thirty years. At the same time, the proportion of crime solved by police reached a thirty-year high.

There were over 65,000 "active" police officers on May 15, 2008, two-thirds of whom were employed by municipal police services. However, there were an additional 13,234 "authorized" positions that were not staffed for a number of reasons, including difficulty in replacing officers who had retired or otherwise left the police service, were on maternity/paternity leave, or were on long-term medical leave.

Civilian personnel, such as clerks, dispatch officers, and bylaw-enforcement officers, has increased over the past ten years at a rate more than twice that of police officers. In 2008, there were over 25,000 civilian personnel accounting for 28 per cent of all policing personnel or 1 civilian per 2.5 police officers.

Chart I: Rates of police officers and civilian personnel, 1963 to 2008

1 Includes: special constables, native special constables, security officers/guards, bylaw enforcement, parking control officers, cadets/trainees, communications dispatch, management/professionals, clerical support, school crossing guards, and other civilians.
Source(s): Statistics Canada, Canadian Centre for Justice Statistics, Police Administration Survey.

Over the past ten years, all provinces and territories, except the Yukon, recorded increases in the rate of police officer strength. The largest provincial increases were in Newfoundland and Labrador (up 21 per cent) and Nova Scotia (up 17 per cent).

Chart 2: Police officer strength among the provinces, 2008

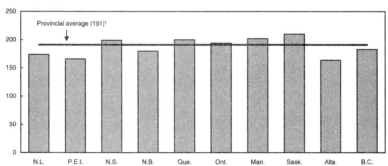

1 The provincial average excludes the territories and Royal Canadian Mounted Police Headquarters and Training Academy. The territories are not shown on this graph as their sparse populations result in considerably higher police strengths than the rest of Canada.
Source(s): Statistics Canada, Canadian Centre for Justice Statistics, Police Administration Survey.

As is historically the case, police per capita in 2008 was highest in the territories, where crime rates are well above the rest of the country.

Among the provinces, Saskatchewan reported the highest rate of police officers for the eighth year in a row, while Alberta and Prince Edward Island reported the lowest.

Over the past decade, all twenty-seven census metropolitan areas recorded increases in police officer strength, with the exception of Victoria. The largest gains since 1998 occurred in Sherbrooke, St. Catharines–Niagara, and London, all up by more than 20 per cent.

In 2008, Thunder Bay had the highest rate of police officers, followed by Saint John and Regina.

Among Canada's nine largest metropolitan areas, the rate of police officers was highest in Montreal and Winnipeg. The rate of police strength in Toronto, where crime rates were among the lowest, was also above average compared to the other large cities. Quebec reported the lowest rate of officers as well as one of the lowest rates of crime.

The rate of female officers grew at a faster pace than their male counterparts in 2008, continuing the rise in female recruitment that began in the mid-1970s.

In 2008, females accounted for almost one in five officers in Canada compared to approximately one in eight a decade ago. In 2008, Quebec and British Columbia reported the highest proportion of female officers among the provinces. The lowest proportion of female-to-male officers was found in Prince Edward Island.

After adjusting for inflation, police expenditures rose for the eleventh consecutive year, reaching $10.5 billion in 2007, or $320 per Canadian. Total spending was 4 per cent higher than in 2006 and 43 per cent higher than in 1997.

Generally, about one in every three police-reported crimes is cleared, by a charge being laid or by other means, perhaps lumped in with other similar cases that have been closed. In 2007, the proportion of crime solved by police went up for the third consecutive year, reaching a thirty-year high of 37 per cent. Police strength, the volume and type of crime and the complexity of police investigations are among the many factors that affect clearance rates.

OVERVIEW OF POLICING IN CANADA

Policing in Canada is the responsibility of all three levels of government: federal, provincial/territorial, and municipal. While the federal government is responsible for criminal law, under the *Constitution Act* (and dating to the *British North American Act* of 1867), each province and territory assumes responsibility for its own policing at the provincial, territorial, and municipal levels. Further, many First Nations communities also administer their own police service.

Federal Policing

The federal government, through the RCMP, is responsible for the enforcement of federal statutes in each province and territory, and for providing services such as forensics laboratories, identification services, the Canadian Police Information Centre (CPIC), and the Canadian Police College (CPC).

Provincial and Territorial Policing

Provincial policing involves enforcement of the *Criminal Code* and provincial statutes within areas of a province not served by a municipal police service, as in rural areas and small towns. In some cases, police boundaries may overlap. For example, in some areas provincial police perform traffic duties on major provincial thoroughfares that pass through municipal jurisdictions.

Newfoundland and Labrador, Yukon, the Northwest Territories, and Nunavut are the only areas in Canada without municipal police services. In Newfoundland and Labrador, the Royal Newfoundland Constabulary, which is a provincial police service, provides policing to the three largest municipalities—St. John's, Corner Brook, and Labrador City—as well as to Churchill Falls. Newfoundland and Labrador contracts the RCMP to provide policing to the remaining municipalities and provinces' rural areas.

The RCMP provides provincial/territorial policing and community policing services in all provinces and territories except Quebec and Ontario, which maintain their own provincial police services: the Sûreté du Québec and the Ontario Provincial Police, respectively. In Ontario and Quebec, the RCMP only provides policing at the federal level. Where a provincial policing contract is granted to the RCMP, the RCMP automatically assumes the provincial policing powers. In the provinces and territories where the RCMP is contracted to provide provincial-level policing, the provinces are billed 70 per cent of total contract costs in most cases. The remaining funds come from the federal government.

Municipal Policing

Municipal policing consists of enforcement of the *Criminal Code*, provincial statutes, and municipal by-laws within the boundaries of a municipality or several adjoining municipalities that comprise a region (e.g., Durham Regional Police in Ontario) or a metropolitan area (e.g., Montreal Urban Community [MUC]). Municipalities have three options when providing policing services: to form their own police force, to join an existing municipal police force, or to enter into an agreement with a provincial police force or the RCMP. In cases where the RCMP is granted a contract to police a municipality, under the billing agreement, municipalities with a population below 15,000 are billed 70 per cent of total expenditures, and municipalities of 15,000 and over are billed 90 per cent of total costs.

First Nations Policing

In addition to federal, provincial/territorial, and municipal policing, various types of First Nations policing agreements for Aboriginal communities are in place across Canada. The federal government announced the First Nations Policing Policy (FNPP) in June 1991 in order to provide First Nations across Canada (with the exception of the Northwest Territories and Nunavut) access to police services that are professional, effective, culturally appropriate, and accountable to the communities they serve.

The FNPP is implemented across Canada through tripartite agreements negotiated among the federal government, provincial or territorial governments and First Nations. The agreements are cost shared 52 per cent by the government of Canada and 48 per cent by the province involved. Depending on the resources available, the First Nation may develop and administer its own police service, as is the case in most of Quebec and Ontario, or it may enter into a Community Tripartite Agreement (CTA). Like self-administered agreements, CTAs are negotiated between the federal government, the province or territory in which the First Nation is located, and the governing body of the First Nation. Under such agreements, the First Nation has its own dedicated contingent of officers from an existing police service (usually the RCMP). Best efforts are made for these police services to be staffed by Aboriginal police officers.

On April 15, 2009, in his op-ed piece for the *Ottawa Citizen*, Liberal senator Colin Kenny appealed for even more police rather than for the new prisons offered by Prime Minister Stephen Harper's Conservative government. Discounting statistics indicating that crime rates had dropped in recent years, Kenny argued that "yesterday's statistics won't tell you what is happening today" and challenged their accuracy for not reflecting crimes that go unreported "because victims know that the police are stretched too thin to deal with them." That unhappy reality was compounded, he said, because too often police were forced to act as social workers in their communities. He warned Canadians to prepare for more break-ins, more robberies, and more violence in these tough economic times.

"Drug addictions breed thievery," Kenny wrote. "Gangs breed thievery. Recessions breed thievery. And right now Canada—like most industrialized countries—is having significant problems with all three of these: drug addiction, gangs and one whopper of a crime-breeding recession."

He noted that more police are also needed at our airports, seaports, border crossings, and on the Great Lakes—all areas of mutual concern to Canadian and American security officials.

As chair of the Standing Senate Committee on National Security and Defence, which has publicly called for up to 6,500 more Mounties to boost the 17,000 now in uniform, Senator Kenny argued that this was needed to make Canadians more secure in small towns and big cities, offering facts to "make your head swim":

- The U.S. Coast Guard patrols the Great Lakes with 2,200 officers; there are fourteen Mounties and the RCMP doesn't have the budget to provide more;
- We are 900 Mounties short to police our ports and airports;
- The Mounties can keep tabs on one-third of the criminal organizations *it knows about*;
- The *Charter of Rights and Freedoms* requires more officers to spend more time doing paperwork that one officer used to be able to complete in less time.

In short, there were too few officers to patrol too many areas while these officers were buried under too much paperwork. Suggesting that the police may attract more recruits in tough times, Kenny concluded: "Canada needs more good cops...I say stop pontificating about tougher prison sentences. Give us more quality humans to fight the good fight for a humane society."

Three days later, the senator was back with another opinion

piece, repeating his call for more police officers and warnings of rising crime to come, saying: "It's clear as the recession comes we're going to see more break-ins, more organized crime operating simply because people will find it an economic necessity to do that. The right way to deal with it is with more police."

The *Citizen* article reported that the economic downturn was also creating an ideal breeding ground for violence, often against employers and families, citing sharp spikes in the overall crime rate during the last two recessions: "In 1991, in the midst of the deep recession of the early 1990s, the crime rate rose nine per cent in one year, the biggest single-year hike since the mid-1970s," according to Statistics Canada.

Such were the realities of policing in Canada nearly forty years after James Ahern advocated turning policing in North America "upside down" to fix it, and weeks after David Brown bluntly reported that, given prevailing conditions, the police cannot do their job. No matter how rosy the numbers seemed to be, very senior police officers were painting a far grimmer picture for Senator Colin Kenny and the Standing Senate Committee on National Security and Defence he chairs.

ONE

STORM WARNINGS

Parliamentary testimony from three top law enforcement bosses reveals police no longer have the capacity to deal with the sort of crime and emergencies facing the country.
—*Vancouver Sun* columnist Barbara Yaffe, "Thinning Blue Line a Scary Prospect," published in CanWest newspapers February 26, 2008

On February 25, 2008, former RCMP commissioner Giuliano Zaccardelli, OPP commissioner Julian Fantino, and Edmonton police chief Mike Boyd presented a united front and common message to Kenny and his panel of senators: Pierre Claude Nolin, a Quebec lawyer and deputy chair of the Special Senate Committee on Anti-Terrorism; Hugh Segal, a noted public-policy analyst from Ontario; Rod Zimmer, a Winnipeg businessman and philanthropist; Tommy Banks, a celebrated musician and entertainer from Alberta; Joseph Day, a New Brunswick lawyer; and Wilfred Moore, a municipal activist from Halifax with a seat on the board of governors of Saint Mary's University. None were optimistic about our chances to fight organized crime or protect ourselves from terrorists.

The committee members had invited the trio to brief them on developments, since they had published what Kenny termed a "comprehensive report" on Canada's national preparedness to re-spond to manmade and natural disasters. That 2004 study, *National Emergencies: Canada's Fragile Front Lines—An Upgrade Strategy*, had painted an unsettling picture of the country's inability to respond in a productive or timely manner to any natural or manmade dis-aster or terrorist attack. Chapter titles like "We Scramble to Survive," "Canada's Fragile Front Lines," and "An Unready Nation" consti-tuted a litany of confused reporting structures, funding concerns, and equipment failures, most notably two-way radios, vital for the first wave of emergency responders to communicate with each oth-er and their command centres.

The standing committee's 2005 interim report on the status of Canadian-American border security was discouraging. The title gave it away: *Borderline Insecure*. (There were similarly alarming reports confirming penetration of our ports and airports by organ-ized crime. Senator Colin Kenny, a week after British police arrested twenty-four suspects believed to have been plotting to blow up British airliners flying to the United States in August 2006, used his website to cite our vulnerability in these key areas as the real Achilles heel in our counterterror operations. And in its 2004 National Intelligence Priorities report, the Criminal Intelligence Service of Canada [CISC] foresaw no end to the criminal exploitation of our ports and airports by organized crime since it first sounded the alarm in 1998.) The 2005 interim report bluntly asked why there was such a lack of urgency to fix the problems, and tried to anticipate, from a national security and economic viewpoint, what would hap-pen if they weren't fixed. Further, it implied that the main difference between twentieth- and twenty-first-century terrorist threats is that now Canada and the United States could be *joint* targets.

Conventional wisdom held that terrorists struck where the media were concentrated, which meant Toronto. Pearson International Airport and the CN Tower, possibly the Ontario legislature, had been considered more likely targets than even the Parliament Buildings or other institutions in the nation's capital. There was also the theory that Canada was not a high-risk target because so many terror groups based their agents here for easy and ready access to the prime target—

the United States. In other words, you don't foul your own nest or do anything to draw attention to yourself where you are trying to hide while plotting to strike more distant targets. Quite simply, it was, until recently, how the Taliban managed to grow stronger using bases in neighbouring Pakistan from which to attack targets in Afghanistan.

But now, with Canada allied with the United States so clearly in the war on terror being waged in Afghanistan, and with Internet and twenty-four-hour news networks thirsting for news anywhere in the world, would this new threat seek a vulnerable target that could hurt both allies? As the 2005 standing committee report concedes, the Parliament Buildings, the James Bay hydroelectric project, and the Pickering nuclear reactor were all good targets— but not the best. "If somebody really wanted to tear into Canada's political and economic future and wound the Americans at the same time," the report concluded, "an optimal target might well be the Ambassador Bridge in Windsor, Ontario."

Acknowledging that "some limited progress" had been made to reduce the odds for disasters at such international crossings, and that more assistance had been promised in the federal government's 2005 budget, the report concluded: "However, our general assessment is that much more progress should have been forthcoming by now, on both sides of the border, in the more than three and a half years since 9/11."

With Senator Kenny conceding that the earlier reports had "clearly indicated" the country was not well prepared to deal with national emergencies, he and his standing committee were now seeking feedback to gauge the country's current emergency-response capabilities and the pace of progress from all levels of emergency-response organizations, from local to federal. If they were hoping to hear some good news from Zaccardelli, Fantino, and Boyd, they were about to be disappointed. A diverse audience was about to hear a unified tale of misery that basically said the police couldn't do their job and protect Canada and her citizens.

"We also hope to hear his [Zaccardelli's] opinions on how resources, or the lack thereof, impact the RCMP's ability to deal with emergency management and organized crime," Kenny added. (No one at the hearing or in the media seems to have questioned why the former commissioner was attending rather than the serving commissioner, Bev Busson.)

Zaccardelli spoke first, assuring the panel that while he was no longer RCMP commissioner, his passion for protecting Canadian citizens and communities remained very much intact. He got directly to the point: "From the outset, let me assure you that my perspective is that we are approaching a crisis point, and we may already be there in certain parts of the country. This crisis requires extensive integrated effort on behalf of all the key stakeholders in the police sector."

It got worse from there, as he outlined police strength across Canada. To give the panel "the big picture," Zaccardelli estimated there are 89,000 people employed in public policing across Canada— with at least the same number working in private security. Of those 89,000, he suggested 64,000 are sworn officers of whom roughly one-third are Mounties. Of other 222 police services, boasting 46,000 officers, he suggested more than 85 per cent are small services employing fewer than 300 people, with more than half having fewer than twenty-five employees. In other words, Canada comprises nine large police services employing more than 1,000 people with four larger ones employing more than 5,000 officers, plus the RCMP.

"That means there are over 170 police services that are quite small and insular and have no resource flexibility," he said, warning that the smaller forces—the overwhelming majority—are barely able to meet the demands placed upon them. "That is not a model that ensures that every Canadian in this country is safe and secure in their communities or that there is a common standard of policing."

Such inadequacies did not come cheaply. In his statement to the committee, Zaccardelli observed that Canadians spend almost $10 billion on community policing—more than $300 per year per Canadian—and that did not include the additional costs for national agencies like the RCMP, Customs, Immigration, Transport, and Corrections to enforce federal statutes, which are not binding on provincial and municipal police, but which often assist the feds who cannot do it all alone. Nor does the $10 billion include costs Canadians pay for private security. The former commissioner estimated total expenditures in "the neighbourhood of $30 billion." And, Zaccardelli reasoned, that cost would climb as police chiefs requested increased funding, before he asked: "Is there any citizen in this country that would not be willing to spend more than $300 a year to ensure the safety of their property and children?"

Throwing money at a problem—a long-accepted government solution to almost any problem—was not working for the police. While the budgets were constantly rising, they were a fraction of what the police required to protect Canadians. Staffing levels have dropped significantly from 1975—Ahern's era—when there were 206 officers for every 100,000 Canadians. "Today," Zaccardelli said, "there are 195 officers for every 100,000 Canadians. That is the smallest number of police officers to population ratio in any of the twenty-five major developed countries in the world." (Online statistics compiled by www.nationmaster.com, a site reputed to do a better job than the CIA World Fact Book for comparing data to make it more relevant and which is highly praised by several major U.S. media agencies, list Canada as forty-second among forty-eight countries in per capita policing, albeit at 171 officers per 100,000 population, leading only Zimbabwe, Finland, Zambia, Papua New Guinea, India, and Costa Rica.)

Zaccardelli put the blame squarely on the politicians, citing the cutbacks of the 1980s and 1990s, noting that crime did not take a cut and that the police fell behind because government funding priorities "are not based on need or demand; unfortunately, they are based on politics." That, he said, has resulted in a 10 per cent reduction in "real capacity" to do police work over the last decade. "The cost and workload of policing has outpaced any budget increases. Organized crime has grown; policing has not."

Zaccardelli recalled the headlines he made a few years earlier when he admitted that the RCMP lacked the resources to investigate more than 30 per cent of the known organized crime organizations.[1] "That was the known crime," he stressed. "What is the potential impact on our lives of what we do not know? What are we doing about it?" The problems for the police, he emphasized, go far beyond budgets and staffing.

"Every time a piece of legislation in Canada is passed, policing becomes more difficult," he said, citing a recent study that showed police responses are increasingly selective. "Why? Every time there is new legislation, every time there is a new court decision, it puts pressure on and increases processing time for the police."

His statistics must have chilled—or at least numbed—the Senate panel. Over the past decade, the average time required to investigate a simple break-and-enter has increased by 58 per cent; an impaired driving charge increased 250 per cent; a domestic assault increased 964 per cent. No corresponding budget increases were given to the police every time a court decision or a new piece of legislation increased the processing time for these crimes.

"All of this [the growing gap between stalled funding and increased demands on the police] took place in a policing environment of more public oversight, more media scrutiny, and more public expectations for an accountability bar set higher than [for] any other profession," Zaccardelli said. "If that does not cause you concern, let me add [that] a report to police leaders stated … [they] will have to prepare for massive turnover in leadership ranks and compete for, attract, develop, and retain the next generation of talent in a highly competitive labour market.

"That report came out seven years ago. That was before 9/11 and since then the police role in protection against terrorism has increased exponentially."

Switching gears, Zaccardelli cited the Police Sector Council, an Ottawa-based agency he described as "a new collective of police leaders looking at the long-term sustainability of policing." He explained that the council was calling such challenges a "perfect storm" for policing. They, like he, deemed these realities a call to action to respond to the converging triple threat to public safety.

"First, you have the changing face of policing demographics," he explained. "In the next short while, 40 to 59 per cent of senior leaders in policing will be retiring. Second, less than 3 per cent of a diminishing youth cohort is interested in policing today. Third, the changing work, increasing demands, complexity of crime, changing management, budgets, governance are other factors."

Zaccardelli estimated that each fully equipped police officer had cost Canadians $67,000 in 1993. That already exorbitant amount soared to $107,000 in 2003 and to almost $150,000 today in urban centres.

"This situation has been getting worse for the last seven years and the future is not looking bright," he concluded, predicting that policing was doomed to fail if the course is not altered.

"The report goes on [to say] that if the status quo does not change, the public may come to this realization through a failure of policing," he warned. "Such a collapse may not happen tomorrow, it may happen in a couple of years, but it will happen ... brought on by a failure to take collective and timely action to solve the [staffing] issues that have eroded the effectiveness of police services for the better part of the last decade. When this happens, the public will demand solutions from senior levels of government..."

Suggesting that government would then impose solutions, Zaccardelli cautioned the committee members to be prepared to answer some tough questions: "Do we want every police service to be fighting or poaching each other for best candidates? What happens to all those 170 small services? How do they keep pace? Do we as Canadians want have- and have-not policing depending on where you are lucky to live in this country? Policing is jurisdictionally silent; crime is not. Why is it we can collaborate on operational files and joint forces operations but we cannot collaborate on a strategic framework for policing, or even consider a new model?"

Perhaps because he was no longer RCMP commissioner, and therefore freer to challenge the political elite, Zaccardelli questioned the Conservative government's resolve to step up and do what needed to be done.

"The federal government [speeches] suggest they were embracing a law-and-order agenda," he said. "Where is the meat? They offer 2,500 new officers on the street but we need 5,000 in the next three to five years just to replenish the retirements let alone deal with increasing transnational, organized and technology-enabled crime."

Zaccardelli could never have dreamed that, almost a year later, the federal government's response would be to announce that it was freezing the Mounties' wages—this after Treasury Board had earlier refused to pay candidates in training, as almost every other police force does—potentially making them the least desirable option in an incredibly competitive market for recruits. As for the 2,500 promised recruits dutifully reported by the media, no journalist seems to have asked just where the government thinks it's going to find that number of candidates. Equally hollow promises were made earlier, often at the provincial level, that thousands of doctors and nurses were going to be hired—far more than the number available in Canada. Again, the stories ran without question.

Zaccardelli concluded with a single question: "Where is the leadership?"

That prompted Senator Banks to focus the discussion solely on the RCMP: "To your knowledge, to what extents and how is the RCMP itself prepared, able or doing something to address those issues?" Zaccardelli replied that a holistic approach is needed, that fixing one level of policing is not the answer to the problems facing those sworn to serve and protect the public and Canadian borders.

"The RCMP has been very effective, but that does not at the end of the day deal with the problem of the gap that exists and the gap that is widening," he said. "In 1975, I said we had more police officers in this country per 100,000 than we have today. Just look at the nature of organized crime and the impact of the threat of terrorism, let alone the level of sophistication of the crimes. In 1975, the notion of gangs drawing huge amounts of resources from our municipal police forces did not exist; today, it is a serious component of the crime in our communities.

"We simply have not kept pace. I think we can do a better job if we all come together and recognize the challenges and work together to overcome them."

Senator Nolin turned the conversation to the recently released Brown report on RCMP governance before Senator Segal asked how assuming provincial and municipal policing duties affects the Mounties' ability to perform their duties as a national police force.

Zaccardelli explained that much has changed because organized crime, terrorism, and computer crime transcend police jurisdictions and national borders. "Until the 1960s, the RCMP basically was responsible for all the drug work in this country," he recalled. "Then municipalities and provincial police forces had to come in because it [transnational crime] overwhelmed us all, so we integrated and worked together." He added that everyone has to understand how what is happening around the world affects all Canadians, not just the police, but argued that getting out of contract policing—viewed by many as the Mounties' bread and butter—would not give the RCMP more money to spend on federal policing.

"The fact is that policing would be much more costly in this country," he said. "Do you know what Treasury Board would do? Do you think they would transfer the money? A lot of it is not transferable because it is infrastructure money." Zaccardelli cautioned the senators to be "very leery" of such arguments.

Segal asked about recruiting applicants from the military or CSIS, but Zaccardelli replied that it's not that simple, noting: "Recruiting is probably one of the biggest challenges of all police forces today, not just in this country but around the world. The RCMP is facing it because of demographics and so on. We encourage men and women, no matter where they come from, if they meet the standard, to come and see us."

The major "inhibitor" to others transferring to the RCMP, or Mounties leaving to join other police forces, is that municipal and provincial pensions are not transferable to the federal government. Changing that would cost the government nothing, so why, Zaccardelli wondered, is nothing done?

After discussing the staffing commitments to northern policing, border security, and overseas missions to train foreign police, Senator David Tkachuk asked why policing is now so much more time consuming, citing earlier testimony to the committee of a 250-fold increase in the time to process a drunk driver. Zaccardelli explained that it is the result of complying with court decisions and policies to respect charter rights. As a young constable, he recalled, he could prepare a five- or ten-page affidavit for a wiretap authorization in a half day and present it to a judge for approval. "The average affidavit on an organized crime group today will literally run into the hundreds, if not thousands, of pages," he explained. "This means that you need a team of police officers, along with a team of lawyers, who will spend weeks and weeks on it. We have to do it because the court has required us to do that. However, while the group is working on the affidavit, they are not out there doing police work.

"When a police officer picks up an impaired driver, you can kiss his shift away because it will take that whole shift to process that one impaired driver. That is the reality of the work. The way the processes have evolved has encumbered the police officers' ability to be out there on the street doing what he or she needs to do."

Senator Nolin wasn't totally sympathetic, noting that everyone must change with the times. To him, the key was knowing whether the almost 100,000 Canadians "responsible for protecting the rest of us" can adapt to that new reality. Zaccardelli assured him that the police are very capable and have adapted, but stressed again that the time consumption has risen markedly with no corresponding increase in resources.

"The fact is that when the Supreme Court issued a certain decision like *Stinchcombe* on disclosure, disclosure takes a lot of time. [The 1991 ruling compelled the police and prosecution to share their information with the defence, a procedure that had been voluntary under common law.] You have to deal with that reality; however, I do not think any police force in this country got additional resources when the *Stinchcombe* decision was handed down ... [but] those decisions have a direct impact on our ability to be on the street and do the investigations that the public is demanding of us."

Nor was Zaccardelli encouraging when Senator Tkachuk asked him if the federal funds were helping. The former RCMP commissioner was unsure if the funds, as a percentage of the federal budget, were more or less than they were twenty years ago, but he was pretty sure they were still inadequate.

"[The] RCMP is seriously deficient when it comes to terrorism," he said. "Two years ago when I came here, I said we can only deal with about 30 per cent of all the organized crime groups that we know. I am afraid it is probably getting worse. We are talking about huge gaps that have to be overcome. The gap will not be closed by small incremental increases. There has to be a serious recognition of the problem.

"We talked about the different border points of entry in this country. This is a field we have never tackled before and never considered as a threat. Now we know those are vulnerabilities that put us at high risk and we are not putting the resources there yet. They are being considered. However, they are not there."[2]

Julian Fantino, the OPP commissioner who had been chief of several police departments, including Toronto's, picked up where Zaccardelli left off.

"The police beat of today is no longer local; it is international," he began, noting that increased specialization is needed to combat crime and that more complex crime means more time taken to comply with evidentiary requirements—all part of the increasingly "reactive" nature of police work. The creation of so many new specialty units to respond to specific government funding for policing ranging from community policing to catching suspected terrorists, coupled with waves of retirements, too few recruits to fill the void, and the rise in secondments to everything from international peacekeeping to providing security for the 2010 Vancouver Olympics, left too few front-line officers with too little time to consistently "show the flag" by being visible and proactive in the community.

"There is a blurring now of what is organized crime or criminal activity with that which morphs into terrorism," Fantino claimed. "[Not] all criminals are terrorists, but certainly, terrorists are criminals. Much of that evolves around the whole notion of organized crime and how organized crime is able to provide finances or is used to obtain finances to achieve that end goal for terrorists as well."

Fantino noted that the proliferation of gangs and guns also added new demands on policing: "The availability of firearms is a serious issue. We see handguns in the hands of these young people, who have a total and absolute predisposition to using these firearms and are prepared to die in the process—something that is very strange to us and difficult to understand. Nevertheless, it is something that we must tackle. We can talk all we want about doing away with firearms, but we must start talking about what is happening to our young people, who are turning to this lifestyle."

Beyond the increased potential for violent crime, Fantino drew attention to the increasingly difficult white-collar criminals, explaining: "Our fraud investigations consist of very complex, multijurisdictional and transnational fraudulent schemes that result in significant financial losses to individuals, corporations and the various levels of government." Seniors are often high-risk targets. Agreeing that the police need to find new ways to do their job in these changing times, he cited the impetus of the philosophy of Jeffrey Robinson, international bestselling author of more than a dozen books, many dealing with international organized crime and money laundering: "As long as we live in a world where a seventeenth century philosophy of sovereignty is reinforced by an eighteenth century judicial model, defended by a nineteenth century concept of law enforcement that is still trying to come to terms with twentieth century technology, the twenty-first century will belong to transnational criminals."

With so many investigators spending so much time on labour-intensive drug and weapons investigations, Fantino commented that even routine traffic stops are turning up ever more contraband valued at hundreds of thousands of dollars with links to organized crime. However, the police don't get "one red nickel," prompting his comment: "If we are doing the work, we should be compensated in some way."

This didn't appear to be a mere cash grab as Fantino outlined the problem, explaining: "Child sexual exploitation work on the Internet is a difficult and serious issue. You saw what we were able to do recently through a significant collaborative effort. We were able to do the work because, in our case, the provincial government dedicated $5 million to enable us to put our best investigators forward to deal with these dastardly crimes committed against children—the most vulnerable people in our society."

The demands on policing seem endless: child exploitation, Internet luring, child pornography, and identity theft.

"That is the kind of work that we face," Fantino said. "Our

capacity to support these investigations is a major concern because we need to dedicate people to this kind of work. This capacity is also predicated on how much work we have to do to prepare these cases for court.... All of these resources are not on the street because they have been sucked up by this exponentially growing, labour-intensive and highly technical work that our people need to do. It is not just the police officer on the beat but it is all the dramatic increases that we have to deal with." To underscore his point, he cited the seizure of 4.3 terabytes of data that had to be reviewed. "That represented 160 stacks of paper, each the height of the CN Tower."

Almost as an aside, Fantino told the committee that the OPP had received 207 requests for assistance from foreign partners in 2005—most presumably from the United States—and that such appeals have increased dramatically since then. "That," he concluded, "is what we have to deal with."[3]

Edmonton police chief Mike Boyd, who went west after serving as Toronto's interim chief after Fantino left, offered some breathing space for the beleaguered panel by assuring the senators that the police are on the cutting edge of social change "whether we want to be or not." As far as Boyd was concerned, the police had a four-part mandate: crime prevention; the maintenance of social order; law enforcement; and the provision of public safety. Admitting that funding is a vital factor to success, he insisted that law enforcement is not all about the money: it is about leadership. Noting increased co-operation between Canadian and American emergency responders since the terrorist attacks on September 11, 2001, Boyd further cited the increased unity among police, firefighters, and paramedics to have elected officials better understand their world and their efforts.

"What we really need now is to have the different orders of government come together the same way that the police, fire and EMS [Emergency Medical Services] communities have done at the different levels so that we can move forward on the things that are not yet done and very seriously need to be looked at," he said.

Senator Nolin asked what challenges the police faced at the provincial and municipal levels to attract recruits. Boyd said that a "significant number" of his officers have retired over the previous three years and agreed with Zaccardelli's contention that replacing them was a problem with fewer people interested in a policing career.

"Many of us are recruiting at the same time, we are all recruiting from the same pool of people across the country, and that is making it [staffing] very difficult," he explained. "We are achieving our numbers and we feel that we are lucky in doing so. However, I know there are other police services that are struggling. Therefore, we need to be thinking about the future of policing as the world changes."

Fantino recalled losing roughly seven hundred officers in 2003–2004 when he was chief and Boyd was his deputy. It was, he admitted, a daunting challenge to replace them. What Toronto experienced then, other forces are experiencing now, he added. As commissioner, Fantino found that First Nations policing was a huge challenge, with the OPP having direct responsibility for 19 of 134 Native communities, and empowered to respond to emergencies at any of the other 115, although such responses onto Native land could get complicated. "In an emergency situation, we most definitely will respond," he confirmed, "but it gets into a grey area beyond that because it is sovereign territory. There are all kinds of historical agreements."

Senator Segal brought the discussion back to the "challenge of choices" that set police priorities. Citing his youthful experience as a researcher for Quebec Solicitor General Claude Wagner, Segal recalled asking his "crime-fighting" mentor how he assembled his campaign to fight organized crime. "[Wagner] replied that it was simple: you get the guys from homicide, vice, and anti-racketeering and you put them all together in a task force and you go at a particular group of suspects as best you can for a period of time. You invest heavily and arrest some kingpins. You break up some networks and push the forces of darkness back. Then you have to put those people back where they were in homicide, in vice and in anti-racketeering because no one can afford to give you those people all the time. They have another job to do, which is just as important."

After admitting that getting drunk drivers off the road is an important mission, Segal asked Fantino if international organized crime might not pose a greater threat to Canada. Was it not the commissioner's choice how best to deploy resources?

"If you had the freedom to deploy more people on the drug side or on grow ops or the anti-gang squad, would you?" Segal asked. "Are you constrained by limited resources? Are there ever enough resources in that context?"

Fantino insisted there were never enough resources and then ignored Segal's organized crime reference to focus on the drunk-driving crusade, noting that impaired driving is the leading cause of criminal death in Canada. "It is something we have to take into account," he argued. "The death from a traffic fatality results in a $2 million hit on the community and the family through the loss of productivity, health costs, etcetera. We have to stay focused on this very serious crime. In that context, we have made every OPP officer responsible for traffic safety in the province, whether it is a detective, a commissioner or whoever. It is a matter of harnessing the resources you have to focus on this particular issue. Clearly, drugs are a problem. Gangs and guns are a serious issue."

That raised other problems. CISC had redefined organized crime as three or more people gathered together to commit a crime. That blurred the line between the handful of criminal elements that had historically been deemed "organized" and the growth of street gangs who could be little more than a rabble. The only "gang" in the past had been the bikers and only the Hells Angels, who had copyrighted their logo, could be easily proven in court to be an organized crime group. For everyone else, the prosecutor could spend hours or days trying to persuade a judge that the accused who was not an Angel could also be considered a member or associate of a recognized crime group. Hundreds of hours and thousands of dollars were wasted arguing the same things over and over at each trial. Aside from the biker gangs, everyone else was a member of a society or a clan, a triad or a posse. The problem for the police was that just because they had a name for a crime group did not mean the members of that group called themselves the same thing.

About the only criminals who could not be considered part of organized crime were those who made the individual decision to get behind the steering wheel and drive drunk. Two incidents of stopping suspected intoxicated drivers drew media frenzies as first Fantino, then the Ottawa chief Vern White, stopped drivers on the suspicion they had been drinking. The media loved it, never asking if Ontario taxpayers were being well served by having such handsomely salaried police leaders (and presumably Fantino's detective-level chauffeur) sitting around a courthouse for a day waiting for the slow wheels of justice to grind their way. Whatever the cost, however, it complies with basic political and police math that investigations cost money; traffic tickets generate revenues—for the government, not the police. Nabbing a drunk driver removed a public threat and could be investigated by the arresting officer, thus removing only one investigator from the road to complete paperwork.

With no senator interrupting or challenging him, Fantino continued not talking about organized crime, stressing the need for more outside involvement to help the police do their job.

"This cannot be left to the police," he insisted. "There is a huge expectation on the police that we deal with this whole crime issue, law and order and public safety. In actual fact, we need to move to a more strategic place and find the mechanism in our society to do more prevention and education. We need to ensure that we have the infrastructure and resources in place to keep young people from turning to these non-productive and often criminal ways of life. That is the big challenge for us. If there is one entity that is working very hard, it is the men and women in the trenches doing the heavy lifting."

Having commended his front-line officers, Fantino echoed Zaccardelli's earlier point that the police need more community partnerships because they cannot do it all. "We are social workers, psychologists, psychiatrists, counsellors, medics and on it goes. There is too much of an expectation for a young police officer to be all those things and not ask the question where is everyone else?"

Thus, thirty-six years after Ahern wrote that police are frustrated cops, not wannabe lawyers, or social workers, or anything else, the commissioner of the Ontario Provincial Police seemed to be telling members of the Senate of Canada that is exactly what police in that province—perhaps nationwide—have become. No one asked why that was or how it had come to pass.

Senator Tkachuk was curious as to whether, as he had heard from a peace officer in Saskatoon, the problem was less a case of spawning new criminals than of recycling old ones through the justice system, because "if you come out at night the chances are that 100 per cent of the calls will be [concerning] someone who is out on bail, on parole, just out of jail or a repeat offender."

Curiously, that statement brought the discussion back to organized crime and Fantino's belief that a "whole new set of criminals" is emerging whom he considers "more violent, more predisposed to gun use and looking for quick ways to make a buck."

"Organized crime," he warned, "is very much aware of that and that is where they [the police] are working to recruit and bring people on board." Alas, apparently not drunk drivers who seem easier and cheaper to catch.

Fantino's observation brought Boyd, the Edmonton chief and his old colleague from Toronto full circle to "social disorder," one of the four-part policing mandate that he had outlined in his opening remarks.

"There is another kind of fear that is very relevant to your questions tonight," he told the panel. "There is the crime that needs to be attended to, but then there is this other issue called social disorder.... When police agencies are stretched to do so many different things, they try to deal with what appears to be the most important thing." That, he concluded, is the crime that is occurring at any given point in time.

"What we have learned is that it is very important to deal with the social-disorder concerns in communities because those social disorders, although they may not be crimes in and of themselves, have an eroding effect on countries and on cities," Boyd explained. "We have seen this across our country. It is the graffiti; it is the aggressive panhandling ... It may be the prostitution. Forget for a moment the issue of prostitution and the selling of one's body as an adult. It is the issue of prostitution when it occurs along with drug dealing. This makes the community a magnet for undesirable conduct. The relationship between crime and social disorder creates the fear.

"We have learned that lesson in this country. When we are stretched so thin, it is very difficult to tackle that as well as the crime. It is all about trying to maintain or build a good quality of life for people in our cities and communities."

Everyone in the room, with rare exception, seemed to talk around the key issues. To tackle organized crime and international terrorism meant essentially waging low-intensity warfare. Whether that was better suited to the police or the military was moot. Both forces were stretched so thin by their existing commitments and limited resources that it would be an uphill battle for either—or even their combined efforts. God knows there was precedent for the latter. Although all major forces had developed their own heavily armed tactical units decades ago, the military had been there to assist and advise the police in almost every major operation they had conducted over the past half century, beginning with Cold War survival preparations starting with the Cuban Missile Crisis of 1962. Since that time, the military worked with the police at the 1976 Olympic Games in Montreal (the OPP Tactics and Rescue Unit [TRU] and soldiers patrolled the sailing events held in Kingston, Ontario), in ongoing counter-narcotics operations and in the 1990s during major Native standoffs at Akwasasne, Oka, Ipperwash, and Gustafsen Lake.

Ironically, if the Senate panel and the police chiefs were looking for a template for combatting international terrorism and organized crime, they have had to look no further than their own archives. On June 21, 1966, Lieutenant General Jean Allard, commander of the recently created Mobile Command for prompt deployment to any emergency, anywhere at any time, appeared before the standing committee to explain how the military was to be restructured for low-intensity operations against "protracted revolutionary war" against national liberation fronts. Their first test came four years later when Pierre Trudeau invoked the *War Measures*

Act and sent the army after the Front de libération du Québec (FLQ), at the request of Quebec premier Robert Bourassa, who claimed he had lost faith in the RCMP and Quebec police.

But even with a template on file that could be adapted to meet police needs, success would still require strong political will and determined police leadership. Brown had not found much of either in his study of the Mounties.

TWO

CRISIS IN COMMAND:
Looking Out for Number One

In an already fractured culture, senior management was projecting an attitude of disinterest and callousness ... In the process, the commissioner lost his troops.
—David Brown explaining the demise of morale in the RCMP

David Brown's back-to-back reports in 2007 and 2008, which condemned former RCMP commissioner Zaccardelli's "autocratic" leadership style and discovered a federal police force in desperate need of repair, should have been a wake-up call to senior police managers and their political overseers everywhere. The perceived failures of any one person paled beside what seems to be a larger systemic failure created by the very politicians who are responsible for keeping the police on track—while not meddling in operations. In the end, the politicians who failed in their responsibility to oversee the police tried to undo their errors by naming Brown to determine what had gone wrong and how to fix it.

With only five months to conduct interviews, Brown's task force met with thousands of RCMP members and employees at detachments across the country, as well as with senior officials at Mountie headquarters in Ottawa and cadets training at Depot Division in Regina. They visited with federal departments and agencies involved in any aspect with the RCMP, including the Canada Public Service Agency, Treasury Board Secretariat, the Office of the Public Sector Integrity Commissioner, the RCMP External Review Committee, and the Commission for Public Complaints against the RCMP; they also interviewed federal and provincial Solicitors and Attorneys General, deputy ministers, mayors and city councillors. The task force even reached out to the public, inviting Canadians to comment online, by letter, phone, or fax. In addition to the interviews he conducted with both serving and retired RCMP members and employees, Brown reported receiving another 500 confidential emails and correspondence.

"All of this led us to conclude that there is a need to radically overhaul the way in which the RCMP is governed," Brown reported, while also "significantly" improving accountability of the RCMP to the public, to elected political leaders, and to the members and employees of the Force. Brown observed that merely treating the symptoms would not produce sustainable improvements; that a more fundamental approach was essential if they were to create a new independent body for complaints and oversight of the RCMP. The massive changes they proposed would be disruptive, but Brown advocated that the task force's recommendations be implemented quickly by a new implementation council to provide leadership and guidance. To underscore the imperative, and to explain why he believed there was no time to spend on a formal inquiry, Brown offered some insights into the complexities of Canada's federal police force.

"The RCMP is, arguably, the most complex law enforcement agency in the world today, including Interpol, which is primarily a clearing house for information shared among police forces worldwide. The RCMP provides, under contract, rural and municipal policing services in all but two provinces (Ontario and Quebec), in all three territories and in approximately 200 municipalities and Aboriginal communities. It also provides federal and international police services, national police services, and protective policing.

"There are currently more than 27,000 members and employees

of the RCMP comprising regular and civilian members of the Force and public servants. The approximately 17,000 regular members are trained as qualified peace officers, are entitled to wear the uniform and to carry weapons. There are also approximately 3,000 civilian members of the RCMP who are not trained as peace officers. Civilian members provide specialist support to the Force in areas such as forensic science and technology. Additionally, the RCMP employs approximately 4,700 public service employees who are not members of the Force, but who provide specialized services in key areas such as human resources and financial management. They also provide critical operational and administrative support in detachments across Canada, in divisional and regional centres, and at headquarters in Ottawa. Finally, the RCMP employs approximately 2,000 temporary civilian employees to perform an array of clerical and support functions. The Force is also supported by several hundred municipal employees, auxiliary constables, and volunteers.

"The RCMP operates with an annual budget of approximately $4 billion, paid through appropriations from the federal government and on revenues from its contracting provinces, territories, and municipalities. The commissioner, appointed pursuant to the *Royal Canadian Mounted Police Act*, heads the police and reports to the minister of Public Safety and Emergency Preparedness. The Force is organized into detachments within districts, which comprise provincial and territorial divisions, ultimately reporting to the commissioner. Overlaid on this organization is a structure that divides the Force into regions for administrative purposes."

Any organization that large and unwieldy is not going to easily change direction. Brown acknowledged that some critics of the RCMP (usually politicians, pundits, and academics) have suggested "breaking up" the Force to address its complex structure and vast and diverse law enforcement responsibilities across Canada and overseas, but he said that such debate exceeded the mandate of his task force.

How had the Mounties, a cherished Canadian icon respected worldwide, become so tarnished? How had their image and the morale of their members fallen so far so fast? Surely someone should have been watching. Every regulated profession has its oversight agencies, normally comprising peers for judges, lawyers, physicians, and nurses. Even the media are answerable to provincial press councils and national watchdogs for broadcasting standards for television and radio, as well as the Canadian Radio-television and Telecommunications Commission for the latter outlets. The police are the exception, with layer upon layer of internal and external oversight and a variety of opportunities for anyone to lodge a complaint, which will be thoroughly investigated and a hearing held if it is determined that charges are warranted. Moreover, there are no negative repercussions against anyone who files a nuisance, frivolous, or vexatious complaint. It is the good cops who catch the bad cops, yet only the police are challenged for investigating their own despite being answerable to legislation, regulation, and policy, all the while trying to navigate the power of the press and the court of public opinion. There is evidence to suggest that neither the public nor the politicians have a thorough understanding of who the police are and just what they do, seemingly drawing their insights from American television dramas and Hollywood movies. One thing was clear, the majority of federal parliamentarians had little experience or understanding of how policing work or are organized.

On May 4, 2009, the Ottawa-based Public Policy Forum (PPF), an independent, not-for-profit think tank that aims to improve the quality of government in Canada through enhanced dialogue among the public, private, and voluntary sectors, issued the results of its updated demographic study which found that a "stunning" number of federal politicians lack political experience. Although no links were drawn to policing by the report *(Less) Male, (Even Less) Educated, (Even Less) Experienced and (Even More) White*, there were some striking similarities between the police and elected officials. Given the number of new recruits replacing retiring police veterans, it was noteworthy that two-thirds of parliamentarians had less than five years' experience in politics. Police rookies were often considered veterans by that point, although many may have suffered from lack of training owing to "operational needs" to keep them on active duty. While still rating education highly, police recruiters had begun looking for life experience in their candidates, who could still join many forces with high-school credits. It was just the opposite for elected officials.

"The old complaint used to be that there were too many career politicians," PPF chief executive David Mitchell told *Ottawa Citizen* reporter Joanne Chianello the day before the study was released. "We got a little jaded that they had little or no real life experience, but now we've gone the other way. The stunning lack of experience and hence memory of Parliament as an institution provides the context for the acrimony we see in the House on a day-to-day basis."

Mitchell also suggested that their lack of understanding might also explain parliamentary committees grilling deputy ministers and senior bureaucrats as if they were part of the "political process" rather than "an independent profession," explaining: "There's a lack of appreciation for what the public service does." Certainly the public servants in police uniforms could relate to that sentiment, which seemed very similar to political confusion at times by the "guardian" agency claim for the RCMP (denoting an institution devoted to protecting the public interest), and the arm's-length buffer that is to protect all police forces from government intrusion into operational decisions. The study, without ever referring to the police, underscored that the police, like the military, are the professionals, and their political masters, while duly elected, are the amateurs. Ultimately, the police and the military are public servants who are guided by government policy but who must be free to determine how best to implement their tasks.

Yet the Mounties in particular, and provincial and municipal police across Canada in general, were being pressured by their overseers to operate as businesses, with a greater eye to the financial bottom line than preserving the peace. Consequently, there were police detachments where constables ended up working alone at night since their superior refused to bring an off-duty constable because they would have to pay overtime. Happily, this did not seem to be widely practised, but that did little to console the hapless constable who had no hope of backup. Suggestions that constables stay in the office and do paperwork were fine until the first call for assistance came in requiring a prompt response to a traffic accident or domestic dispute. Yet no one at any level of police management seems to have challenged their political overseers, arguing that public and officer safety should trump budget concerns. The problem went beyond politicians who knew little if anything about the police or what they do.

To make matters worse, these inexperienced elected officials were being guided, advised, and protected by a core of equally inexperienced young aides. Invariably described as young, confident, and aggressive, these twenty-something Millennials (also known as Generation Y, defined by the *Canadian Business Journal* [CBJ] as those born between 1981 and 1999 [others range from 1979 to 2003]) are bright, articulate, and well educated, but questions arise about their common sense and life experience. These "Kids on the Hill," as the *Ottawa Citizen* headlined on June 21, 2009, came under media scrutiny in the wake of the resignation of Jasmine MacDonnell, the twenty-six-year-old who resigned as communications director for Natural Resources minister Lisa Raitt for accidentally leaving her tape recorder behind in a washroom. (She was hired soon after by Ottawa mayor Larry O'Brien for essentially the same job she had just vacated).

MacDonnell's career move might have been inevitable regardless of the circumstances. The Gen Ys are, among other things, job hoppers, predicted to have ten to fourteen jobs during their working life and less likely than previous generations to see their employment in terms of a paycheque. In an interview entitled "The kids are alright: What Generation Y brings to the workplace," written by an anonymous Millennial author for the July 2009 edition of the CBJ, some light is shed on the new wave of employees flooding the workplace by entrepreneur Ray Williams, who offers leadership training, personal growth, and executive training through his companies in Vancouver, British Columbia, and Phoenix, Arizona.

"They will be productive if they believe the work is significant, they are not expected to be married to their job, and if their workplace is structured in such a way that shows them respect," he observed, complementing the author's opinion that Millennials are "characterised by their technological savvy, self-confidence and affinity for collaboration." They do not, he stressed, require managers to cater to them; they essentially want to know the plan, how they fit into it and to be respected for their contributions. He concluded that Millennials are willing to work hard, but in a different way.

"Many professionals from this generation are highly educated," Williams told his interviewer, "so they are less likely to tolerate a command-and-control, top-down leadership style. Instead, they want to give input and get feedback as a part of a company that respects their ideas."

In short, they want to be treated like human beings. That's a crucial distinction for police managers to grasp, particularly those who rose through the ranks from the old-school paramilitary mindset. The police are recruiting from the same talent pool, and while many of those attracted to the profession are performing their duties admirably, there are too few candidates. Policing is simply proving not to be a career of choice for many young people. For a brief time, the police ranks also reflect the unprecedented anomaly that, for the first time in history, there are four generations working together in the same field at the same time: the vanishing Greatest Generation (Second World War and Korean War veterans), the retiring baby boomers (born between 1947 and 1964), Generation X (born between 1965 and 1980), and Millennials (born between 1981 and 1999). What veteran officers may mistake for rudeness or self-serving attitudes are merely the natural result of a generation reared by doting baby boomers who assured them that they were special and valued. As the CBJ article notes, they were not usually required to "pay their dues" for rewards and recognition. It may be more important than ever to have leaders, not managers, calling the shots who, even if they can't relate to the Millennials' priority for balancing work with life, can be inclusive and nurturing as well as mentors.

That's leadership, and leadership is the key. The trick is to find leaders. American business guru Lee Iacocca literally wrote the book on that issue: *Where Have All the Leaders Gone?*

"We've spent billions of dollars building a huge new bureaucracy, and all we know how to do is react to things that have already happened," he wrote. And that was before Wall Street brought the American economy to its knees and weakened the rest of us as collateral damage. Iacocca laments that we are governed by politicians who can't react to a crisis and captains of commerce who have recently been carted away in handcuffs. Instead of greedy and entitled, Iacocca believes leaders are curious, creative communicators, have strong character, are competent and boast courage, conviction, charisma, and common sense.

Have managers replaced leaders and, if so, at what cost? Leaders appear to be an endangered species in an age when bean-counters have come to the fore, where a human-resources career can trump an operational background in the rise up the police ladder, and where advertising and marketing and political spin drown out real news. It wasn't always this way. There was a time when policing was run by rank in a rigid paramilitary structure. James Ahern, author of *Policing in Trouble*, was one of those leaders whose life seemed to crystallize in one moment in history. Lucky or unlucky, Ahern's seventeen-year policing career came down to a single confrontation with the militant Black Panthers protesting the trial—the longest in Connecticut history—of their party co-founder and ten other members accused of murdering an alleged informant. The whole nation was watching and holding its breath that May Day weekend in 1970.

As the New Haven police chief, Ahern rose to national prominence by keeping the Yale University campus cool when all around him risked losing their heads. Standing alongside his police officers, who numbered far fewer than the estimated 600 journalists who descended on what threatened to be a major riot tinged with racism, politics, and open warfare, he was determined to avoid the mistakes made by the Chicago police who violently beat protesters, journalists, and spectators at the Democratic National Convention in the Windy City two years earlier. That incident was ultimately classified as a police riot. Having studied police strategies and tactics used in other clashes in burning cities across the United States, Ahern devised a system of squads, pairing less experienced officers and "hotheads" with calmer, older veterans, ensuring not only that his 450 men could contain and control the expected hordes joining the planned Black Panther protest, but that the estimated 15,000 protesters had clear escape routes to the Yale campus. If things turned ugly, it was imperative that the demonstrators, perhaps choking and bleary eyed from the effects of tear gas, had a clearly marked exit away from his thin police ranks. State troopers and National Guardsmen posted out of sight would give him an edge if it was needed, but Ahern's ability to persuade his political superiors who controlled the state troopers and the National Guard commander to follow his lead paid off. He had avoided the mistakes and violence of Chicago. The hardest part for Ahern was getting the 300 state police he needed—and convincing President Richard Nixon and the New Haven mayor that he did not need the thousands of soldiers, paratroopers, and marines they tried to force on him.

In the end, while there were tense moments, Ahern's strategy was an unquestioned success as the police response, with assistance from Yale officials and students, and even some Black Panthers, defused potential violence wherever and whenever it threatened.

"We watch mass confrontations like spectators at games," Ahern recalled in *Police in Trouble*. "The moment when rocks and bottles fly across no-man's-land and fall into police lines, we film, we write in notebooks, and we remember. The moment when police charge and shoot tear gas or fire their guns we also keep. The moment they do nothing—when they stand gauging the dangers and weighing all the complex factors of their responsibility—is not capturable. The moment when they act well is lost."

Ahern's words were prophetic. On May 4, mere days after his officers triumphed, demonstrating the restraint of referees and shunning confrontation, Ohio National Guardsmen were pulled away from a violent clash with striking teamsters and marched onto the Kent State University campus with bayonets still fixed to their loaded rifles to confront students protesting the invasion of Cambodia. Thirteen students were gunned down—four of them died. Several had nothing to do with the protest.

The crisis in police leadership in Canada came to a head in 2006 when the commissioners of the Royal Canadian Mounted Police and the Ontario Provincial Police resigned within months of each other. To understand why, we need to examine the roots of the problem.

Prime Minister Brian Mulroney's 1987 appointment of Norman Inkster as RCMP commissioner is well remembered by some who shared their predictions around the water coolers in farflung detachments and in the offices of the federal Solicitor General. There was widespread speculation that the new appointee was lobbying to have his position become a deputy ministership, which most believed would undermine the independence of the office and effectively result in the Mounties' relinquishing their traditional investigative independence. The Mounties soon found themselves in the absurd position of having to advise anyone on the Hill they intended to investigate.

As one former investigator recalled: "The need to keep Parliament informed came in three forms. One was an almost daily briefings to the Deputy Criminal Ops or the commissioner of what the investigative unit was working on which in turn formed the basis of briefings of the Solicitor General or the Prime Minister's Office. Second, any Information to obtain a search warrant had to be presented in advance to the Speaker of the House of Commons. This turned out to be really important as it turns out for most if not all warrants we didn't actually search we were simply presented with the material we had asked for in the information to obtain. Turns out for years we were not getting what we asked for because most of the documentation related to Parliament had ceremonial names. You could describe the document to a tee and still not get it because you did not use the right name. You received nothing and no explanation or help as to what was required. That ended when the legal counsel for Parliament (an old Liberal appointment) gave us a list of the correct names. We used them for a warrant on two particular Conservative MPs and the speaker almost fell off his chair. A few months later, Parliament passed a law precluding the RCMP from doing financial investigations without their authority and the legal counsel was fired."

There were other concerns for the Mounties. New management styles and buzzwords were replacing actual operations as the police were lumped in with the trendy private-sector business plans to downsize, rightsize, and eventually capsize. Front-line officers were increasingly frustrated and resentful. Criteria for promotions rested less heavily on years of service and career record, replaced by new "enlightened" management techniques and priorities—often bilingualism—pushing many to the edge of revolt.

This was the culture Phil Murray inherited when he replaced Inkster as commissioner in 1994. Things were about to get worse as word spread across RCMP divisions that the Mounties were to be included in the federal government's recently announced wage freeze for the federal public service. This process had begun under Progressive Conservative prime minister Brian Mulroney and continued under his Liberal successor, Jean Chrétien. Coupled with a new promotion system that greatly diminished operational experience as a key to advancement, revolt began to simmer in the ranks. The Mounties expected their new commissioner to fight the inclusion. Murray agreed to meet with the distraught officers, unaware just how badly morale had soured or of the open revolt that awaited him.

Mounties posted elsewhere across Canada describe E Division as "Texas"—big, brash, and loud. The first meeting with their divisional representatives (the RCMP, unlike any other police force in Canada, was forbidden by statute from having an association for collective bargaining) to hear what was happening and what, if anything, could be done to stop it, had to be rescheduled as the chosen venue could not handle the overflow crowd. Two weeks later, more than 1,000 angry Mounties from Surrey and nearby detachments descended on Shannon Hall, lining up at the two microphones set up at the front and rear of the hall. In the crowd was Jane Hall, one of the first women to join the RCMP in the mid-1970s, who had been recently promoted to corporal. As she recalls in her memoir, *The Red Wall: A Woman in the RCMP*, "Rank did not matter that night. Thirty-five year staff sergeants stood beside two-year constables. We were still a troop of one."

The commanding officer of E Division and the officer in charge of Surrey were invited to attend; the media showed up, but were sequestered outside the meeting. Hall records that the Mounties appreciated the honesty of the presentation, if not the message, but even those willing to fall on their swords for the good of the bankrupt country drew the line at freezing incremental raises. Junior constables stood to lose the most because they would not receive pay increases as they rose in rank to first-class constables. In a show of solidarity, senior officers appeared to accept their lot, but made it clear, as they lined up at the microphones, that they expected their superiors to fight for the junior members whose salaries didn't match the cost of living in the most expensive housing market in Canada. They also expected management to resist the new promotion system that gave precedence to political gamesmanship and language skills, so common to working in Ottawa, which many members believed fast-tracked francophone officers with little or no time in the field over years of service and actual investigative accomplishments. The unhappy veteran officers at the meeting believed that the new system clearly undermined operational excellence—and they wanted headquarters to fix that.

The second meeting was held at the North Surrey Senior Secondary High School auditorium on June 9, 1994, and drew an even larger crowd than the first meeting. Early optimism that Murray and his onstage entourage represented sufficient clout to at least modify the new promotion standards faded as it became evident that Inkster's heir apparent, who had been appointed but not yet sworn in as commissioner, thought he was there to discuss another local issue. Frustration and tensions rose as Mountie after Mountie spoke into the microphone, and the police sensed that Murray and his contingent failed to understand their point, responding with what Hall calls "warm and fuzzy" platitudes. The room fell silent as everyone in the crowd seemed to realize the magnitude of the irreconcilable differences that separated them.

Finally, an unnamed staff sergeant, described by Hall as "well-respected" addressed Murray: "Sir, you have inherited a demoralized, fractured force." Speaking his mind freely, and accepting that his career was probably over, he turned his back to the senior officers from headquarters, imploring the young constables to decide what they wanted from the RCMP. The staff sergeant concluded with apparent respectful insubordination, advising those on-stage: "It is time for you to leave, sirs."

No one moved or spoke.

The staff sergeant repeated his suggestion.

Hall recalled the moment, writing that one Mountie rose and began clapping a slow cadence. Others followed spontaneously until the entire auditorium stood shoulder to shoulder, clapping and singing in unison: "*Na-na-na-na, na-na-na-na, hey, hey, hey, good bye.*"

Murray led his contingent offstage without a word. Transfers and early retirements ensued for some senior divisional staff in British Columbia's E Division. The unprecedented event, Hall wrote, could not have been imagined ten years earlier. But membership discontent did not stop there. A decade later, through public hearings and commissioned studies, the much-vaunted Royal Canadian Mounted Police were shown to be a broken culture in dire need of repair. In June 2007, David Brown, former head of the Ontario Securities Commission, reported a host of internal allegations of possible violations of the *RCMP Act*, the *Public Service Staff Relations Act* and the *Criminal Code of Canada*, prompting the *Globe and Mail* to editorialize: "Mr. Brown focuses on the paramilitary way the RCMP is run, with members required to obey every lawful order of a superior officer, however questionable, without suggesting the order might be flawed. Blowing the whistle has been a quick ticket to demotion or transfer. If the force's senior executive committee had had any 'challenge function,' rather than meekly accepting Mr. Zaccardelli's edicts, the RCMP might have been spared this present ordeal."

The former commissioner also found himself at the centre of the storm raised by retired staff sergeant Ron Lewis and a small cadre of colleagues who doggedly followed the money in the RCMP pension and insurance fund scandal, ultimately setting the stage for David Brown's damning reports with their testimony to Parliament's powerful all-party Public Accounts Committee. Autocratic leadership was cited in virtually every woe endured by the Mounties.

By contrast, in his memoir, *Soldiers Made Me Look Good*, Major General (ret'd) Lewis Mackenzie identifies leadership as the ability to get people to do what they don't necessarily want to do—and enjoy the experience. His top-ten skills of a good leader are:

1. Being yourself
2. Leading by wandering about
3. Listening
4. Setting difficult, but achievable objectives
5. Accepting responsibility
6. Thinking outside the box
7. Striving for ethical decision making
8. Having the courage to disagree
9. Preparing and training your subordinates
10. Being an actor

Mackenzie believes that all these abilities contribute to the ultimate encompassing leadership trait: approachability.

What is truly remarkable in a book about soldiering and dedicated to soldiers, written by a man who hails from an era as a young soldier when local troops showed up with brass knuckles and belt-buckled fists to help the outnumbered local police deal with a biker problem, is that Mackenzie's prime example of leadership is a police story. In 1982, as an International Fellow studying for a year at the U.S. Army's War College, an American colonel persuaded Mackenzie to help him conduct a field study at a New York Police Department (NYPD) precinct in Harlem. There had been more murders there the previous year than were committed in all of Canada—all but one involved nomadic, nocturnal drug traffickers. If Mackenzie felt he knew what leadership was, it was there that he confirmed what it looked like.

Mackenzie found the precinct a depressing environment. The police viewed themselves as cogs in the "revolving door" justice system: arrested users had no rehab programs that they could attend, voluntarily or otherwise, and so were often released. Pushers who could afford good legal counsel could return to business as usual.

On their final day at the precinct, the police invited the soldiers out for a farewell drink—a classic smoker, with plainclothes cops (marking them as detectives) swathed in a shroud of tobacco clouds. A thirty-five-year-old detective at the event told him a story that Mackenzie still vividly recalls.

The young detective, unlike most of his colleagues, had moved his family into the area when he was first posted to the precinct in 1979. One day while riding the elevator with his wife and two young children up to their tenth-floor apartment after a shopping trip, they were joined by a "scruffy" man.

"When he saw me—and perhaps recognized me," the young police officer told Mackenzie, "I'll never know—he pulled out a pistol and shot at me."

The scruffy man missed. The detective did not: "A split second later, I shot him three times and killed him in front of my family."

Mackenzie asked if he was paid extra. No, the cop told him. He was paid the same amount as someone his rank directing traffic in downtown Manhattan. Mackenzie was stunned.

"Look, Detective," Mackenzie observed, "one of your colleagues told me less than five minutes ago that you'd just asked for a two-year extension with this precinct. In God's name, why?"

Mackenzie recalls the detective smiled, rose on his toes, and scanned the room until he located a man standing in a distant corner with a handful of others. Mackenzie described the man as "short, overweight, balding, disheveled and smoking a massive cigar, which I discovered later kept him permanently covered in ash."

The young detective identified the man as his boss and explained, "I'll do anything to keep working for him, no matter where he goes or what he does. And he is going to be here for another two years."

As a career soldier attaining general-officer status, Mackenzie was well versed in leadership traits. And whether you're a soldier, a cop, or a captain of industry, leaders have a knack of paving the way and others just tend to follow. Those who rise through the ranks on the backs and shoulders of their subordinates are the antithesis of leadership, and the consequences of that are documented in a 1978 book entitled *Crisis in Command: Mismanagement in the Army*.

Co-authors Richard Gabriel, then a major in the U.S. Army reserves, and Paul Savage, a retired army lieutenant colonel, concluded with great precision how the American army officer corps had failed miserably in Vietnam. There were stellar exceptions, of course, but overall performance had been abysmal. To their credit, the authors offered possible solutions, including an Officer's Code of Honor:

- The nature of any command is a moral charge which places each officer at the center of ethical responsibility.
- An officer's sense of moral integrity is at the center of his leadership effectiveness. The advancement of one's career is never justified at the expense of violating one's sense of honor.
- Every officer holds a special position of moral trust and responsibility. No officer will ever violate that trust or avoid his responsibility for any of his actions regardless of the personal cost.
- An officer's first loyalty is to the welfare of his command. He will never allow his men to be misused or abused in any way.
- An officer will never require his men to endure hardships or suffer dangers to which he is unwilling to expose himself. Every officer must openly share the burdens of risk and sacrifice to which his men are exposed.
- An officer is first and foremost a leader of men. He must lead his men by example and personal actions. He cannot manage his command to effectiveness ... they must be led; an officer must therefore set the standard for personal bravery and leadership.
- An officer will never execute an order which he regards to be ethically wrong, and he will report all orders, policies, or actions to appropriate authorities.
- No officer will willfully conceal any act of his superiors, subordinates or peers, that violates his sense of ethics.
- No officer will punish, allow the punishment of, or in any way discriminate against a subordinate or peer for telling the truth about any matter.
- All officers are responsible for the actions of all their brother officers. The dishonorable acts of one officer diminish the

corps; the actions of the officer corps are only determined by the acts of its members and those actions must always be above reproach.[1]

Gabriel and Savage also addressed the question of what makes a good officer and suggested criteria for selecting the "best men for the right job":

- Distrust any officer with a perfect or near perfect record of efficiency reports. He is conforming to the existing value system and will have no interest in changing it.
- Look carefully at a man who gets low marks on "tact" and who "deviates from accepted doctrine." He may be creative.
- An officer who gets low marks on loyalty is especially valuable, for he is unwilling to acquiesce in his superior's policies without debate. He is likely to have an independent mind.
- Be suspicious of any officer who has accumulated awards for valor without having sustained any physical injury. Trust a Purple Heart wearer.
- Distrust any officer who has had "all his tickets punched" and who sports an array of staff awards on his chest. He is likely to be a manager playing the system.
- Distrust all officers who use "buzz words" and who have a poor vocabulary. They tend to be managers of the most obsequious type. True leadership is likely to be foreign to them.
- Trust a man who heads for the sounds of the guns and who has repeated tours of combat and command at all unit levels; it is preferable that he have only minimal exposure to staff work.
- Trust an officer who was seen by his men in combat and whose command performed well and showed low rates of drug use, fragging (the wounding or killing of an unpopular officer in the field by his troops), body counting, etc.
- Search for the officer whose readiness reports indicates a high percentage of equipment which is deficient. He is a man addicted to the truth.[2]

Not all such military applications translate as well or easily to policing. However, there is a clear message in the above criteria that those in command are responsible for the welfare of their subordinates; that those with great power must look after the needs of those with less authority. That's not always the case in policing. Mackenzie, the retired major-general, also notes a key difference between military and police commands: it is safer to be a Canadian general officer criticizing the United Nations in distant New York City than for a police chief to quarrel with his mayor. Moreover, according to Mackenzie, no military commander has ever had to deal with a members' association as they do in policing. Yet both police and military recruits are invariably all volunteers. In fact, no police officer has ever been conscripted, as troops were during both world wars. Police officers have always joined their profession because they want to, never because they have to. The presence of an association does not excuse a superior officer from being responsible for those on the front lines. There should be a moral imperative for senior officers to monitor and ensure, as much as possible, the welfare and safety of their troops and constables, just as any manager in the private sector remains responsible for his or her staff.

In many ways, *Crisis in Command* provides common ground for the military and the police in an era when they seem to be switching roles. Policing in Canada became more militaristic with the creation of the first tactical-response teams in the wake of the kidnapping and mass murder of Israeli athletes by Palestinian thugs at the 1972 Munich Olympic Games. At the same time, our military earned an international reputation for its prowess in peacekeeping. Today, our troops in Afghanistan are trying to defeat the Taliban insurgency by winning the hearts and minds of the local population, doing everything they can to avoid inflicting civilian casualties, and spending more time with the locals to win their trust and respect. It marks the third stage in regaining trust for the Canadian Forces, preceded by reconnecting with troops, then all Canadians. As former chief of defence staff Rick Hillier (ret'd.) recalls in his 2009 memoir, *A Soldier First: Bullets, Bureaucrats and the Politics of War,* "The perception across the junior ranks was that we, the leaders, had broken faith those we led."

The military may have been even harder hit than the Mounties by the 1994 federal wage freeze as it came at a time when our forces were facing a crushing increase in United Nations– and NATO-sanctioned international missions. The police are increasingly being seconded to international peacekeeping missions, further depleting their front lines but saving their departments a lot of money as their salaries are covered by another police force or agency, such as the United Nations. But in the fallout of recent events, even the can-do Mounties are pushing a little harder for their rights.

An unintended consequence of the recent reviews of the RCMP—the sole police force in Canada denied a professional association by government legislation—was the court ruling in early 2009 that such denial violated their charter rights. But no court order can substitute for leadership that abandons its rank-and-file members. It then falls to the association to act. That seemed to be the case during the initial days of the Native land claims protests in Caledonia, where the Ontario Provincial Police Association accused Commissioner Gwen Boniface and her cohorts of sacrificing their officers to preserve the image of the force. At least one detachment formally voted "no confidence" in their leader. Over time, even the citizens of Caledonia, initially dismayed and upset by the lack of OPP resolve to enforce the law when Natives began digging up the highway, which the community insisted had nothing to do with the land-claims issue, turned their wrath from the officers in the field and put it squarely on Boniface and her headquarters staff in Orillia.

When her resignation was announced on July 26, 2006, the media initially reported that she would stay on the job until October before assuming her new role as one of the top three police veterans hired to oversee the Garda, Ireland's national police force. The Ontario government also denied her resignation had anything to do with her response to the Native land-claim occupation at Caledonia. Perhaps, but she clearly had not resigned to protest government intrusion or obstruction. Nor had Zaccardelli. But there was precedent for that with the Mounties, dating to the earliest days of what was then the North West Mounted Police. The RCMP Directorate of History at national headquarters in Ottawa confirms that between 1876 and 1886, three of the earliest commissioners of the North West Mounted Police—George Arthur French, James Farquharson Macleod, CMG, and Acheson Gosford Irvine—all resigned, at least the first two resignations believed to be over disputes with Ottawa concerning government's meddling with the Force.

In 1959, Leonard Hanson Nicholson became the fourth RCMP commissioner to resign when Ottawa refused a request from the Newfoundland government for police reinforcements at a logging strike. Nicholson didn't quit because he believed the police should break the strike, but because he "had always operated with a clear recognition that the province was responsible for law enforcement within its own borders and that these things were not subject to control from Ottawa."

Zaccardelli, the fifth to resign, had been on the hot seat in several areas, including the membership pension funds scandal and the Mahar Arar case, in which a Canadian citizen claimed he was surrendered by the Mounties to U.S. authorities, who shipped him to Syria where he was imprisoned and allegedly tortured. What wasn't analyzed nearly as closely by the media was the appointment of outsiders to take command of the RCMP and OPP. Was it lack of talent in the wings? A desire for a fresh approach by an outsider? Or simply an effort to tighten the leash on the police? Ontario premier Dalton McGuinty's Liberal government had seemed happy with Boniface's performance. In fact, the government had recently renewed her contract. The situation was all a bit curious. Boniface had never campaigned to become commissioner; had never sought the office. And yet, there she was—the first woman to command such a major police force. Her appointment broke with another OPP tradition: historically, commissioners came from the investigative side, normally having done a stint in the Criminal Investigation Bureau (CIB). That should have made Wayne Frechette, a proven investigator and former CIB head, the logical choice for the appointment. When Boniface got the job, Frechette moved down the road from the OPP Orillia headquarters to become police chief in nearby Barrie. Several members of an OPP elite Tactics and Rescue Unit followed a short time later.

Many saw Boniface's departure as an opportunity for Deputy Commissioner Jay Hope to become the first black OPP commissioner. As acting commissioner, his effort to calm rising tensions in the Native land-claims standoff in Caledonia consisted of a statement that ran as part of a *Globe and Mail* article, which reported that Haldimand County mayor Marie Trainer was prepared to declare a state of emergency in response to a planned rally she feared would turn violent. McGuinty had already confirmed that his government would not intervene. Hope's prepared release stated that police were "well prepared to deal with any situation that may arise as a result of this weekend's anticipated rally," adding that the OPP would not allow the "hard work and commitment to ensuring a long lasting and peaceful resolution to be derailed."[3]

Such vague assurance may have been a wake-up call to Trainer and any other elected official who believed the OPP are *their* contract police force. Whatever the terms of their contracts, Hope's words and inaction left no doubt that Orillia headquarters, not locally elected officials, would call the shots on police deployments— just as Mounties anywhere in Canada ultimately report to headquarters in Ottawa, not to locally elected officials who have contracted their services.

As deputy commissioner, Hope had been responsible for Native affairs. No one disputes that he "oversaw" the OPP role there, but no one can recall ever seeing him actually show up in Caledonia. There certainly seems to be no public or media account of his presence. Boniface did attend the scene, perhaps precluding Hope's presence. No matter. None of this seemed to tarnish his chances at the brass ring. Then, incredibly to most police observers and the cops themselves, McGuinty announced that Julian Fantino, the controversial career city cop, would leave his job as head of Ontario's Emergency Management agency to serve as the new OPP commissioner. Hope got Fantino's old job where he would be expected to co-ordinate the provincial response to a declared emergency and times of crisis.

Giuliano Zaccardelli, a self-confessed autocrat, fared less well as RCMP commissioner. On December 6, 2006, he submitted his resignation letter to Prime Minister Stephen Harper, citing the fallout over the Arar case. Zaccardelli's resignation was immediately accepted, followed by a public statement from Harper, which praised the RCMP as one of Canada's "most respected and important institutions," adding: "It is important that the men and women of the RCMP know that they continue to have the full confidence of the Government of Canada as they work tirelessly to keep Canadians safe and secure."

Beverley Busson's appointment as RCMP commissioner quickly proved just how much could be accomplished in a very short time if you had the right person at the top. Although the media chronicled her place in history as the first female RCMP commissioner, there was a sense that Busson was being dismissed as a mere caretaker commissioner. That may have been unfair. She acted quickly and firmly to address the lingering problems associated with the RCMP pension and insurance fund scandals, rewarding those few who had persevered to uncover the accounting irregularities—some of them at great personal and professional cost. Mountie insiders also swore that Busson had been offered the post of commissioner earlier by Prime Minister Jean Chrétien, but had turned it down for personal reasons, opening the door to Zaccardelli.

Busson's appearance gave the Mounties new hope for the future. They had no idea that their tradition of appointing their commissioner from within the ranks had run its course. In 2007, Harper named William Elliott, a career pubic servant, to the post—the first civilian commissioner in the history of the Royal Canadian Mounted Police. There were widespread grumblings among the RCMP membership that a perceived crisis in command had just been made worse. Others worried that Elliott's appointment was a blatant political ploy to gain even more civilian control over an already short arm's-length relationship between police and politicians. While the jury is still out on that decision at the time of this writing, there may be a hopeful precedent. Lawyer Eric Silk had served long ago as commissioner of the OPP and there were old-timers who swore he might have been the best they ever had. His service, which included surviving a provincial Commission of Inquiry by Justice Campbell Grant into alleged links between the OPP and organized crime, is commemorated at Orillia headquarters where the OPP library bears his name.

On June 16, 2007, Elliott transmitted his first "rally the troops" email:

> The Royal Canadian Mounted Police is a proud organization with a history stretching back almost to Confederation. I am deeply honoured to become a member of the RCMP and to take on my responsibilities as the 22nd Commissioner.
>
> Much has been made of what distinguishes me from my predecessors and from the other men and women who serve as regular members of the RCMP. More important is what unites us: a commitment to protecting and serving Canadians and providing them with the best possible police service.
>
> My first priority is to support the women and men of the RCMP, who provide exemplary and essential services to communities across Canada. My first order of business is to meet and talk with you to discuss your priorities and concerns. I began this important work last week when I met with Commissioner Busson and the RCMP's Senior Executive Committee and with the National Executive Committee of the Staff Relations Representative Program.
>
> I recognize the importance of gaining a better understanding of the important work you do. I want to hear your concerns and answer your questions. I'll have questions for you as well, and I look forward to our discussions. I am committed to visiting detachments, offices and work places across the country as often as possible, and commit to doing so, at the very least, twice a month, beginning immediately.
>
> As one of my first acts as Commissioner, I am very pleased to announce that Deputy Commissioner Bill Sweeney, has agreed to leave his current position as Deputy

Commissioner, North West Region, on a temporary basis, to take on an assignment in Ottawa.

This assignment will be for an initial period of up to eight months. During this period, Deputy Commissioner Sweeney will provide invaluable assistance to me in my new role as Commissioner. Bill will play a key role in relation to operational matters. He will also work with me and with the senior executive committee to lead our efforts in relation to the task force the government is establishing to study RCMP issues, including governance and organizational issues.

I am committed to working as hard as I can to carry out my responsibilities as a member of the RCMP and as Commissioner, to respect and demonstrate the values of the RCMP, and to live up to the highest standards and the proud history and traditions of the RCMP.

With your help, I am confident we will make the RCMP an even stronger and more effective national police service. I thank you for your ongoing efforts, and for your service to the Force and to Canada. I look forward with enthusiasm to a bright future together.

William J.S. Elliott
Commissioner

Many Mounties had thought Sweeney would be the next commissioner, just as many OPP had expected Frechette to lead them. But it likely matters less who is named top cop anywhere than who is the political power standing behind him or her. There may be a valuable lesson for the police to learn from the military experience, where command officers believe that not only are they accountable to their civilian overseers, but also to their troops. It has become fashionable for police to distance themselves from their paramilitary roots, calling themselves a "service" rather than a "force" (except the Mounties who are a Force under the *RCMP Act*). They have adopted buzzwords like "community policing" for programs that seem ill defined and difficult to measure for success, and boast of mandates and values and mission statements, none of which seem to mention catching bad guys. And they pride themselves on their recruiting efforts to become more representative of the communities they are sworn to serve and protect. Most commonly, that means creating outreach programs to attract more women, visible minorities, and First Nations recruits.

The military also seeks to be representative, but in a broader context. Unlike the police, and their well-intentioned outreach programs to attract non-traditional applicants, the Canadian Forces reach out continue to appeal to *all* Canadians to enlist in the armed forces. Their priority is to reflect the values of the society they serve and protect in Canada and abroad. In his memoir, Hillier writes, "[W]e had lost contact with Canadians, and if we were going to survive, [we] had to win back their respect.... That recruitment had to be done from a basis of credibility." As historian David Bercuson writes in *Generalship and the Art of the Admiral: Perspectives on Canadian Senior Military Leadership*, for a military to effectively serve "a dynamic and creative" society like Canada, "it must mirror the talent, creativity, ambition, drive, educational achievement and technological competence, even the humanitarianism of that society. If a military is properly organized, administered and led, then the goal of keeping the armed forces and society united is achievable. From the recruitment process to the system of promotion to the highest ranks of general officers, selecting and educating leaders is the key to that objective because the higher a man or woman is in rank, the greater is his or her potential impact on the process of ensuring that the military evolves in parallel with society."

That goes beyond the apparent police and political preference to equate representation with perpetrating racial and gender profiling at the recruitment, and, some argue, promotion stages. If the police are not truly representative of society's values, they risk becoming occupiers rather than liberators or protectors. While the military trains its rising stars at staff college, the police send theirs to places like the Police Leadership Program, touted as the only MBA-style program in Canada. Developed jointly by the Ontario

Association of Chiefs of Police and the University of Toronto's Rotman School of Management, the intensive course offers a customized curriculum that covers strategy, financial management, human resources, leadership, police-service delivery, community knowledge, political astuteness, and communications—all deemed to be key to police-service succession planning. The program appears to be limited to commissioned officer ranks of inspector and higher, causing some in the ranks to suggest that it should also be offered to sergeants and staff sergeants who are the heart of the chain of command in policing and the military. The classic test for police leadership is whether those in charge will prioritize officer safety above budgetary concerns, perhaps simply by spending the money to call someone in on overtime to provide timely backup. Failure to do that can create what internationally renowned management consultant Eli Sopow has termed "corporate personality disorder"— a situation where good people are crushed by poor leadership and bad planning and policies.

In June 2007, the British Columbia Organizational Development Network (BCODN) reported on Sopow's case study, entitled "The RCMP as an Emotional Organization" in its June newsletter. The BCODN is an online community for organizational development practitioners employed by private industry, non-profit organizations, and government agencies. Sopow's study confirmed that a culture shift was under way within the Mounties, known, like most law enforcement agencies, as a "para-militaristic, command-and-control entity." Now, he reported, the RCMP is exploring how best to engage their employees in the workplace—not just to learn how to motivate them to perform well, but to "understand" what they need to do to excite their personnel about their jobs. That approach is a far cry from the traditional, even historic, structure common to all police and paramilitary agencies where superiors barked orders and underlings jumped into immediate action with no questions asked.

Sopow's provincewide research, which began in January 2007, focused on gaps between public, client, and staff involving the RCMP, their contract municipalities, and the front-line officers who actually policed the communities. The research was conducted through public and personnel surveys of all parties, one of which focused on how the Mounties felt about their workplace as a source of "emotional and knowledge fulfillment." Managers were surveyed in May on how they would rate themselves on predefined emotional and knowledge factors that help measure their leadership abilities. Knowledge factors included active listening, active sharing of information, personal accountability, and sharing of power. There was a good response as 120 of 150 "leaders" completed the online survey, suggesting, Sopow wrote, "a strong commitment by RCMP organizational leaders and managers to further explore their own leadership attributes and create the climate for culture change on an organizational level."

This shift within Mountie management persuaded Sopow that organization development "was on the radar." It had since become a standing strategic objective that influences the RCMP's larger strategic plan. Fairly early in his research, Sopow detected what front-line officers needed to feel "engaged" in their work and workplace. Key themes included:

- Where personnel would get information is not necessarily the most preferred source. Most RCMP personnel get their information from colleagues, but would prefer that senior levels of the organization provide it.
- Recognition, professional development, and personal satisfaction with one's job are key factors that foster engagement in the workplace.
- Balancing a work and personal life may or may not make a difference in workplace performance or the ability to influence others.[4]

Staff were also asked if leadership:

- Recognized the knowledge and emotional needs of staff.
- Demonstrated emotional intelligence indicative of a changing workplace.
- Demonstrated the emotional skill required to lead effectively.[5]

Sopow insists that without both engaged employees and leaders, you cannot effect change within an organization. Improved emotional traits for a manager would also improve their leadership style and key leadership attributes, which he views as being "indicative of a learning organization."

"By developing a leader's emotional skill, [the Mounties] will be able to help engage employees in the workplace," Sopow concluded, noting that his interim findings have enabled the RCMP in British Columbia to recognize opportunities to change their overall structural model.

Proactive steps were already being taken to involve employees in the organizational development process to help make the RCMP a better place to work. In other words, change, ideally improvement, was based on consultation with everyone affected—staff and management.

"Together," Sopow wrote of the next steps, "staff and leaders will also look at short- and long-term wins, and how structural issues in the organization can be changed in the long term. Staff across the organization will also work together on strategic planning to determine how to move the recommendations from the research forward."

The study's findings seem even more relevant in light of the Brown reports, which called for immediate action to fix the demoralized Mounties. Ironically, further evidence suggests that the police can learn from the military experience, which seems to be modifying its traditional "command and control" mindset to a more inclusive "consultation and collaboration" structure—a system that may bring women to the fore. There is evidence to suggest that women may be better supervisors than men. In his presentation to the 2008 National Forum on Women in Policing, held in Ottawa, Sopow cited the findings of a wide range of empirical surveys that show women are better at empathizing, listening, conciliation, networking, communicating, team building, and emotional awareness.

The last point may be the greatest challenge to traditional police structure, which has traditionally been based on knowledge, not emotion. Yet that is the strongest trait Sopow identified for police leadership to adapt to its new challenges and changing demands and external expectations, concluding: "In general, women are more intrinsically aligned with 'emotional intelligence' than males."

So, why are there so few women at the top?

It may be simply that many don't want the job, at least not at the price historically exacted from them to rise through the ranks in policing or the private sector. Many policewomen seem to eschew the privileges and power of rank because of the demands that can impact heavily on a healthy lifestyle. Interestingly, their priority for finding balance in their lives seems to have been embraced by both men and women in the latest generations to enter policing. The days of blind obedience are gone as many new recruits seek answers to the reasons for their assignments, and for their superiors' expectations, and try to understand where exactly they fit into the plan. In the extreme, some may even wonder what's in it for them.

Retired Mountie and author Jane Hall has applied a number of academic studies to her own experiences as a former policewoman. On July 15, 2008, she presented her findings to the International Consortium for Public Safety Leadership, in Tallahassee, Florida, in a speech called "Changing the Face of Leadership from within: Gender Differences in Leadership Styles."

Defining "positional leadership" as a person's ability to influence his or her organization by virtue of rank, she immediately cited the "looming leadership crisis" in Canadian policing, with up to 50 per cent of existing executives (positional leaders) due to retire. Ever the optimist, Hall sees the crisis as an "unprecedented opportunity to rethink" who should replace them. Noting the lack of women in these positions, particularly in larger police departments, she asked: "Have large policing agencies in Canada been operating on traditional male assumptions of motivation, values and ethics resulting in an under-representation of females as positional leaders?" If so, "What can be done to correct the imbalance?"

Noting that Vancouver City Police, which hired their first woman in 1912, is now 21.61 per cent female, Hall observed that 24.25 per cent are constables, but only 2.8 per cent at the officer level—a lone female at the lowest commissioned-officer rank. By contrast, in the

RCMP, her old employer, which hired their first female regular members in 1974, women now account for 19.7 per cent of the Force, 23 per cent of whom are constables. Men make up the 92.3 per cent of superintendents and higher ranks. Is that situation due to sexism or is it that women simply aren't interested in promotion? Hall cites British sociologist Catherine Hakim's conclusion that female employees can be divided into three categories: 20 per cent are career oriented; 60 to 80 per cent are "adaptive"; and 20 per cent are home centred.

"The 20 per cent who are career oriented are the ones who don't get distracted by marriage and/or children; and even if they do have children, they often cut their maternity leave short to return to work," Hall explained. "They will hide health problems, even heart attacks and a cancer diagnosis, because it will negatively impact careers.

"The 20 per cent who are home centred focus on success in their private lives. If they work, it is an end to a means, not a means to an end.

"The 60 to 80 [per cent] majority, the adaptives, are looking for balance between family and work ... happy doing meaningful work so long as they don't sacrifice their children or families on the altar of their career ambitions."

Conceding that career-oriented women can shift their priorities if they start a family, Hall confirmed that the adaptives are most likely to voluntarily self-limit their careers or want out at one point, at least for a while. This majority of females and a growing minority of male professionals seek a healthy work-life balance. That's certainly not unique to policing. Hall cited the experience of Deloitte and Touche. In 1991, the international accounting firm employed about 29,000 people in the United States and a total of 95,000 worldwide, but only 5 per cent of corporate partners were women. Despite hiring more women, only 8 per cent of the new candidates promoted to partner were female. A task force determined that most women were leaving the company before they were qualified to become partner—and that they were leaving in droves, roughly 33 per cent annually. But they weren't leaving the workforce, just the company, citing their lack of interest in an eighty-hour workweek or a male-dominated work culture. The company began offering new workshops and training, flexible workweeks, and reduced travel expectations. The result was that by 2000, in less than a decade, the number of female partners had risen to 14 per cent and the turnover dropped for women and men. The changes proved that organizations could have more proportional female representation at higher levels if they made the changes to hire women.

Hall recalled the psychologists who descended on the first few female Mounties to study their stress levels and reactions, gender-specific work expectations, and occupational adjustments. Everything was monitored and documented. The most comprehensive survey of female Mounties was conducted in 1985 by the RCMP in British Columbia. In hindsight, Hall said the results supported Catherine Hakim's theory of adaptive dispositions and gender differences in career aspirations, identifying "statistically significant differences in career rank aspirations and motivations but also dissatisfaction with a work environment, which was male oriented, occasionally hostile and lacking understanding of female 'issues.'" The authors believed time would change things, but, after nearly twenty-five years, Hall said the passage of time had less effect than expected as far as changing the RCMP. To change, she told the consortium, requires knowledge and the commitment to use it.

Citing a workshop at the 2008 annual Women in Law Enforcement conference in Halifax, Hall recalled an RCMP assistant commissioner acknowledging that women were underrepresented in management and appealed to the audience for solutions.

"This was the most positive, progressive thing I have heard a senior member of the RCMP say," she observed, "since Deputy Commissioner [Thomas] Venner supported the E Division study back in 1985 by writing 'I think we should do something helpful and forward thinking.'"

In 2008, Hall sought statistics on the percentages of women at the different rank structures within the Canadian policing community to determine if the trend of bottom-heavy female percentages was consistent for police agencies outside of the RCMP. The results left her wondering if smaller police forces have done a better job adapting to female employees. Hall cited Saskatoon staff sergeant

Shelly Ballard as an example that confirmed the adaptive theory, even though Hakim's work was unknown to her, when she told the consortium: "There are several female sergeants who are certainly in a position to be able to write for S/Sgt [positions] but have chosen not to as they are enjoying the investigative positions they are in."

Hall's findings all seemed to tie in nicely with the three suggested solutions advanced by the Police Sector Council's Policing Environment 2005 survey of 184 Canadian police: 1) that three immediate challenges had to be met by new strategies to cope with up to 50 per cent of senior officers retiring by 2010; 2) that current recruitment levels would not fill the ranks; and 3) that the police were finding it hard to sell themselves as a career of choice.

Commenting on the first point, Hall remarked that the future is even bleaker when you realize that 74 per cent of serving police officers have less than fifteen years' experience—and other studies confirm that a great number have five years or less on the job.

"Public Safety work is not a 'plug and play' career," she said, noting that replacements "cannot just be hired off the street or out of a University and expected to replace a seasoned police officer's operational and cultural knowledge."

The Mounties used to sign members to five-year commitments—because that's how long it was calculated for a raw recruit to repay the RCMP for its investment of time, training, and equipment. But even if enough recruits were found today—which no police force seems to have achieved—the new blood would fill holes in the front lines, not replace the accumulated skill and knowledge losses. And how are you going to find new recruits with pay that pales compared to better-paying and less-dangerous careers in the private sector? And what about retention? Tough economic times can attract recruits to secure jobs, but will they stay when the good times return? In his memoir, Hillier freely admits that what prevented a "mass exodus" from the Canadian Forces during their most trying times of budget cuts and ill-fated missions was that the economy was slow to recover.

Hall sees no silver bullet to cure these woes, but believes the police can buy some time if they can slow the retirement rate, ensure existing staff are properly employed to match their training and skills, and attract recruits who are motivated by something other than the size of a paycheque—in other words, those for whom policing and public service are callings, not just careers.

It would also help, she adds, if organizations and employees better understood and adapted to gender differences, noting: "The answers to today's and tomorrow's problems won't be found with yesterday's thinking."

Part of the problem, Hall suggests in her presentation, is that upper managers can be unaware or indifferent to the fact that staff may already look to these lower-level employees for leadership. Management must also accept the scientific evidence that men and women learn and remember in different ways.[6] Noting that the addition of stress generally improves male scores, but has the opposite effect on female performance, she adds: "It is unclear if the women are afraid of losing; or of winning." In other words, will women pay a price for outperforming male co-workers?

Despite their differences, Hall rejects the notion that women are less intelligent, less capable, or less qualified than men to assume leadership roles, insisting that women *choose* not to pursue some leadership roles. Bev Busson's declining the offer to be named permanent RCMP commissioner underscores that point, as do similar stories about female jurists who declined the opportunity to be named the first woman to the Supreme Court of Canada. That choice plays a significant role in a woman's decision to pursue leadership positions seems more positive than the reasons for women leaving policing, which were cited in 1996. That year, roughly a generation after the first female Mounties graduated in 1974, Canadian Police College researcher Marcel-Eugène LeBeuf, reported in his paper "Three Decades of Women in Policing: A Literature Review" that it was not simply because women could not adapt or fit into police life, but that women were more likely than men to resign from policing, citing the attitudes of their male colleagues and superiors, sexual harassment, family/career conflicts, and family/maternity issues.

Today, with women accounting for approximately 20 per cent

of police officers across Canada, roughly mirroring the percentage of female federal politicians and in non-traditional jobs, it seems they've come a long way.

Maybe.

THREE

WOMEN:
You've Come a Long Way, Maybe

For the first time in my service, I had found myself on the outside of
the Red Wall with no way of getting over it ... I could continue to
throw myself at it and break completely, I could mark time and
become bitter, or I could walk away. I was looking for a fourth path.
—Jane Hall, *The Red Wall: A Woman in the RCMP*

Women were first admitted in significant numbers to the RCMP,
the OPP, and the Canadian military in 1974. The aftershocks still
resonate today.

The first female troop to report for training at RCMP Depot
Division in Regina learned quickly just how much mental toughness, courage, and physical stamina they would need to earn their
spurs. There was no free ride for them; no coddling. It is one thing
to create a policy that women will be admitted, quite another to
have everyone buy into that concept. The female cadets were
expected to excel—to pay their dues and take their lumps—along
with the male cadets, playing by rules devised by men for men.
There were, to be fair, some male officers who resisted the inclusion

of women in the Force because they simply did not want to expose the sometimes sad and dark world of police work to "the fairer sex," insisting theirs was not a job they wanted for their own wives and girlfriends and daughters. Paternalism and chauvinism were alive and well in policing.

The unspoken rule in those early days was that female officers never showed fear and males never cried. Very few ever broke that code, no matter how demanding or demeaning their circumstances, as they lived a new variation on the police reality that those first through the door confront the greatest risk. But their gruelling schedule left little time to ponder their future legacy as the women who kicked open the doors for others to follow in a traditionally male-dominated career. Their focus was just to survive the ordeal. They persevered to earn the grudging respect of their tormentors, as they would have to do again at each posting during their early career. Jane Hall recalls in *The Red Wall* that most of her female troopmates were warmly received to their first posting, but also recalls the outraged NCO who was ordered to accept a female officer over his objections. When he learned she was pregnant, he wrote to the *Pony Express*, the RCMP national newsletter, insisting she be charged under the *RCMP Act* with "conduct unbecoming" a police officer or "a self-inflicted wound" and dragged before a disciplinary service court.

Graduation was a major achievement for these young women whose mothers had few job options or career aspirations beyond teaching, nursing, the steno pool, and homemaking. Their mothers had enjoyed brief liberation during the Second World War when women were hired to fill the jobs left open by the men who had gone to war. Those who enlisted in the military were barred from combat-designated operations, although many braved danger and death in their supporting roles, most often as nurses, ambulance drivers, or even pilots ferrying aircraft to the rear lines.

There had been some good news for women in policing as they were promoted or assigned to specialty units. It had taken seven years for Diane Wright to be promoted to first female corporal in the RCMP, in 1981, the same year that Constables Chris Mackie and Joan Merk became the first women to join the Musical Ride, the RCMP link to its past as a mounted unit that tours Canada and beyond to thrill audiences with highly trained steeds performing a series of intricate formations. Seven years later, ten female corporals were training instructors at the academy. By 1988, there was also a woman in the RCMP Band, a female senior constable pilot in Air Division, and two women serving with the national recruiting team. In 1989, Corporal Patricia Anne Harrish was the first woman to command an operational detachment, at Arviat in G Division; another was appointed to the United Nations contingent in Namibia. In 1990, Sergeant Diane Pilotte was the first woman delegated to a foreign post, in Lyon, France. Two years later, Bev Busson, a graduate of the first female RCMP troop in 1974, grabbed the brass ring, to become the first woman promoted to commissioned officer as an inspector, rising to superintendent in 1996. Five years later, she was appointed the first female deputy commissioner, commanding E Division in British Columbia—home to more Mounties than any other province or territory—and would become the first woman to head the federal force when Giuliano Zaccardelli resigned in 2006.

Such recognition was not restricted to the RCMP. Liz Scout became the first female police chief in Canada when she was named to head the Blood Tribe Police in Alberta, in 1988. She was followed by two women from rural Ontario: Lenna Bradburn, who was appointed chief in Guelph, in 1993, and Christine Silverberg, who was the first woman to lead a major police department, assuming her role in Calgary in 1995. More recently, Inspector Kathryn Martin, a twenty-four-year veteran of the Toronto police, was promoted in February 2009 to head the fifth-largest homicide squad in North America—a position that launched Julian Fantino and his successor, Bill Blair, to chief of police. And, for good measure, Commander Josée Kurtz became the first woman to take the helm of a major Canadian warship, HMCS *Halifax*, in April 2009.

So what's changed? Is policing better today? It's certainly changed, and one of the greatest changes is recounted in the report of the 1997 federal Commission of Inquiry into the Deployment of Canadian Forces in Somalia and retired Mountie Jane Hall's 2007 memoir, *The Red Wall*. Both offer compelling evidence that while male Mounties and soldiers may resent the presence of female colleagues as an additional burden to protect, the presence of women amongst their ranks can also have a calming and settling influence in a hostile confrontation. Physical force can be less often the first response. So how were these discoveries being applied to policing?

The most recent effort to check the pulse of women in policing was the National Forum on Women in Policing held in Ottawa in mid-October 2008 to address "key obstacles through proven models." Organized by Vancouver's Summit Institute, the two-day event drew scores of female police officers from forces across Canada to hear the who's who of well-known speakers ranging from retired and serving senior officers to civilians expert in police issues. There were reasons to question just how far women had advanced in policing over the preceding decades. Among those with concerns was Ottawa deputy police chief Sue O'Sullivan, who co-chaired the forum with RCMP superintendent Shirley Cuillierrier. Just fourteen months earlier, when O'Sullivan had been the acting chief in Ottawa during the search for a replacement for former chief Vince Bevan, an internal members' survey had indicated that harassment and discrimination were still too prevalent in her workplace. It seemed debatable just how much progress women had made since Canadian Police College researcher Marcel-Eugène LeBeuf had reported his 1996 findings that women were leaving policing because they could not adapt to the life.

The Ottawa police results made headline news in April 2007 when the majority of the 921 officers who completed the online survey (well over half the 1,750 invited to participate, including eight out of ten women) claimed to have experienced or witnessed such bad behaviour over the preceding four years:

- 52 per cent had experienced sexual harassment or discrimination.
- 54 per cent had experienced personal harassment or discrimination.

- 28 per cent had witnessed sexual or personal harassment or discrimination.
- More than eight in ten women and six in ten men had experienced either type of harassment or discrimination.
- Only 13 per cent of victims reported the harassment to managers.

That final statistic may have actually been the most disturbing, as less than half of respondents felt safe reporting the harassment or discrimination to their superiors; only one-third were satisfied with how management responded to complaints of harassment and discrimination.

The survey also confirmed a lack of confidence in senior management in other areas:

- 15 per cent agreed and more than 50 per cent disagreed that promotions and transfer decisions are made on the basis of individual skills and experience.
- 80 per cent did not agree that senior management follows through on promises made to members.
- 40 per cent disagreed that senior management's decision-making processes are transparent.

Respondents overwhelmingly claimed to love their job, but little more than 50 per cent believed they received the training and resources to do it properly:

- 83 per cent were satisfied or very satisfied with their jobs.
- 87 per cent said their work unit worked well as a team.
- 64 per cent said they had adequate resources to do their job properly.
- 65 per cent said they get the training they need to do their jobs.

This was the fourth internal survey for the Ottawa police on this topic and, with eight out of ten women reporting they had experienced sexual or personal harassment in the previous four years, management was probably hoping for better results. The results clearly disappointed Police Services Board member Jim MacEwen who told the media: "This will not be tolerated in this day and age and I'm angry. I can't believe these figures. I think that's appalling, especially in a public organization like this."[1]

But Ottawa was not unique. Almost exactly a year earlier, the *Vancouver Sun*, citing an internal poll obtained through a Freedom of Information request, had reported similar results for the RCMP in British Columbia, noting "a serious gender gap" where female members were "far less likely" than male colleagues to believe their rights are respected. In the Vancouver Island district, only 36 per cent of female officers surveyed agreed that "everyone is treated fairly" compared to 60 per cent of the male officers; in the North district, less than half (46 per cent) of the women agreed that their "personal rights and values are respected" compared to 65 per cent of the men. The report also cited sexual harassment claims dating to 2002.

Robert Gordon, head of criminology at Simon Fraser University and a former police officer, told the *Sun* that women face daunting challenges in policing, explaining: "I think the role of women in policing … has always been one that has been fraught with difficulties around acceptance and an unwillingness on the part of more conservative police officers … to accept women as equals." Stating that this problem exists in all police forces, he suggested that the RCMP's strict paramilitary structure makes it "a tougher fit" for women than municipal forces like the Vancouver Police Department—the first to hire women constables in 1912. With 75 per cent of male officers versus 62 per cent of female officers in the North district agreeing that "the RCMP works to ensure that I am provided a harassment-free environment," Eli Sopow, who conducted the survey, told the *Sun* he expected those numbers would be similar across the province.

While Ottawa police trotted out a new policy to help create a more respectful workplace, the RCMP seemed to be stalled at focus groups. But the Mounties are a resilient bunch; by March 2008 they were back in the saddle and media across Canada were reporting that the federal police were actively recruiting women. Times had changed—again—but had the corporate mindset kept pace? Doubts were raised by those attending the National Forum on Women in Policing as they listened to Sopow try to assure them that sometimes those who felt underappreciated were often good employees trapped in the miasma of corporate personality disorder.

As head of organization development and research for the Pacific Region RCMP, Sopow has received three national awards from the Mounties for excellence in issues management. In 2000, he was awarded the international Howard Chase Award, presented in Washington, D.C., by the Issue Management Council. He also seems ideally situated for police research. British Columbia has the largest RCMP division in Canada (E Division), which represents a third of the total national police force. E Division provides federal, provincial, and municipal policing across the province within four districts or regions, each with a distinct work culture. There are 150 leaders and managers; staff consists of 5,900 police officers, 1,700 civilian members and public-service employees, 1,200 municipal workers, and 1,200 auxiliary constables. Sopow believes that beleaguered employees can survive and actually help revive their ailing organizations. His topic at the Ottawa forum, "Women and Organizational Climate Change in Policing," confirmed just how many external factors have an impact on organizational growth within the policing environment. Among them are legislation, public needs, news coverage, court rulings, technology, demographics, politics, and social, economic, and ecological issues.

Sopow reviewed the current policing environment from the perspectives of the public and the police then addressed trends in crime and other issues.

Eighty-five to 90 per cent of the public surveyed has a high level of trust in policing and still equates police visibility with good policing. The fear of crime is shaped chiefly by sensational media coverage, thus expectations gallop ahead of police inability to perform. This results in private security staff outnumbering sworn peace officers.

As for the police, 70 per cent have less than five years' service and 18 per cent are women, a statistic that remained unchanged over several years. Young recruits have very different expectations, seeing policing as a job as opposed to a career. Officers also retire earlier compared to their peers in other fields, which leaves a huge loss of institutional memory that is vital to retaining a sense of identity and tradition, and to avoid repeating mistakes because no one can remember how they had resolved the same issues in the past.

These perspectives are compounded by trends in crime and other issues, notably the increasingly sophisticated, complex, multicultural and transnational high-tech organized crime and international terrorist groups who now had worldwide reach, wherever they were based. As a result, Canadian police would be increasingly required to join forces with other domestic and international partners to track such criminals and their crimes. Otherwise, they were doomed to simply apprehend the foot soldiers, never the high-ranking leaders, and would simply put a dent in their criminal operations. It would slow them down, but only temporarily, and sadly, would never stop them.

Arrayed in a thin bruised line to respond to those issues and concerns are the police, a culture that Sopow defined as paramilitary by necessity. Thus, policing is based on knowledge, not emotion, with a historic can-do attitude, leading to a never-say-no mentality and a conservative culture. That, he explained, begets conservative structures that spawn conservative workplace cultures, not open to creative thinking to find new solutions to old problems. And, he concluded, presumably no surprise to the female police officers in his audience, policing is still very much "testosterone driven" and dominated by male thinking. Employing everything from a Dilbert cartoon, to national survey bar charts, to demonstrate how management and employee engagement works (or doesn't), Sopow identified five essential leadership attributes: strong communication skills, team building, fairness, situational leadership, and trustworthiness.

Police leaders uniformly believe their job requires excellent listening skills, fair treatment of everyone, strong ethics, excellent communication skills, concern for workplace morale, and collaboration and teamwork. Equally, police officers seek fair treatment, collaboration with their superiors, help, support, and feedback to their leaders that is taken seriously, clearly defined expectations, expeditious resolution to workplace conflicts, and the assignment of leaders they can trust and respect.

Distrust of senior police managers to respond to complaints seems widespread among both male and female officers. However, the findings of a survey of the RCMP membership, representing the national average of all categories, showed that on basic issues, men and women really weren't divided on their opinions of management, with a few glaring exceptions. Men agreed far more than women that the Force respected rights and values (67 versus 55 per cent) and that management shared information well (68 versus 54 per cent). Women were far better than men at adopting a work-life balance (69 versus 55 per cent). Roughly 50 per cent of both genders believed that everyone was treated fairly and that they have input to decisions. A little less than 60 per cent of men and women agreed there is recognition for a job well done. And that was about as good as it got. Roughly one-third of men and women believed there is accountability for actions, and 31 per cent of women and 22 per cent of men agreed that supervisors take their feedback seriously—about the same percentage who agreed that the RCMP develops capable leaders. But for all those laments, an astounding 84 per cent of women and 83 per cent of men rated the RCMP as a good organization for which to work.

Sopow expects management survey results to change when more women crack the glass ceiling and move into leadership positions. But, as Hall has pointed out, it will be interesting to see how many women take advantage of the offer. Bev Busson was a keynote speaker at a 1997 Women and Policing workshop for policewomen held at the Canadian Police College, in Ottawa. Who better than she to ask the question back then: Are women truly being integrated into policing?

Acknowledging that women had certainly made advances in their first twenty-three years in policing, she was quick to note that men had also come a long way in "overcoming the minefield" of stereotypes and the traditional view that considered it "improper" for women to work outside the home. She recalled that prior to her joining the RCMP in 1974, the few women working in police operations were often office staff seconded to act as "window dressing" to add a touch of reality for an undercover operator who needed a female companion.

"From the training experience on, there was a feeling that we were treading on hallowed ground," Busson said. "For me, I felt a kind of benevolent skepticism. Was it possible for a woman to be a viable member of the Royal Canadian Mounted Police? I think that the decision to accept women was more political than we realized at the time, but we were all, in that first class, committed to doing the best job that we could. We shared none of the skepticism, but were eager to show our stuff as we were posted."

While the early Mountie philosophy was to make the training as similar as possible for men and women, there were still lingering stereotypes—like the women reporting for work with their guns in their purses.

"It didn't take us long to realize that the credibility gap would be almost insurmountable, even before we finished our first shift on the road, if we showed up for our first day at work with a purse," Busson said, adding that if that seemed to be a small issue, it was "evidence of how difficult it was for the institution of policing to accept that women could actually stand side by side with their male partners and get the job done."

The purse story had a happy ending, she recalled, as her troop convinced their superiors that "the liabilities, never mind the appearance" of a police officer with a loaded weapon in a purse was not a good idea. The community seemed to accept policewomen more quickly than the police accepted them, and Busson noted that she never felt unwelcome or unduly scrutinized by those she was sworn to serve and protect. Initially posted to a small town in the British Columbian interior, she benefited from her male colleagues teaching her what she needed not only to survive, but to thrive, in the police environment, lamenting that some of her female colleagues did not fare as well. As both sexes grew comfortable in their roles, she suggested it was time for the women to embrace their "femaleness," conceding it had not always been that way, likely because the women were trying to police like men, who were their only role models, doing their job the way it had always been done. By 1997, Busson believed that women were now much more confident and able to use, rather than excuse, their female talents.

"Women have never been the sole repository of characteristics such as compassion, caring, concern, and emotional support," she said. "These things, I believe, are equally distributed amongst both sexes. However, women have always been more comfortable in showing these emotions, and thus using them in their everyday life and their work. This in turn, I believe, has created an environment where males may feel more comfortable in showing their human side when fulfilling the duties of the police profession."

That sentiment was echoed by two male speakers at the conference, Bob Lunney, former chief in both Edmonton and Peel Region, just west of Toronto, and Sergeant Syd Gravel, of the then Ottawa-Carleton police (renamed Ottawa Police when the city was amalgamated in 2001). They agreed publicly with what they confided was a growing number of male officers who were learning to talk rather than scuffle their way to resolution.

Busson identified the final barrier to promotion for women as the one unique attribute they had different than men: motherhood. (At this time, there was no such thing as paternity leave.) There was still work to be done to convince the decision-makers back then of the need for more flexibility to allow policewomen to be wives and mothers as well as peace officers, and to accept them as full participants in society. She suggested job sharing or fully trained reserves to reduce the stress created directly or indirectly on women officers by the feeling that they had let down their partners or shift members by leaving them a person short. Given the evidence that nurtured children cope better with life, Busson's suggestions were strategic as well as tactical: allowing women to remain Mounties *and* moms could at least help ensure that their kids wouldn't become the delinquents they were chasing. In that way, Mountie moms were helping to lower future crime rates. At work, they were stepping into leadership roles.

"As women progress through the ranks in the various police

forces, communities continue to be very accepting of women as not only street cops, and detectives but as leaders," Busson observed. "I believe too that our male counterparts are supportive, so long as we earn the credibility and respect that is required of anyone whose role is to lead others.

"One cannot be mandated as a leader without that corresponding credibility. It is what we expect from, and of, each other, and is not unreasonable," Busson concluded. "I truly believe the days are gone when we have to make excuses, or create special opportunities or criteria for advancement for women in police work or elsewhere. So long as we have a process that is accountable in the selection of those most capable in the field, women will be able to take their place, alongside of others in any role they choose."

Bob Lunney's presentation that day, "Women's Influence on Police Members' Responsibilities," also touched on leadership and promotion opportunities for women. Praising them for achieving full parity and acceptance at the patrol level "in all but the less enlightened forces," he noted that they had gone on to establish their competence in a variety of specialized investigative roles, and crossed "the last frontiers" to join tactical squads, use-of-force trainer positions and canine handlers, years earlier. They also gravitated towards "inside day jobs" in specialty roles that had been the exclusive domain of female officers before they were integrated with male officers, usually clerical and other deskbound duties. He was less sure that women sought their roles with crime prevention, drug education, sexual assault investigation, child abuse and frauds, or administrative work in court because they wanted them or were handed them by "gender stereotyping" male managers.

"There exists a certain degree of ambivalence among women officers towards this tendency," he said. "The more assertive and ambitious regard it as evidence of a glass ceiling or exclusionary decision making, or being diverted from the core policing roles where unreserved recognition is available. Others may perceive those factors, but actually perpetuate the stereotype by seeking out the day jobs, away from the front-line action, because it suits their personal desires, social needs or family situations."

Lunney considered these to be difficult choices for women "aspiring to promotion" to the backrooms where police culture required boldness, the willingness and ability to do the "dirty work"—which often involved physical confrontations—as the prime asset for acceptance and promotion. Time spent in a "day job" might be a comfortable backwater, but also "detrimental in the competitive career process." Qualified women, he said, had raised the bar for recruitment, routinely bringing to the table academic qualifications superior to those of their male counterparts, thus injecting more "knowledge and enlightenment" into policing, while edging out men with minimal education. The Canadian public was the beneficiary of increasingly intellectual policing.

"At the risk of creating yet another fallacy of stereotyping," Lunney said, "it was my observation as a police executive for twenty-three years that women's attributes are exceptionally valuable at the supervisory and middle-management levels. The women who have earned promotions to the middle ranks almost universally have proven adept at managing detail and any task requiring precision and accuracy. Where men tend to generalize and take unwarranted risks, women focus meticulous attention to detail. This ability, combined with a willingness to accept accountability, produces highly effective and dependable performance."

If the jury was still out on whether women had actually changed the structure of policing, Lunney was adamant that they have had a definite positive impact upon the character of policing by increasing civility in the workplace and inducing an environment of respect, while blunting at least some of the "macho-male aggressive" attributes of the culture. All that had combined to force a re-evaluation of gender stereotyping.

"This influence on organizational character is perhaps the major impact of women to this point," Lunney said, regretting they had still not vanquished "destructive" sexual harassment—and perhaps never would.

"During the early years of integration, women were forced to contend with a strong internal police culture entirely male dominated, with every process determined by male tendencies," the retired chief recalled. "Even today, women most often get ahead by relying on male models of power or hardball strategy. They bully, or they blend in; they negotiate or compromise. Negotiation always results in compromise. Women mistake survival for success. They complain about the glass ceiling, but they have helped erect it, by accepting an unauthentic heritage of men's fighting strategies."

After twenty years, Lunney suggested it was time to evaluate the past and plan progressively for the future, perhaps by allowing men and women to reclaim, understand and celebrate their differences as opportunities for learning and growth.

"Let us put gender competition to rest, and relieve women from living out male behaviour patterns in policing," he urged, suggesting different approaches to take advantage of what he perceived to be the natural attributes of ordinary and exceptional women.

Lunney hailed women for their caring and nurturing abilities, their positive influence on socialization and civility, and their "natural ability" to introduce negotiation and non-violent conflict-resolution methods to street culture; all of which would help ease the conventional police tendency to meet all challenges with the "aggressive fighting stance" used in the past.

"With the immensity of change overtaking the traditional role of the public police, leadership will need much more open, flexible attitudes from their partners to ensure functional survival," he said. "Women's characteristics have the moderating effect that is needed. Every woman in policing has a role to play in influencing cultural change. Persistence and encouragement from leadership is a key factor in accelerating the process.

"The exceptional woman has a responsibility to establish new templates for behaviour for both women and men in policing," Lunney continued, adding that she must create a "new paradigm" for police leadership, encompassing such attributes as the ability to think strategically over the long term on critical issues confronting policing. "They should not use the warfare-oriented thought patterns of men, but adapt women's innate capacities to satisfy their personal desires in any given situation, and demonstrate how to prevail through personal example and apply insight into the critical elements of situations and people."

The exceptional woman was also well qualified for a leadership role.

"The capacity for superior intuitive powers is commonly attributed to women. Intuition is the sum of applied knowledge and practical thought, processed through the subconscious capabilities of the mind," Lunney said. "Intuition is a prime ingredient of strategic thinking. It can be consciously learned, improved and tested through decision making. Leadership candidates among both women and men should focus on development of their intuitive powers. But women may have an innate ability ... I would expect from the exceptional woman a superior degree of social intelligence. I would expect her to have the ability to understand how and why individuals and groups behave as they do, and how to effectively work with them to achieve the desired goals."

The workshop could be a watershed moment for women in policing, he said, adding: "Women's destiny is largely in your own hands. You cannot expect a male-dominated culture, however well intentioned its leaders or sympathetic its partners, to willingly surrender to change the methods and attitudes that have perpetuated its existence. You must achieve the next progressive steps not through reliance on legislation and regulation, but by bold and determined action on your own terms and in your own way: Use the educational skills that many women possess in abundance. Use unique approaches to problem solving and innovation occurring to women by nature. Demonstrate persistence, determination and energy."

The next speaker, Syd Gravel, the Ottawa sergeant, spoke from the heart. The veteran's old-school no-nonsense view of policing perhaps best underscored just how far female cops had advanced. He conceded early that the priority for bulk and brawn that favoured his selection when he applied to be a police officer in 1978 had kept out a few good men and virtually every woman from following that dream. In fact, even at six foot two and 170 pounds, Gravel had been deemed too light for policing and almost never got to fill out an application and claimed he loaded his pockets with metal ball bearings to pass the minimum-weight requirement.

No one knew if he was joking, then or now.

"My first impression was that it appeared to matter little how stupid I might be, as long as I looked good in a size 42 uniform," he quipped, recalling the training progression back then—basic training at the Ontario Police College, working with a coach officer, then back to college for more training. After graduation, he was assigned to walk a beat, which was when the mentoring began. In the early days, that was the biggest difference between male and female officers aside from their gender. The women simply had no female role models and any mentoring, no matter how well intentioned, was, of necessity, from the traditional male perspective.

"I was expected to learn from the older officers already on the beat," Gravel recalled. "It wasn't long before I learnt that I had a turf in which I was supposed to reign supreme. If anyone tried to challenge me, then I was supposed to do whatever I had to do to get respect."

That sometimes meant diving into the middle of a "donny-brook," or brawl in some neighbourhood bar to show the citizenry that you didn't mess with Syd. His beat required him to stare down local toughs with enough menace to "burn a hole" through them if they pushed you too far. If push came literally to shove and he found himself losing the battle, Gravel recalled that he was expected to take a few pokes to the nose before calling for help. "Anything less than that is being a coward," his older colleagues had warned him.

"I was well on my way to becoming a grizzled old dinosaur," Gravel said, conceding that he had learned to play his tough-guy role so well, he was nicknamed "Syd Vicious"—an ironic reference to the punk rocker. While he had earned the alias honestly through rough-and-tumble policing, he confessed to his audience that he was now a little ashamed of how proud he had been of it then. Nor could he easily overcome his initial shock when the physical standards for recruitment into the police force were lowered for beat cops to allow women into front-line policing: Whose idea was that?

"My immediate reaction to this was to cry foul to anyone who would listen," Gravel recalled. "I even went as far as making an appointment with my family lawyer ... to advise him that if I should get hurt at work because I ended up with a woman partner who couldn't fight her way out of a paper bag, then I wanted to sue not only the Ottawa Police Force for being so spineless, but every women's lib group who, in the end, forced this dreadful situation upon us, and also the entire provincial government for giving in to the fanatics and activists. I was very angry that my life was going to be endangered and, consequently, my family's also."

It seemed safe to assume at this point in his presentation that Gravel was far and away one of the least embracing male officers at the time women were admitted to policing. It was two worlds colliding.

"I am not ashamed of the way I reacted because that was the nature of the beast then," he said, "but I am very sorry that it happened at all because I have seen and learnt so much since. Everything about what I was about then was wrong with regards to attitude and opinion about women in policing."

All that changed, he explained, the more he worked with the first women constables.

"Attitudes are changing with regards to the integration of women in policing because of the women who were hired in that first wave back in the seventies and eighties," he said, admitting that it had not begun well in his personal experience. One of the first policewomen he worked with "failed miserably" on her first opportunity to prove herself.

"The story was that she just stood by while her partner fought with some big burly wife abuser who just didn't want to get himself arrested," Gravel recalled. "I was there. I ran by her to help her partner and then, after it was all over, I walked away thinking ... 'I'm glad she's not my partner.'"

In hindsight, Gravel was more understanding: "The bottom line was she got scared. It was the worst thing that could have happened because from there, everyone had been watching, and when the story got around about how she had screwed up, then all women police officers were screw-ups."

In time, Gravel found himself feeling sorrier for the policewoman than for the partner she had failed to help. Remembering times he had been afraid, he reasoned that being scared was OK if you learned from it. It seemed she had. She was a changed woman at the next call they worked together—a brawl in a known biker bar. The alleged diva had been transformed into a dervish.

Gravel followed the first responding officer into the bar, then paused to let his eyes adjust to the dim light. The policewoman shoved him aside, "jumping ahead to get first crack at the idiots fighting on the floor. She went in there kicking, punching and yelling like a trooper." In fact, Gravel was so surprised by her aggression that he did exactly what she had done at the domestic—stood there and watched. From that point, he knew she could deal with the worst parts of policing. He found himself liking her. His attitude began to change. And then he found himself respecting her—and, in time, learning from her.

"[As] admirable as she was in being willing to do grunt work, she didn't keep the fighting attitude with her," he recalled. "When I was on the street, I wanted to be tough all the time—fighting or not." He got a reality check from his wife when she told him she'd seen him walking his beat one day, but didn't stop because he looked too "unapproachable." He had shrugged it off at the time, saying: "When I'm working, I'm always working."

He realized now that he had been wrong—that many of "us old toughs" were wrong. He recalled that the policewoman viewed by many to be a problem was able to speak gently to people and calm them down. She brought a warmth to calls that Gravel had never experienced before, allowing him to watch people react in positive ways that he had also never seen before.

"It was a class act and I started to see where this stuff could work for me," Gravel said. "The community seemed a better place because of her approach. And, as I copied off her, my job got easier. I got into a lot less fights. My arrests were still good and my enforcement still happened, but now I started to develop relationships with the community."

It didn't end so happily for the policewoman. She lasted another couple of years on the job, but the damage was done. Gravel tried to talk her out of quitting, but she couldn't shake the rumours from her first call, regardless of how many times or how many ways she vindicated herself. It got to her. Gravel vowed then to never again lose such good officers as her to "such petty harassment." Slowly, over the years, he observed other male officers change their ways of doing things—less "a force to be reckoned with" than "a force to work with."

"I can tell you that the officers of the modern police service are the officers that are committed to the concept of working with the community and smart thinking as opposed to having the 'toughest guy wins' attitude," he said. "There is still a need for tough action at times, but with intelligent, resourceful and sensitive methods of attack as opposed to the 'bull in a china shop' approach. I personally feel that women in policing had a great deal to do with the refinement of the police attitude in Canadian society today. Those officers will continue to grow successfully in this community."

That was a vital consideration for Gravel who realized that without a proper link to the community and the skills for problem solving, "officers will sink." By adopting the ways of the policewoman whom he had urged to "stick it out," Gravel said he learned to calm people using a soft voice, to be "firm, yet caring, strong, yet sensitive." That, he said, had made him more of a peace officer and less of a goon.

His reading habits may have changed as well. Citing the article in the May 1997 edition of *Chatelaine* about Christine Silverberg, whose appointment to chief in Calgary was the first for a major city (as mentioned earlier, Lenna Bradburn was the first female chief in Canada in Guelph, Ontario), Gravel praised her efforts to push the city towards recognizing the root cause of problems and solving them in co-operation with the community.

"This is a wise move," he said. "The front-line officers are tired of the struggle. They are tired of communities thinking that the police can fix everything. Problem-oriented policing tactics under the community-based policing structure is smart policing ... Problem-oriented policing is smart policing with strong partnerships within the community, with officers developing strong ties within the communities in which they police. Where, in this model of the future, is there any room for anyone who has strong biases against women and minorities?"

Another article in the May 1997 edition of *Canadian Living* magazine, chronicling the struggles Silverberg had faced trying to work her way into a male-dominated environment resonated personally with Gravel.

"I recognized much of what she described . . . from the wrong side of the fence," he said. Addressing the room, hoping she was attending the workshop, he added: "I would like to take this opportunity to apologize for whatever it was I might have done to make you feel unwelcome and thank you from the bottom of my heart for sticking it out, in spite of guys like me!"

Gravel had changed and he saw better days ahead for policewomen and policing.

"The negative perception of female officers within the police services is fading, I think. There are now more of us who can see the value of having women as partners than there are that can't. There are more of us who need you and want you. You have more friends out there than you may think!"

He was seeing the change first-hand in Ottawa, citing Sue O'Sullivan as one of the "most brilliant" inspectors any officer would be proud to serve.

"It wasn't unusual for her to get out with me and try to scoop some bad guy," he said. "It was always interesting for me to see how she could talk some bad guy into the cruiser after arresting him, while I would have had to [fight] him using the old ways. So, who is better for the change?"

In 2008, O'Sullivan was deputy chief in Ottawa where she co-chaired a two-day national summit to check the pulse on women in policing. In the interim, she had tackled sexist stereotyping by writing to object to a TV car ad for Kia Canada featuring an actress playing a police officer in a hot embrace with the Kia driver whom she had pulled over. "Women have worked long and hard in this profession to earn legitimacy and have certainly proven their abilities to do this job and do it well," she wrote.

Just how long and just how hard was perhaps evident back in 1996 when "Policing and Aboriginal Women" was the focus of a workshop at the twenty-second annual general assembly of the Native Women's Association of Canada (NWAC) held in Winnipeg. The same year that Canadian Police College researcher Marcel-Eugène LeBeuf had reported his findings on why women were leaving policing, the NWAC wanted to improve their "very complex relationship" with the police and learn how more of their daughters could join the force.

Native women felt such changes would help them transform their lives and overcome their historic struggles connected to deprived rights, collapse of their families and traditional communities, violence, substance abuse, and poverty. Being frequent victims and occasional perpetrators of crime further complicated their relationship with the police. The conference, it was hoped, would give Native women a chance to speak with the First Nations constables in attendance, to find ways to improve policing and enhance the safety and security of their communities.

The Solicitor General's Aboriginal Policing Directorate, which was one of the sponsors of the conference, advised attendees that there were then about a hundred Aboriginal women police officers in Canada who brought a new problem-solving approach to the table. It was further noted that these policewomen often seemed more comfortable than their Aboriginal male counterparts in policing even potentially volatile situations.

Prior to the Solicitor General assuming responsibility for First Nations policing, the Ontario Provincial Police had, since 1975, appointed, administered, and supervised officers who were assigned to police more than eighty First Nations communities. The approach seemed to make sense, but Native officers soon found themselves trapped between OPP guidelines and commitment to their people. First Nations across Ontario moved to take policing matters into their own hands, leading to the creation of self-managing First Nations policing authorities with equal status to other Ontario forces, both municipal and provincial. But, as the conference heard, that still left many concerns with policing, notably that mainstream police did not do enough to protect Native women and children, nor did they seem to look very hard to find them when they were missing, or their killers when they had been murdered.

The women suggested that the police should hire constables or at least interpreters who could converse with tribal elders in their own language, and noted that relations with the Aboriginal Women's Policing Association would improve if First Nations policewomen were allowed more input and invited to more forums where they could make presentations about their work.

They also urged that Aboriginal policewomen be viewed as role models: "Just by their nature, Aboriginal policewomen approach policing in a unique manner. The impact of their contributions is remarkable. Aboriginal women in policing play an important part in the communities."[2] They should also be promoted to higher ranks; there was a sentiment that they faced the double whammy of being both Aboriginal and female. They also complained of sexual harassment and of having nowhere to turn for support.

Finally, they asked that politics be kept out of policing, noting: "A true and honest police service is one that is fair and equitable to everyone. Politics must recognize and respect the philosophy of policing and should not interfere with police matters."[3]

That last point should have resonated with peace officers from constable to chief or commissioner across Canada.

FOUR

INTRUDER ALERT:
Oversight versus Politicization

Contain and negotiate a peaceful resolution.
—Peter Edwards describes the primary objective of the OPP Project Maple in
his book, *One Dead Indian: The Premier, the Police and the Ipperwash Crisis*

The most publicized clash between the roles of the police and their
political overseers must certainly be the 2003 Ipperwash Inquiry
into the 1995 land-claims standoff between Native occupiers of
Ipperwash Provincial Park and the Ontario Provincial Police that
resulted in the shooting death of Native protester Dudley George
by a police marksman.

No one disputed that Acting Sergeant Ken Deane had fired the
fatal shot, but the inquiry commissioner, the Honourable Sidney B.
Linden, found, as had the relatives of the dead man long before,
that Deane had been put in a place he should never have been.

"There is no doubt that [Deane] shot and killed Mr. George
and nothing in this inquiry challenges or undermines this conviction," Justice Linden said in a prepared statement when he released
his findings on May 31, 2007. "However, [he] should not have been
in a position to shoot Mr. George in the first place."

George's family had demanded an inquiry soon after the incident, and repeatedly offered to terminate their civil lawsuit against then premier Mike Harris and others who had held key positions in his government or with the OPP at the time of the shooting. But the Progressive Conservative government, by then headed by Ernie Eaves, balked, citing that suit—although *Toronto Star* journalist Peter Edwards noted in his book, *One Dead Indian,* that "a raft of civil suits certainly hadn't stopped an inquiry on the Walkerton water deaths" where, in May 2000, tainted water killed at least seven people and sent many more to hospital. Civil suits weren't justification for blocking that inquiry.

The Mackenzie King Liberal government of the day had taken the land at Ipperwash for military use during the Second World War, promising to return it after the cessation of hostilities. Fifty years after the war had ended, the local Kettle and Stony Point First Nations were still waiting to get their land back. When the last summer campers left, they simply strolled into the park and settled in. The OPP response was prompt but not threatening. Commanded by Acting Superintendent John Carson, who would retire a decade later as a deputy commissioner, the OPP launched Project Maple, putting more than a dozen negotiators on alert, no simple task on a Labour Day holiday. The response seemed neither rushed nor threatening.

"The premier [Mike Harris] and his executive assistant Deb [Hutton] had a different perspective than the OPP on how the occupation should be handled by the police," Justice Linden continued in his statement. "The OPP's wish to pursue a 'go-slow' approach contrasted with the government's desire for a quick end to the occupation. Civil servants agreed in principle with the OPP's approach but deferred to their political masters on questions of policy."

And the clock began to tick for Dudley George and Ken Deane.

As Edwards notes in *One Dead Indian,* "In mid-May 2002, Liberal MPP Gerry Phillips released a previously secret government memo from a high-level meeting of various ministerial staff just hours before Dudley George was shot. The handwritten memo said the OPP was pushing for a go-slow approach, advocating 'removal later (ASAP)' or 'when feasible, i.e., injunction.' Under a reference to the Premier's Office are the words 'removal NOW.'"

But Linden wasn't pointing any fingers.

"It is impossible," he said, "to attribute Mr. George's death to a single person, factor, decision or institution. On the contrary, it was the combination of these that made a violent result more likely, particularly when they all came together in the space of a few short days and hours in the context of a highly-charged confrontation. Individuals and institutions need to be held accountable for the consequences of their decisions and actions, whether those consequences were intended or not."[1]

It was unclear who should be held accountable: Harris or Hutton, whoever had actually given the police their marching orders; or the OPP for agreeing and moving in on the protesters. It turned out no one seemed to be taken to task.

"The provincial government's imperative for a speedy conclusion to the occupation was difficult to justify by events on the ground," Linden continued, noting that the park was closed for the season, that there were no campers there, nor any evidence that any "substantial risk" existed to public safety. So why the urgency? The question seems rhetorical, as Linden continued: "It is clear that the provincial government had the authority to establish policing policy and there is no doubt that the premier wanted the occupiers out of the park as soon as possible and the occupation ended …"

If that seemed to be a reprieve or validation for the police, given their stated "go-slow" approach, which they presumably tried to share with the occupiers, and the police intent to negotiate a settlement rather than mount a tactical assault to forcibly resolve the standoff, it did not indict the political response as Linden concluded: "The evidence does not support the claim that he [Harris] interfered with the OPP's operation."

The inquiry commissioner did determine that he believed Harris and Chris Hodgson, his minister of natural resources, made "racist comments," although he noted both had denied during their testimony ever making "these offensive comments." In addition to implying that their testimony was not accurate, Linden also cited Harris for thwarting any hope for a peaceful resolution.

"Notwithstanding the government's authority to establish policy, including policing policy, these comments and the speed at which the premier wished to end the occupation created an atmosphere that unduly narrowed the scope of the government's response to the occupation," Linden observed. "The scope of the government's response to the occupation, the premier's desire to see a quick resolution closed off other options endorsed by civil servants, including … negotiations, the appointment of mediators and the opening up of communication with the First Nation *(sic)* people, thereby creating a barrier to peaceful resolution."

Which was, of course, the exact resolution that Acting Superintendent John Carson and the OPP had sought.

"Further," Linden continued, "the interaction between police and the government was not conducive to a peaceful resolution. There was considerable lack of understanding about the appropriate relationship between police and government, which had significant consequences. Lines of communication and chains of command were blurred. There was also a lack of clarity between the relationship of the political staff and the civil servants, which created the appearance of inappropriate interference in police operations."

That was a vital distinction. Everyone, most certainly the police, accept that their elected overseers have the right and the power to set policy; but police operations have historically been considered to be at arm's length. Harris and his minions had every right to tell the police they wanted them to get the Natives out of the park; the police had every right to determine the best way to do that. And they had opted for a peaceful solution.

Linden lauded Carson's plan to contain and negotiate a "peaceful resolution." But he also identified relatively minor deficiencies in its limitations for communications and intelligence gathering, requiring Carson, whom he considered a "conscientious and competent incident commander and a man of integrity," who clearly sought a *peaceful* resolution [emphasis his], to rely on unverified and sometimes inaccurate intelligence. The police were further chastised for making racist remarks during the occupation and creating coffee mugs embossed with insensitive slogans to commemorate their time at the standoff.

To be fair, there would seem to be a world of difference between opposing sides tossing inappropriate epithets at each other across no man's land and a provincial premier announcing at a high-level meeting that he wanted "the fucking Indians" moved out, as was testified to at the ensuing inquiry.[2]

Events at Ipperwash also triggered several academic papers for a symposium co-chaired by Margaret Beare, the director of the Nathanson Centre for the Study of Organized Crime and Corruption, and Tonita Murray, the former director general of the Canadian Police College. As co-editors of the 2005 edition of the *Canadian Review of Policing Research*, Beare and Murray explained why it remains imperative to review the roles played by the police and the state: "Questions of police governance, accountability, and independence have been subjected to thorough research before, most notably in the McDonald Commission of Inquiry into Certain Activities of the Royal Canadian Mounted Police. That the issue still draws critical attention more than twenty years later suggests that understanding and a resolution to the issue still eludes us. Despite the modifications to police practice that the *Charter of Rights and Freedoms* has brought, there is still concern over the degree of independence the police exercise, and debate over where the line between legitimate government direction of the police and illegitimate political interference should be drawn. Perhaps there is no ideal relationship between governments and the police, and perhaps leaving the situation fluid is the only solution...."[3]

Linden also devoted considerable effort to explore and help resolve the always tricky relationship between politicians and the police. He warned that the increasing complexity of policing and governing means that the apparently clear and simple differences between police operational responsibility and government policy and decision making may no longer be sufficient to guide those on both sides of the issue.

"Police and government decision-making will always intersect and policy and operations will always be fluid concepts, subject to reasonable interpretation and re-interpretation depending on the context. And this is particularly true in the case of aboriginal occupations and protests where lines between policy and operations are often blurred."

Linden recommended adopting reforms to significantly reduce the "perception and fact" of "inappropriate" government interference, suggesting that clearer rules will "promote accountability, transparency and public confidence in key democratic institutions and leaders." This, he explained, required that care be taken to ensure transparency and clarity so that the police and governments can be held to account for difficult and controversial decisions, no matter what balance is struck between them.

"When something goes wrong, as it tragically did at Ipperwash, the public has a right to know who made the key decisions and why," Linden concluded. "In an ideal world, proceedings such as this inquiry would not be necessary."[4]

His words remind us of just how imperfect the world can be for our police. They are clearly held accountable for their actions or inactions and can be compelled to explain why they did or did not do something as required by the laws of the land or the rules and regulations of their respective *Police Acts*. They can be compelled to explain themselves at internal disciplinary hearings within their departments or to their police boards. They can be made to testify to city councils, or to provincial or federal oversight panels, committees, and commissions of inquiry.

Ironically, the OPP were still answering for their actions at Ipperwash while confronting another Native land-rights claim at Caledonia, which sparked an occupation of the disputed property on February 28, 2006. But this was different. This time, the unrest affected local homeowners and developers. As tempers flared on both sides, the police, caught in the middle, were ordered to stand down even as lawful protest was marred by blatant criminal acts, such as destruction to property that included digging up a section of public highway with a backhoe.

Gwen Boniface had replaced Tom O'Grady as OPP commissioner and asked much of her front-line officers in her bid to avoid escalating violence at Caledonia. This time, many would criticize the police for not moving in. Hostile Internet websites sprang up, media scrutiny intensified (if only because Caledonia is much closer to the major news outlets in nearby Toronto and Hamilton), and officer unrest became more evident as time passed. Ontario premier Dalton McGuinty did not push for an early resolution and tried to mediate by having his government buy the disputed land from the developer trying to build new homes, many of them already bought and paid for.

When Boniface was replaced by former Toronto police chief Julian Fantino, he took a more rigid stance, but was quick to remind politicians, through the media, that issues like Caledonia were never going to be resolved by the police. At best, they could provide a temporary solution and apply sufficient pressure to keep the lid from blowing off the simmering violence just a spark away from igniting. This time, the OPP found themselves talking to another judge in his chambers, trying to explain why they seemingly defied his court order to move in and move the occupiers out.

It's never easy being the cop.

Oversight involves letting or making the police do their jobs. The fine line between civilian oversight and political intrusion is blurred and concealed by the myriad ways politicians and their oversight committees have of controlling the police and their effectiveness. The police are the handmaidens of the law and were once answerable primarily to the law, instructed to protect the peace without fear or favour. The courts determine innocence or guilt and the appropriate punishment for the latter. If the courts release them too quickly, or sentence them too leniently for the public's liking, the police get to arrest them again because, if they are truly bad people, they are likely to break the law again. For that to work, the line between enforcement and harassment has to be clearly viewed and accepted by the police and their overseers with stronger support for the front-line officers most vulnerable to public complaints.

The police take such complaints seriously and some provinces have created special units to investigate incidents involving police that result in injury or death to an officer or member of the public. Manitoba was the most recent to take on this initiative, unveiling its new approach to investigating the police in April 2009. Some complaints can be numbing, but are eventually deemed to be unfounded, perhaps vexatious; no one ever seems to be charged with mischief or is, in any other way, deterred from idly, mischievously, or maliciously tying up already limited police resources with groundless accusations. If the issue goes to a human-rights tribunal, the sense is that the accused is presumed guilty until proven innocent. True or not, the perception is widely held. That was also the sense among police officers in the early days of Ontario's experiment with an independent body, the Special Investigations Unit (SIU), created in 1990 to investigate alleged police wrongdoing, when an incident involving police resulted in the death or serious injury of a citizen, or a public complaint of a sexual nature. In 1999, then chief of York Regional Police and the outgoing head of the Ontario Association of Chiefs of Police (OACP), Julian Fantino, formally complained about the SIU on behalf of the OACP to Premier Mike Harris. He leaves no doubt in his memoir, *DUTY: The Life of a Cop*, how he felt about the agency created to investigate the police with questionable investigative techniques.

"In the first nine years of its existence, the SIU had nine different directors and was a totally inept organization. It had incompetent investigators muddling through very complex cases and then passing judgments on the actions of the police. Policing was an organization they knew very little about."

Fantino believes there was a presumption of guilt and "preconceived notion" within the SIU that the officer they were investigating must have "done something." But things got better and Fantino now views it as a model for other provinces, praising its "excellent and timely" investigations, its well-trained investigators, and "solid" directors.

Not everyone seemed to agree.

In October 2008, one of the top media stories in Ontario was the release of provincial ombudsman André Marin's damning review of the very changes Fantino was praising. In his report, "Oversight Unseen: Investigation into the Special Investigations Unit's Operational Effectiveness and Credibility," Marin noted that, since its inception, the SIU has opened and closed 2,771 cases, but laid just 73 charges—an indication of what a "toothless" agency it had become.

In the *Toronto Star*, columnist Rosie DiManno wrote, "The probers arrive late, are often confronted with compromised crime scenes, laggard in interviewing witness officers, easily obstructed by department chiefs and union lawyers, impotent in the face of police resistance and too closely associated with cop culture to boot." While she questioned Marin's accuracy in some areas, DiManno agreed that the perception that cops are treated differently when they are investigated was true. Perhaps the real significance was that you had to read almost to the end of the 884-word opinion piece to learn that Marin was once the head of the SIU—in fact, in the immediate years before Fantino had formally complained to the premier on behalf of the police chiefs' association.

Could Marin's former position with the agency he was reviewing cloud his perception? Certainly, concerns were raised a year earlier in the *National Post*, when Marin announced his intention to conduct a "systemic investigation" of the SIU and to review "specific cases" and what he had cited as a "troubling increase" in the volume of public complaints.

"Craig Bromell, former Toronto police union president, and defence lawyer Edward Sapiano differ on the need for a probe, but they both agreed it should not be led by Mr. Marin because of his past role with the SIU," the *Post* reported. "Marin was the director of the SIU for 21 months between 1996 and 1998. As well, the current director of the Ombudsman's special response team is Gareth Jones, who was a senior SIU investigator when Mr. Marin was director."

Bromell, who had been a contentious and confrontational association president, claimed there is "an industry complaining about police" and hinted that, if Marin was empire building, what better way than to review the SIU?

"If he could not fix what ails the SIU while at its helm, why would I have confidence in his ability to fix it in his capacity as Ombudsman," Sapiano asked. "Something else is going on," he added, noting that "conflict arises from a perception of bias" and suggesting it would be valuable to know if the number of complaints against the SIU is greater now than it was when Marin headed it.[5]

Bromell seemed to agree, claiming that the percentage of SIU investigations in which charges were laid had been constant since 1995 and suggesting that to identify any possible systemic problems would require looking back beyond Marin's February 2003 cut-off, and should include the data from when the ombudsman had headed the unit.

Police associations were known for not co-operating with the SIU when Marin was in charge and he was twice sued by officers for malicious prosecution during his tenure. He was absolved in one case after a long civil trial; the other was settled out of court without going to trial. There has been push back, but seldom blatant defiance, from the national and provincial associations of police chiefs, the police associations who represent the rank and file, and sometimes more senior officers, when they believe politicians or their staffs are not acting in the best interests of public safety—or their own well-being. The Ontario Association of Chiefs of Police has an "Eye on Queen's Park" section on its website, an information tool that lets the provincial government know that the chiefs are watching those who watch the police. Bromell, as president of the strong Toronto Police Association, had led his members into uncharted waters in 2000 overseeing their controversial telemarketing campaign, Operation True Blue, during which donors were given stickers they could place on their vehicle's windshield, raising more than $300,000 for the association. Critics accused the union of building its war chest to target its political opponents. Toronto City Council condemned the campaign as "an affront to democracy." Bromell replied by releasing a list of seventeen councillors he urged police to support in the municipal elections. Two years earlier, there was major media coverage of the association's demand for a provincial investigation into comments made by Councillor

Judy Sgro, then vice-chair of the Police Services Board, for criticizing its planned aggressive ad campaigns against candidates they viewed as anti-police.

When Charles Momy was head of the Ottawa Police Association (OPA), he explored a similar possibility in the 2006 municipal election campaign. When he announced his plan to question candidates on law-and-order issues in March, he, too, was denounced as "an affront to democracy" by Paul Copeland, representing the Law Union of Ontario and Criminal Lawyers' Association. Momy killed the plan less than a month later, but the candidates had taken notice.

Whatever differences the police association and police leadership may have, they have also demonstrated they can work together. Fantino endorsed the Toronto association's $2 billion lawsuit in 2002 against the *Toronto Star* over racial profiling allegations, and, in Ottawa, Chief Vern White extolled the virtues of Momy and his group when they were honoured by the Salvation Army for their good deeds. Reviewing the professional services it provides to its membership, White, a former Mountie who sat on the NWT Salvation Army board when he was posted to Yellowknife, noted that the association does many good deeds for which it receives little notice.

"It would be easy for the OPA to throw money at the community and call it a day, but they become involved . . . by becoming personally involved in their community and in organizations," which the chief claimed added value to those organizations in a personal way. Specific examples included their commitment to youth and sports, fundraising for charitable causes, and volunteer work in the community.

"The work of this association and its membership has been tremendous for and in our community," White concluded. "Congratulations to all on a job well done and done well. I am proud that I have Charles, his team and the Ottawa Police Association as my partner in the city of Ottawa, working to make this city safer every day."[6]

Yet there are still those who blindly distrust the police; it doesn't seem to matter whether the issue is an internal probe or if outside investigators are brought in from another force. Quite simply, there is a sense that the police will protect their own. Perhaps. But the opposite is more often true: the police tend to eat their own, underscored by the member surveys that rate organizational stress greater than operational stress.

Statistics Canada reports that between 1961 and 2005, 125 police officers were killed in the line of duty, fifteen of them by gunshot while investigating firearms complaints. StatsCan also lists the following causes:

- Apprehending an escapee   (5)
- Approaching a stolen car   (3)
- Attempting to make an arrest   (10)
- Domestic dispute   (13)
- During a robbery   (14)
- In the police station   (3)
- Investigating a burglar alarm   (5)
- Investigating a firearms complaint   (15)
- Investigating a kidnapping   (3)
- Investigating a non-domestic complaint (7)
- Pursuit of vehicle   (6)
- Questioning suspect   (8)
- Riot control   (2)
- Routine spot check   (3)
- Stopping a suspicious vehicle   (6)
- Traffic violation   (6)
- Transporting a psychiatric patient   (2)
- Unprovoked   (11)
- Revenge   (2)
- Unknown circumstances   (1)

In the ongoing debate about Tasers, it is estimated that in ninety-three of those deaths, the electronic-shock devices would not likely have saved the officer. It should also be noted that while the tragic death of Robert Dziekanski at Vancouver International Airport on October 14, 2007, was exhaustively reported by the media, no one seems to have tried to determine who exactly gets issued with Tasers. In Ontario, for example, no front-line officers carry the conducted-energy weapons. If they require a Taser, they must contact their duty sergeant or commander and ask them to attend the scene. If the threat is real, by the time they arrive, the constable who requested assistance may have already felt compelled to shoot. Police are trained to shoot at the torso, the biggest part of the body and the best odds for hitting their attacker. There are no warning shots as in Hollywood movies.

It wasn't long ago that veteran police officers on forces across Canada could say that they had never drawn their sidearm outside of the firing range during their entire career. Those days are over. It's a different world that, even if we aren't exposed to it, the police are. That's part of the reason, Calgary police chief Rick Hanson told CTV news on December 12, 2008, that he does not plan to take the conducted-energy devices out if his constables' hands, as has occurred in other provinces, explaining: "I would feel very uncomfortable removing Tasers as a tool for our officers on the street. I can tell you that our officers are faced with situations where the opinion is either Taser or deadly force and I can tell you I'd rather have our officers default to a Taser."

Although front-line Mounties are issued Tasers, other (city) police in Saskatchewan (and Ontario) are not. Another overlooked question by the media report alleged abuses: Who exactly is wielding Tasers when they are used? Deskbound sergeants? Older constables no longer willing to mix it up, or younger, smaller, less confident constables who resort too quickly to anything short of a gun to resolve a situation? No one knows because no one's asking, including politicians and civilian overseers.

To better understand the life-and-death split-second decisions peace officers often face daily (and nightly), *Regina Leader-Post* reporter Barb Pacholik participated in a simulation at the police firing range. She described her experience in the November 6, 2008, piece "Adrenaline high during dangerous encounters." As her heart raced, she eyed the gun in her target's "steady hand" through the dim "blur of flashing red lights," then was jolted by a booming voice to her left: "He's gonna shoot you!"

She hesitated, lined up her shot, aimed at an elbow … and shot the target in the groin. She was surprised because a short time earlier she hit where she was aiming when she was firing a "surprisingly light but powerful" Glock 40-calibre handgun.

"But this time," she wrote, "the adrenaline is pumping."

To simulate what officers would endure in the instant they see someone bearing down on them with a handgun, she raced up and down several flights of stairs, followed by jumping jacks—the same routine for police recruits. She then had a fraction of a second to gauge the risk and determine if lethal force is justified before deciding to pull the trigger. It was a far cry from the movies, where a running gun battle can last for two minutes or more, involving protagonists shooting at each other from a distance. Constable Dave Scantlebury, a police armourer and firearms instructor, explained to her that in the real world, "most life-and-death confrontations between police and an armed suspect usually occur in close quarters—separated by a mere seven or eight feet (less than three metres)—and the 'battle' will likely be over in under 2.5 seconds."

Police officers in Regina, she notes, are trained to process all that information and to draw and fire, ideally in 1.5 seconds, adding: "Even at the outside—2.5 seconds—there isn't a lot of time to weigh options. That's where training comes into play."

With her shot to the target's groin, Pacholik has answered a common question: "Why not shoot to wound?" Scantlebury confirmed that recruits are taught to aim for the torso, explaining: "Under stress, it's really impossible to teach anyone to shoot for an arm or shoot for a leg. Even if you do hit that individual—say they're armed with a knife or even a gun—that's not going to stop the threat. It may not stop the person coming towards you." Police are not taught to "shoot to kill," Pacholik writes, but to "stop the threat."

There are studies, she reports, that show police "typically" hit their target with one shot out of five, under duress, in part because they may be firing so quickly. The threat and the stress levels can rise even higher if someone attacks the officer with a knife—an assailant charging from twenty-one feet away will be on the constable before they have time to draw and fire their sidearm. Pepper spray, effective up to eighteen feet, is not considered a viable response to a life-threatening situation, nor is it possible to pre-mix a tranquilizer dosage that would work on all body sizes. And so, Pacholik writes, police arrive at the scene and must constantly assess and reassess a situation to determine appropriate force to stop any perceived threat.

The *Leader-Post* article—the fourth in a six-part series about deadly force and alternatives—confirmed that responding officers' actions and reactions are typically determined by what they encounter. Excessive force is forbidden, but lethal force may not be excessive under some circumstances. "We have to pick an option that matches the behaviour," explained Regina police corporal Kelly Trithart, who instructs in self-defence at the Saskatchewan Police College. "There is no one way to deal with a certain thing, and they can change immediately."

All this underscores the value of the simulations like the one run for reporter Barb Pacholik. "We're trying to put them in situations, and have them on the spot make decisions, because they can make mistakes there," explained Regina police corporal Brad Walter, a defensive-tactics co-ordinator who teaches at the Saskatchewan Police College, adding that the suspect largely controls the officer's response: "We don't show up and dictate we're going to use lethal force. It's [the response] based on what we're seeing, and what we're hearing and being told, and what the behaviour is."

Scantlebury, the Regina armourer, offered a simple piece of advice that could save a life: "If you're given a command (by police) to do something—to stop what you're doing—then stop. This will prevent us from having to make that decision where maybe lethal force may be needed."

As if that isn't enough to contend with—split-second life-and-death decision making—the responding officer would also be aware that his soft-body armour—mistakenly called a "bulletproof" vest—would likely stop neither a knife blade nor a high-velocity bullet. As the RCMP conceded to the media in July 2006: "We're outgunned."

"They've [criminals] got the big guns and they're not afraid to use them," said Constable Rip Mills. "So you go to a gunfight with a pistol and the bad guy has a rifle. What do you do with a pistol? Duck and take cover. We've got a pistol and a shotgun. That's not going to cut it. How many more lives need to be lost before we change?"[7]

Constable Pete Merrifield agreed that front-line Mounties need more than one trip to the shooting range each year to keep up their skills, adding: "It ain't getting any better and we're undergunned. We've got old pump-action shotguns and pistols. If you're within 20 metres or less a pistol is OK, but outside of that, how do you face rifle fire with a pistol?"[8]

Most police officers can tell you when they were issued their body armour, especially early women constables who often had to fight to get vests designed for the female form. But ask them why they were issued, what cataclysmic event prompted police forces to issue vests to all front-line officers, and you tend to draw blank stares. Ask them if their vests will stop a bullet and most say no. They will answer, as if by rote, that their vest is designed to stop a bullet travelling at a velocity equal to that of the bullet they fire from their sidearms. That unnerving reality suggests that police responders are safe as long as the only one shooting at them is a colleague who has possibly snapped under the pressures of the job, but aims at their chest, not their head. Not a particularly encouraging prospect for anyone.

In October 2006, the *Ottawa Citizen* reported on a 2005 internal RCMP survey that showed a majority of its officers and civilian employees felt they were undertrained, unmotivated to learn in "concrete ways." Less than 50 per cent of respondents felt respected or trusted by their superiors and a little over one-third felt adequately consulted on decisions and actions that would have an impact on their work. Fewer than half said they were treated fairly and nearly 70 per cent said that poor performance was not dealt with effectively. Little seemed to have changed since the first such internal survey in 2003, including the claim by 88 per cent who said they were proud to be Mounties.

The studies have continued into 2009, when the RCMP in Quebec (C Division) again slammed the Force they remained proud to serve in the results of a study by three professors at the Université de Montréal's Research Group on Language, Organization and Governance. As William Marsden reported in the Montreal *Gazette* on January 8, 2009, C Division was "a mess of bad management, poor employee communications and rotten promotion procedures that reward cronyism and sycophants while keeping good officers down," creating a system that "favors development of careerism, which members explain is a genuine plague that taints relations and decisions within the RCMP."

Explaining that this careerism interferes with sound police work, the report said it "creates 'individualists' that invest in projects and initiatives not out of interest or for their intrinsic value, but simply to garnish their promotion file with 'good examples.'"

Competition for promotion was blamed for destroying teamwork by creating a system where everybody is out for his or her own career interests, creating a system that "fails dismally at 'putting the right people in the right places'" and managers who "turn a blind eye to mediocre performance, incompetence and especially reprehensible actions when it suits them."

Senior officers were accused of being incapable of handling disciplinary problems and of covering up bad conduct to "preserve the image and reputation of the RCMP and avoid, at all costs, conflicts with members that could attract media attention."

The report noted: "From the members' standpoint, 'image policing' weighs too heavily among management's concerns."

The report confirmed the turmoil identified most recently by David Brown's "Rebuilding the Trust: Report of the Task Force on Governance and Cultural Change in the RCMP," and Dr. Linda Duxbury's report, "The RCMP Yesterday, Today and Tomorrow: An Independent Report Concerning Workplace Issues at the Royal Canadian Mounted Police," both of which recommended a reinvented and revitalized national police force.

The authors of the 2009 study determined that senior RCMP officers seemed oblivious to the depth of the internal problems, apparently living in a "different reality" from the front-line officers who accused their superiors of trying to run the Force like a business, apparently forgetting, as one respondent said, "that the essence of their work is to be police officers."

The authors did not sugar-coat their findings: "Our observations clearly reveal that a large chasm separates—more gravely than we initially anticipated—the perspectives and realities of the members and managers in the C Division."

But the problems weren't confined to the Mounties in Quebec. City police in Montreal, weary of being called names by the public, sought bylaw protection that would make it a crime to call them "pig" or "doughnut eaters" or other hurtful sobriquets. Similar bylaws already exist in Quebec City, Sherbrooke, and Trois-Rivières and, as the CBC reported: "Police officers are 'victims of intimidation and threats,' which would be tempered if a bylaw were in place.

"The goal is to encourage respect toward police officers on the beat, especially at night when bars close and during protests," said Yves Francoeur, president of the Montreal Police Brotherhood, the union representing officers. "There is a lack of respect for police officers working on the streets. What we are [experiencing] when they close the bars on St. Laurent Street from Thursday night to Saturday night, there's always trouble . . . It's only a question of respect. We have to respect a code of ethics when we deal with citizens, so they have to respect us too."[9]

Nor were the concerns limited to Quebec. Every police force was suffering the same internal and public-relations woes to a greater or lesser extent. No one seemed immune. Few seemed to know what to do. A couple of exceptions were Edmonton city police and the Morinville, Alberta, RCMP detachment. Both ran similar programs to involve civilians and let them see first-hand what was involved in policing. These "civilian colleges" were successful, changed some attitudes, and even got a few people interested in policing as a career. But while looming retirements makes recruitment a pressing issue everywhere, retaining constables exacerbates the problem.

Forces are stretched to the breaking point. In Edmonton, Chief Mike Boyd has his work cut out for him after the media sounded the alarm in January 2009 that keeping officers might be as immediate a concern as recruiting new ones. The news report concluded that 46 per cent of respondents were either dissatisfied or extremely dissatisfied with workplace morale, and that 51 per cent had seriously considered leaving the force in the previous year. Workplace morale was cited as the primary reason, followed by pay, work-life balance, other job opportunities and career-development opportunities. Boyd said he viewed the findings "very seriously" but didn't seem surprised, noting the extensive changes that had taken place over the previous year. Tony Simioni, president of the Edmonton Police Association, said the report confirms what his members had suspected for a long time, but admitted: "I have to say, though, that I am surprised by the extent of the problem."[10]

Still, there was some good news. Boyd noted that the city had committed funds to hire new officers since the survey was conducted, which he hoped would improve morale. The rank and file certainly seemed to be keen to express their views: more than 1,300 responded of the 1,900 invited to participate. Few seemed to hold their chief responsible for their woes: "I've worked for chiefs who didn't have the respect of members, and believe me, it's a whole different atmosphere," one respondent said. "If there is low morale, it doesn't stem from the chief."[11]

The findings also indicated current satisfaction among officers in other areas. Nearly 80 per cent of respondents were satisfied with their relationship with their supervisor; 76 per cent said they were okay with their current responsibilities, and 74 per cent were satisfied with their work schedule; but 55 per cent were unhappy with their workload, which, combined with the increasing retirements, left those still on the job facing "a never-ending amount of work."

In Ontario, the focus remained on traffic patrol. Ottawa police outstripped all others in the province as their tickets soared 155 per cent, thanks in part perhaps to their new computerized ticketing machines installed in their cruisers, able to churn them out as quickly as the constable can type in the details. The police claimed it enhanced public safety; the public insisted it was a "cash grab," which was denied by city council who happily pocketed the revenues, with a small portion reportedly going back to the police. In nearby Renfrew, five OPP constables told the *Ottawa Citizen* they had been given ticket "quotas," which was officially denied, but the leak was followed by the transfer of the staff sergeant in charge of that detachment. Then, in February 2009, Queen's Park added "smoking police" to the duties of their road cops, legislating stiff new fines for motorists smoking in a car with a minor.

In June 2007, *Ottawa Citizen* staffer Kathryn May reported that the RCMP was "institutionally sick," with the percentage of constables and corporals "committed" to the Force dropping from 67 per cent in 2001 to a mere 50 per cent in 2003: half, it was noted, would never encourage their children to follow in their footsteps into the RCMP because "it is changing for the worse and becoming too political."

Such were the findings of a 2004 study into the management and culture of the RCMP jointly conducted by Linda Duxbury, a professor at Carleton University's Sprott School of Business, in Ottawa, and Chris Higgins, who lectures at the University of Western Ontario, in London. They concluded that front-line officers and middle managers "had lost all trust and faith in their leaders."

Conceding that no one should be surprised by the pension- and insurance-fund slugfest that had erupted into the media spotlight, involving, May wrote, "a parade of officers breaking rank and accusing their senior bosses of corruption and coverup," Duxbury seemed worried that an inquiry at that time might worsen matters. David Brown, the lawyer who was contracted to identify the problems and determine if a public inquiry was required for the RCMP, apparently agreed. There was no inquiry despite Opposition party demands. But that didn't soften the impact of the Duxbury-Higgins report, which the Carleton professor told May was "a big deal because what it signifies is a betrayal of trust." Again, even the most agitated seemed proud to wear the red serge.

"If you look at why many Mounties serve, they are incredibly proud of the uniform, the tradition, their service," Duxbury said.

"They lost the ability to be proud in their uniform, and part of that was the lack of understanding among senior officers what leadership means. People may follow you because of rank or position, but as a leader you have to engage the hearts of the people serving under you. My understanding is that there was a huge betrayal of trust at the top, because when they looked upwards, the behaviour of the senior leadership was against everything they were taught and held to be true." The *Citizen* said the report "flags the stress of mounting workloads, insufficient funding, 'disconnected' senior leadership, poor communication flow between lower and upper ranks and the weak 'people management' of the top bosses." What the press found most startling was the apparent disconnect between lower, middle, and upper ranks, and how they perceived the RCMP was being managed. Only the top brass, superintendents and higher, were happy, feeling content and in full control of their lives. Some griped about the hours they had to work. Everyone else had grown "significantly" discontented, which the report attributed to "circumstances at work," not aging. Hardest hit seemed to be the "bedrock" middle management—sergeants and staff sergeants, who are the heart of any police or military unit—who plummeted from 80 per cent commitment to 59 per cent. If the Mounties had lost them, they were in very deep trouble. As their health deteriorated, due in part to the extra hours required after the September 11, 2001, terrorist attacks, half of the noncoms were identified as "high risk" for burnout. Only 30 per cent felt that their bosses—senior management—were supportive.

Duxbury stated that this "combination of stress, burnout and lack of commitment and high life satisfaction" is typical of disillusioned workers who have "retired on the job," an unhappy and unanticipated end for "former gung-ho, altruistic employees who wanted to make a difference." They gave up, she said, because they felt "betrayed" by the organization and can't make that difference. Re-engaging these workers was critical, Duxbury insisted, especially in the face of a looming labour shortage, because these police officers can easily quit and find other jobs. Such lack of support from above will also turn off new recruits.

"What's scary is that these were the findings before all the muckraking and bad press they have been getting," Duxbury said. "But someone has to stand up and stop painting everyone black because of a few bad senior managers. What is important is for the government to re-engage the bedrock of the force and they can't do that as long as Parliament is playing whack-a-mole with the RCMP in public."

But was the disconnect too large to re-engage officers? How do you motivate people who are told by senior management "just do it" without adequate staff, funds, or equipment, when the managers seem to find plenty of everything for lavish headquarter renovations? It was a classic example of the corporate personality disorder identified by RCMP consultant Eli Sopow.

The Duxbury-Higgins study also found that many Mounties believed that anyone who spoke up risked being punished or shuffled off to another job. That scenario had played out dramatically when a small group of uniformed and civilian members had pursued their belief that senior management was using their pension and insurance funds improperly, leading to David Brown's reviews.

In the end, the Duxbury-Higgins report laid much blame at the feet of the federal government, accusing them of badly managing the public service for the past twenty years, obsessed with budgets, not people. All the Harper government's *Accountability Act* did was manage all bureaucrats like "possible criminals" instead of "cracking down on the bad apples."

The reference to the public service was key. Too many people forget that the RCMP are an arm's-length branch of the government with the unique status of a "guardian" agency. For decades, under successive prime ministers from both ends of the political spectrum, there had been efforts to revive and revitalize the public service. Plans ranged from "make the managers manage" to "let the managers manage." Those same approaches were applied to policing. The trick was to know when the thin line between civilian oversight and political intrusion was being crossed.

On April 8, 2002, Hugh Segal, then president of the Institute for Research on Public Policy (IRPP), addressed police and politicians on their "accountability/independence conundrum" at the

Canadian Police College executive seminar in Ottawa. Recalling being pulled over for speeding "late one evening on a deserted piece of road in Newfoundland," he said his only worry was how much over the speed limit he had been driving.

"We did not worry about being harmed physically or shaken down financially for the officer's personal or political gain," he said. "We did not worry that he did not have a second officer with him. We understood implicitly that he could be trusted to do whatever the highway traffic act and his own legitimate discretion required.

"We took his commitment to the law, the public interest in our safety and his uniform for granted."

Not many countries can claim that peace of mind, he suggested, referring to what we call "democracy." Elected politicians are at the core of that political system, but, said Segal, their only real authority with the public comes from their capacity to persuade. It's a different relationship between the public and the police.

"The police are the front line on crime, and the final resort in terms of addressing public disorder," he said. "No aspect of our social infrastructure has the license to impose penalties as harsh or use as much force as the police" under lawful conditions. "The public understands viscerally the difference between their relationship with elected politicians and professional and disciplined police forces across the country. They have different expectations of each and different levels of trust."

Segal presented a more dogmatic public perception of the police, saying the latter respect the law because they are paid to uphold it, with the use of force if necessary.

"Police are expected to view all citizens equally unless there is hard evidence of malfeasance," he continued. "Police are expected to keep their emotions as human beings, taxpayers, citizens, voters utterly separate from their policing role."

If such expectations seem excessive, he added, they are real.

"Police leadership and political leadership make the same mistake, well-intentioned but potentially quite problematic ... The broad issue of public security is larger than the police oversight and review community; it impacts, and is impacted by, vast areas of immigration, economic and social policy. Often, failures in systems as diverse as mental-health treatment, housing, education and border drug interdiction force the police into difficult front-line roles," usually with too few staff and resources.

Noting that the primary role of the state is to assure citizens the right to go about their lives "unintimidated by crime or violence," Segal said that the traditional arm's-length nature of the police usually means little contact between them and politicians except in times of crisis, and then generally only with those involving policing issues.

"Which is all well and good," he continued, "except that the truly key decisions being made about resources come from finance commissioners, budget committees, finance ministers, premiers and prime ministers." Police leaders, he argued, should then have the same right to advance their "legitimate institutional interests" as the head of any other government department, which depend on public funding and political oversight.

"Police forces and police leadership are independent and must be," Segal went on, "with accountability to the law and the duly constituted civilian oversight organizations that exist . . . because police are not beholden to any group of politicians, any particular political party, any particular minister or prime minister for their authority."

Trusting the police to always act in the public interest requires distance in critical areas, such as who is under investigation, and rigid confidentiality until people are charged, he explained, to ensure the "absolute preservation" of police independence.

"Informal practices that afford people in power any warning at all about pending charges against the strongest, most prominent or weakest in our society are simply a mistake," Segal declared. "Any politician worth his or her salt would much rather find out about this at the precise time that the media and public at large do."

That long-standing tradition had been eroded during the Mulroney era, when many people—and a lot of Mounties—blamed then RCMP commissioner Norm Inkster for changing the rules and agreeing to notify elected officials when they were under investigation. Now Segal seemed to be saying that politicians should have no special rights in that regard and that police must have a say in policies that will affect them, suggesting that when they have legitimate concerns regarding parliamentary debate or public discussion on such issues as immigration, mental-health facilities, legalization of certain substances, highway or housing issues or alcohol abuse, then "uniformed police leadership who have direct contact with street reality must not be excluded from the debate." Similarly, narrowing accountability to the law and the "designated oversight organization" would be a mistake "because that leaves the initiative in everyone else's hands except yours." In that scenario, the finger pointers, politicians, those who always feel wronged by the police "regardless of the facts," and the media critics will always have the initiative, Segal said, conceding that, too, is democracy. Of course, there is also the possibility that the head of an organization is speaking simply for his organization, which was the case when Chief of Defence Staff Rick Hillier spoke freely to the media about military issues and the Prime Minister's Office was accused in the media of trying to "muzzle" him. Hillier, who dubs terrorists as "scumbags" and opinion-makers in Ottawa as "snake-oil salesmen," proved a loyal soldier but a tough man to reign in.

But, Segal concluded, "The most serious risk is that the politicians of any particular government, no matter how popular or well-meaning, become the perceived mouthpiece for the police, or, even worse, the police became the mouthpiece for that government."

In April 2006, the Fraser Institute think tank aired its concerns with the state of federal policing in a much more public forum, issuing its damning report "Bureaucrats in Uniform: The Politicization and Decline of the Royal Canadian Mounted Police." Building its exhaustive case over roughly 100 pages totalling more than 40,000 words, the study concluded: "One way or another, however, it is our contention that de-politicization is the key to halting the decline of the RCMP." Far ranging in scope, the report cited the "unprecedented" centralization of power during the 1990s in the Prime Minister's Office for enabling the PMO and cabinet to largely supplant Parliament, which has become "little more than a focus group," thus undermining the principles of responsible government. Combine that with budget cuts and underfunding, and the report concluded that abilities to tackle organized crime were seriously compromised. That seemed to be confirmed by the 2005 Auditor General's report, which concluded that "too great a focus on contract policing has contributed to relative underfunding of federal policing"; and noting, "Since 2000, the RCMP has, for the most part, met its contractual obligations to provide the required number of peace officers to its clients, but has done so to the detriment of staffing its federal policing activities" And, as the demand for contract policing grew, the Mounties cut back on their federal policing responsibilities.

The Fraser report concluded that the RCMP no longer had "a core competency" in federal policing because it had become a "police-services business."

Similar warnings had been issued as early as 1999, when retired RCMP assistant commissioner Robert Head offered twenty recommendations to address the politicization of the Force:

1. Remove the RCMP Commissioner as a deputy minister and report direct to Parliament.
2. Examine all candidates for commissioner in public session before an all-party parliamentary committee.
3. Give the commissioner of the RCMP the same annual reporting relationship to Parliament as the Auditor General of Canada.
4. Highlight the investigative aspect of law enforcement as a government priority, not to be subjected to the same financial restraints as more discretionary spending.
5. Have the Government of Canada advertise clear support for RCMP federal crime-fighting programs, including illegal immigration, fraud, drug enforcement, etc.
6. Have the House of Commons Justice Committee examine the government policy for financing operations like the Integrated Proceeds of Crime legislation to ensure they are properly financed.[12]

7. Allegations of misuse of public funds by Senators, Members of Parliament and Members of Provincial Legislative Assemblies be subjected to the same rules regarding Warrants to Search as for all other Canadians.

8. Reinforce the RCMP position as a "guardian organization" to direct more policy and personnel resources to law enforcement and crime control.

9. In reference to Bill C-68 on Gun Control, the commissioner's annual report to Parliament should clearly detail (a) the number of instances where rifles/shotguns were used in violent crime offences and (b) the number of instances where the registration system under Bill C-68 has assisted police in their law enforcement duties, and (c) a cost-benefit analysis of the legislation.

10. Amend the RCMP Act to ensure personnel policies, discipline and appeal procedures are simplified and equally balanced between fairness and expediency, more in keeping with the Force's history and organizational structure than to the business style of management.

11. Undertake an independent audit of the new Regional concept of management to determine if it has (a) improved criminal investigation capacity and public service and (b) resulted in more efficient and cost effective administration.

12. Hire civilians into RCMP senior management only when it can be clearly demonstrated that a member cannot be found to fill the position.

13. The RCMP commissioner's annual report to Parliament must clearly explain the impact that *Charter of Rights* decisions and Human Rights Tribunals have on the Force's ability to enforce the law.

14. The commissioner shall be obliged to appeal any pay and benefits issue directly to the government if it cannot be resolved with Treasury Board.

15. Audit the RCMP bilingual program[13] through an independent agency to determine if (a) all designated positions, including those of the senior officers in Ottawa, are still valid, and if (b)

the issue of bilingual bonus pay should be retained, particularly in contract policing situations where the province or municipality is obliged to pay the cost.

16. Review the RCMP overtime compensation system through an independent agency, to determine if (a) members should remain on the 'individual' mode and (b) commissioned officers are being treated fairly by the system.

17. The RCMP shall follow the practice of all major Canadian police forces and subject all member applicants to a polygraph examination.

18. The RCMP shall refrain from discriminating in favour of any particular ethnic or gender group of applicants for membership.

19. The RCMP first draw from a pool of former members of the Force before tapping into the pool of members currently serving (to staff) foreign police duty, and domestically in cases involving field investigations for applicants to the Force and as assistance to members in the areas of stress/trauma.

20. Have the Government of Canada create a separate dedicated agency to handle duties currently performed under Protective Operations of the RCMP.[14]

In December 2007, Dr. Linda Duxbury was back in the news as the media devoured her latest study, which had determined that the RCMP was beyond a "quick fix." This time, she warned that the Force's much-needed makeover was "doomed" if government interfered—and the Mounties as we know them might not even be around in ten years.

Her report, "The RCMP: Yesterday, Tomorrow and Today, a Benchmark for Brown's Task Force on Governance and Cultural Change," said that 40 per cent of RCMP officers plan to find new jobs before they can collect their pensions: "one in five said they were leaving because they aren't treated with respect." In a *Citizen* article, she called for "massive" change, which could take a decade to implement, warning that they "don't stand a chance" if the government interferes.

"This is an organization that has been deeply wounded over time and you can't expect the new guy to fix it overnight," Duxbury said. "It takes nine months to have a baby and having nine women each pregnant for a month won't speed it up. There is no way to speed this up."

Part of the problem seems to be the four-year election cycle, which can mean that a new government minister or commissioner can assume command with big promises and good intentions, but they may be replaced before they can take root, creating a "death valley of despair." Hope falters and productivity falls.

"They are almost ready to crawl out and all the stress and change is about to pay off when a new government comes in, kills it and starts over," Duxbury said. "Do this a couple of times and you wonder why people feel betrayed and don't trust their leaders."

That's why the Brown task force recommended that the RCMP should get out from under the thumb of Treasury Board and appoint new civilian watchdogs and managers so the Force can make its own decisions about budgets, staffing, and contracting.

About the only bright spot for the front-line Mounties in 2007 was the announcement, on December 19, by Deputy Commissioner Bill Sweeney, that the RCMP was implementing a new backup policy after two more Mounties were gunned down and died alone up north within weeks of each other. It would be expensive, requiring more staff or fewer detachments, and no one seemed sure where the funds would come from. But, Sweeney had vowed earlier, that "as an organization, we are and must continue to do everything in our power to support them." And so the Senior Executive Committee would add to the RCMP operations manual that multiple responses would be required for calls of violence, or where violence is anticipated; domestic disputes; an occurrence involving the use, display, or threatened use of a weapon; a situation involving a subject posing a threat to self or others; areas where communications are known to be lacking; or any situation where the member believes a multiple-member response is needed based on his or her risk assessment.

It was too little too late for the dead constables, but would, hopefully, prevent further needless slaughter. And members were still free to intervene alone if they deemed imminent risk for harm or death existed—for someone else.

Do we allow or *make* the police do their job? Civilian oversight is strategic, ensuring that the police are serving lawfully to protect our rights and safety. Political intervention or intrusion is tragic, allowing others to demand how police do their job. No one argues that the police should be monitored and held accountable for their actions—or inaction—within clearly defined parameters. They should be able to explain and justify to politicians, public servants, the media, and the public what they did or did not do and why. Their audience should be encouraged to ponder critically what they are being told or shown. But the key is what questions are asked and by whom; be precise, then listen closely to avoid being "spun" by those schooled by media consultants to give pat answers and stay on message.

In those instances, the media consultants get handsomely paid, and the cop, or whoever happens to be on the hot seat, gets a free pass. We know no more than we did before reading or watching or listening to the interview or article or news clip.

Journalism is frequently accused of increasingly blurring the line between information and entertainment, whether unknowingly or unapologetically, while the political and corporate overlords dominate their pages and broadcasts with their self-serving, favourable, sometimes deceptive, take on things. As the dominance of the print media has waned, radio, television, and the Internet try to reduce very complicated issues and events to short, manageable, seemingly dramatic sound bites. Consider how many times politicians invite the media to a news conference where they offer them a wondrous display of drugs and guns to show the fruits of their latest joint-force swoop and scoop. Then listen very carefully to the charges they claim to have laid. If the word "conspiracy" is not among the charges, all they have done is, once again, target the lowest levels of what may in fact be a widespread organized crime or terrorist organization, and thus a legitimate, perhaps dire and immediate threat, to our safety. It seems that more often, based on media accounts, the police are content to bust meth labs and burn marijuana fields without actually charging anyone, thereby grabbing the media spotlight, public esteem, and political favour without all the fuss and bother and expense of actually conducting an investigation to get bad people off the streets. Increasingly, major police announcements seem to involve tobacco seizures, traffic speeders, and drunk drivers. They are all legitimate targets, but are they the biggest threats to our overall safety and rights? Bringing us back once again to the core questions, we should all be asking: What do we want our police to be and to do? We pay them, we arm them, and we generally obey them, but are they serving in a way that best protects us? And what can we realistically expect them to do? It is their job to get criminals off the streets; it is the court's job to keep them off. A former chief justice of the Supreme Court of Canada has found that in that regard, the existing legal system may be courting disaster.

FIVE

COURTING DISASTER

Suddenly this huge figure filled the doorway ... and I was staring
down the business end of a .303 rifle.

—OPP Inspector (Ret'd) Andrew Maksymchuk from his memoir, *From
Muskeg to Murder: Memories of Policing Ontario's Northwest*

The most deadly call for a police officer can be a domestic dispute.
It is volatile and unpredictable as the officer is often attacked by the
person he's trying to save from a beating by an abusive spouse. It is
a call you don't want to do by yourself, but that was exactly the situation Andy Maksymchuk, known widely as Maks, found himself in
as a young constable at Minaki detachment, the most westerly OPP
outpost. As he admitted candidly in his memoir, his first domestic
call had ended badly for him.

Failing to handcuff the rather large man who had already given
his wife a shiner while they were drinking together, Maks was soon
rolling around the floor embraced in a clutch-and-grab wrestling
match. He wasn't sure he was winning, so he pulled out his billy
club and began hitting the man on his arms and shoulders. The
man recoiled and told him to stop: he gave up. He asked to get his
shoes before they headed out, Maks agreed and next thing he knew,

he was staring down the man's gun barrel. He left and called for backup. But as badly as the call had gone for him, the ensuing trial was worse. The wife of the accused, the woman Maks had rescued, contradicted the constable's testimony and the criminal charge of obstruct police was dismissed. The man was fined fifty dollars for a provincial liquor violation.

It didn't seem much for a guy who'd pulled a gun on a cop.

The police are the front-line public face for the large and at times incomprehensible justice system, which serves to protect our rights, safety, and quality of life. They are obliged to enforce the laws they do not write, and must go call to call with little respite between responses. It is their sense of duty and compassion and doing what must be done no matter the risk that keeps society grinding forward.

While we walk the same streets and neighbourhoods as the police, they almost never see them the way we do. If a van blazes past us on the highway in the dark of night, we are content to let it continue on its way without a second thought. It is the job of the police to pursue, stop, and approach that vehicle, often alone, with no idea of what they will encounter when the driver's window rolls down.

But the adrenaline surge common to police calls is never evident when the drama of the streets and alleys plays out in the ornate sterility of the courtroom, where split-second decisions made long ago by the person on the scene will be reviewed and dissected in painstaking detail—the final act played out in a justice system that has been transformed by the *Charter of Rights and Freedoms* into a legal system where some worry—and not just the police—that the rights of the accused trump the rights of the victim and the safety of society.

We have long accepted that it is better for the guilty to walk free than for the innocent to be condemned, but the concept has gone to new extremes in a system where the burden of proof and admission of evidence has become onerous. The courts are criticized by many in the media and society at large as being too lenient and undermining the efforts of law enforcement. The police also vent their dissatisfaction with the "soft" courts, which are commonly viewed as being more preoccupied with the law than with justice, which too often free or minimize the crimes of felons, sentencing them, as pundits are wont to cite, to luxurious Club Fed facilities where those who actually are sentenced to time behind bars can do so in relative comfort, some would say opulence.

There seems little doubt such rulings discourage police and prosecutors, but the reality is that it is not—nor should it be—the police officer's job to fix what is widely perceived as a flawed system. Even if their complaints are justified, their role is to identify lawbreakers and help, through evidence and sworn testimony, to remove those legitimate threats from the streets. It is the task of the twelve men and women on the jury—or the judge acting alone—to determine guilt or innocence based on what they see and hear at trial. The police are not, and should not, be assigned the additional roles of judge, jury, or executioner, even in a land that long ago banned capital punishment. In our system, even a judge's verdicts can be undone on appeal to a higher court. The verdict and sentence are governed by the law of the land, interpreted and applied by humans, with all the foibles that implies.

Judges in Canada are appointed by politicians, not elected by the public as in the United States. Both systems have merit and shortfalls, and beg the question: How independent are our courts? If, as we have seen, the fine line between civilian oversight and political intrusion into policing has been blurred, how sacrosanct are the altars of our founding philosophies based on the rule of law? It may comfort the police, and the rest of us, to learn that there are jurists working within the system asking these very questions.

Canada's legal system is adversarial by nature, pitting prosecutors against defenders who play for high stakes to determine guilt or innocence. Attorneys for both sides wear the same robes, attended the same law schools, and were taught the same law. It is their personal insights, motivations, and interpretations that guide them to seek "the truth"—or sometimes just find a technicality. The rising use of the latter, commonly raising ever more creative Charter challenges, has lengthened court proceedings to such alarming extents that justices began freeing a disturbing number of accused criminals on the basis that their right to a speedy trial had been violated. David Asper, chairman of the family-owned *National Post*, weighed in on that topic in his January 23, 2009, opinion piece "The problem of lengthy trials needs a Parliamentary fix."

"The phrase, 'Justice delayed is justice denied,' is attributed to 19th-century British politician William Gladstone. But the concept actually first appeared in the 13th century Magna Carta, where it is written at clause 40, 'To none will we sell, to none deny or delay, right or justice,'" he wrote. "This principle has not only stood the test of time and the development of the common law; it has been 'constitutionalized' by our Charter of Rights, which in section 11 guarantees the right in criminal cases to be 'tried within a reasonable time.' Ontarians got to know this provision well when a trial court stayed the corruption charges against six Toronto police officers because of multiple years of delay in their case." (The stay has since been overturned on appeal.)

Commenting that speedy trials are a vital aspect of criminal justice, Asper noted that cases, which once were handled "fairly routinely," had become "monolithic beasts that clog court dockets and judges' calendars, imposing massive systemic costs . . . [and] other cases, new laws have proved fertile ground for abuse, confusion and, consequently, delay. Together, these issues have created the challenge of the long trial."

As we have seen, the increasing complexities of trials originated in the increasing burden placed on the police, multiplying by many times the paperwork and time involved to pursue what had once been relatively simple procedures. It was refreshing and encouraging then to read that Asper was reporting that the alarm bells to fix the ailing system were being "rung loudest by judges."

Asper cited Justice Michael Moldaver, of the Ontario Court of Appeal, as one of the loudest voices calling for reform, beginning with the fuse he allegedly lit delivering the 2005 Sopinka Lecture on Advocacy to the Ontario Criminal Lawyers' Association.

"He pulled no punches about the role lawyers were playing in manipulating the system and unduly dragging out cases," Asper wrote, noting that some attendees resented the suggestion this was a general problem beyond a few practitioners, while others took umbrage that the judge's attack seem to focus on the defence for a problem that they said was "caused at least as much by systemic flaws in the law itself, as well as by other players, such as police, Crown attorneys and judges."

The police, it should be noted, were a contributing "problem" only because the courts, usually in response to defence appeals and motions that often led to new or amended legislation, raised their burden of proof for the investigators. This often mired them in mountains of paperwork to arrive at the same conclusions they had previously reached using a fraction of the time and documentation.

Moldaver, Asper noted, returned with "a tub thumper speech" to the 2006 Justice Summit, concluding: "We have a criminal justice system that, in many respects, is the envy of the world. It is not without its problems though. Complexity and prolixity are the twin demons that continue to bedevil it. The time has come to send them packing."

In that address, which he called his appellate judge's perspective of the state of the criminal justice system, Moldaver also clarified the statements he had made to the defence lawyers a year earlier.

"My message to the Criminal Defence Bar was that the problem was not solely, or even primarily, one of their making. Rather, it was a collective one for which all of the major stakeholders bore responsibility," Moldaver recalled. "For their part, I raised concerns about the proliferation of pretrial Charter motions and the impact these motions were having on the length of criminal trials. In that regard, what I asked of them was to be discerning in their use of such motions, especially where the underlying legal principles had been addressed by the Supreme Court of Canada. Hardly an earth-shattering proposition, or so I would have thought. Hardly one, I thought, that would lead a senior member of the defence bar to describe my address as 'shocking' and a leading academic to chastise me for viewing the Charter not as a 'vital living tree' but as a 'weed to be stunted.' On the plus side, he quipped, such comments proved that Charter-assured free speech 'is certainly alive and well in Canada.'"

Offering to set the record straight, Moldaver continued: "As part of the Constitution, the Charter is the supreme law of the land. It speaks to what we are all about as Canadians and what we aspire to be."

He called the Charter the cornerstone of a justice system that in many ways is the envy of the civilized world—a system that is predicated on the supremacy of the rule of law, that prides itself on an independent judiciary and open courtrooms, and that is founded on the belief that we are all equal before and under the law and that every human being is entitled to be treated with respect and dignity.

"Am I proud of the Charter?" he asked. "You bet I am! It serves as a model for constitutional democracies throughout the world, wherever they may exist and wherever they may take root. Do I want to see it thrive and flourish? Absolutely! As I said in a paper that I wrote in 1995: 'The Charter has the potential to do great good within our society.' Hardly the words, I think you would agree, of a Charter basher. Hardly the words of someone looking to see the Charter shrivel up and die on the vine.

"So let's be clear. Let's get the record straight: Do I view the Charter as a weed whose growth should be stunted? Not on your life. Do I have a problem with counsel who use the Charter to preserve and protect the rights of individuals and minority groups from state excesses? Absolutely not. Do I have a problem with counsel who use the Charter to promote and advance the cause of justice? Absolutely not.

"Now ask me: Do I have a problem with counsel who trivialize and demean the Charter and who use it, not as a means of promoting justice, but as a means of delaying and in some cases obstructing it? You bet I do. Do I have a problem with counsel who clog the courts and tax an already overburdened justice system by bringing Charter and other applications that are baseless? Absolutely. Does it bother me that the antics of these same counsel are depriving worthy litigants from being able to access the courts in a timely fashion? Absolutely. Does it bother me that these same counsel are pilfering precious Legal Aid funds at the expense of needy litigants with legitimate causes? Absolutely. Am I going to give up on my fight against those who would abuse our criminal justice system and make a mockery of it? Never."

The issue, Moldaver insisted, was not, as an assistant professor at Osgoode Law School had recently written, simply a product of "poor judgment by many criminal defence counsel on what Charter issues are worth litigating, as well as a plodding and prolix approach by some in advancing these claims." Nor was it, as someone had said to him after delivering his Sopinka lecture: "'Judge, you only have a problem with long criminal trials because you are on a fixed salary.'"

Vowing never to give up his fight to reform the system, Moldaver said many of his colleagues agreed that the first step was to regain control of their courtrooms.

"On the process side, many believe that we have ceded control of our courtrooms to the litigants and that this has led to delay, inefficiency, waste and all manner of abuse," he said. "On the substantive side, many trial judges complain that the criminal law has taken on complexities and subtleties the likes of which are truly mind-numbing. Few feel confident in their ability to complete a criminal trial from start to finish without committing reversible error. And that, as we all know, translates into new trials and more delays and more expense and more stress on a system that is already overburdened, if not overwhelmed."

To underscore his point, Moldaver referred to Justice David Watt's checklist for what judges are to know before commencing a criminal jury trial, which contained 115 points.[1]

"When I see lists like this and when I think of how cumbersome our criminal trial process has become, and how it often takes weeks and months and sometimes years for criminal trials to complete, I cannot help but wonder whether in our zeal to create a perfect justice system, we haven't instead ended up with one that is on the brink of collapse," he said. "Perhaps this is truly one of those instances where perfection has become the enemy of the good."

In trying to be fair, he asked, had they "bent so far backwards looking for social and economic justice that they just toppled over?"

More positively, he congratulated Chief Justice Heather Smith and her Advisory Committee on Criminal Trials for requiring Crown and defence counsel to focus much earlier on "contentious trial issues" and for requiring trial judges to closely scrutinize pre-trial motions to ensure "that baseless ones are not heard and that those with potential merit are heard in a timely and efficient fashion." Their efforts, Moldaver said, represented a vital new beginning to reduce the length of criminal trials while preserving a high quality of justice.

"Above all else," he observed, "they serve as a sober reminder, to trial and appellate judges alike, that control of the courtroom belongs to the judges, not the litigants ... the time has come for trial judges to regain control of their courtrooms and they deserve our full cooperation and support in this important task."

Hearkening back to a previous decade, when Roy McMurtry was named chief justice of the Ontario Court of Appeal in the mid-1990s, Moldaver drew parallels to the recent committee steps, noting it had been bleak back then too, with a "gargantuan" backlog of cases.

"Civil appeals were taking two to three years from the date of perfection to be heard," he recalled. "Criminal appeals weren't much better. They were being heard one and a half to two and a half years from the date of perfection."

McMurtry refused the "great hue and cry" from the lawyers to name a dozen or more of them judges.

"The problem, he realized, lay with the judges alright, but not because there were too few of us, but because the few of us that there were had given over control of the process to the litigants," Moldaver explained, setting the stage for a blue-ribbon committee to restore the natural order by wresting control back where it belonged—"from the litigants and put it back into the hands of the judges."

That meant challenging those identified by Moldaver who were making fortunes with hefty billings of up to six hundred dollars an hour or six thousand dollars a day in court. If you were among that number, he observed, "you wouldn't be complaining about long trials. You'd want them to go on forever!" Even those raking in only a thousand dollars daily would be happy with preserving the status quo in the courts.

"For those who think that way," he concluded, "the Charter is like a gift from heaven. It is the godsend of all godsends." And it had to stop.

Giving the system a good shake had worked, Moldaver said; within eighteen months, the backlog was gone: "Civil appeals could now be heard within nine to twelve months of perfection and sooner if need be; criminal appeals within six to nine months and sooner if need be." What is needed now is what worked then; a revival of McMurtry's courage, vision and leadership because "the strength of our criminal justice system lies not in rules or regulations or edicts but in the people who serve it." Otherwise, the frustration festering among trial judges will worsen as they ponder their ability to complete a criminal trial "without committing reversible error." Complexity, he concluded, had become a pox on our judicial system.

Moldaver wasn't the only voice in the wilderness. In his column, Asper noted that, in 2007, Chief Justice Beverly McLachlin of the Supreme Court of Canada joined the fray, telling Toronto's Empire Club of Canada that murder trials that used to take five to seven days were now going on for five to seven months or more and that "proceedings in criminal cases are crumbling under the weight of pretrial motions."

In 2008, Ontario attorney general Chris Bentley commissioned a detailed study of large and complex criminal trials under the guidance of the Honourable Patrick Lesage and Professor Michael Code. Their report, published that November, clearly identified the issues that had caused the "complexification" of criminal trials and offered a wide range of solutions. But neither Lesage, a former chief justice of the Ontario Superior Court of Justice, or Code, a former assistant deputy attorney general recognized as one of the province's most distinguished criminal defence lawyers and a law professor at the University of Toronto, harboured any delusion that the courts would ever return to the simpler pre-Charter trials. They concluded that the criminal trial courts have had to absorb "a continuing onslaught of new Charter remedies, new common law evidence principles, new legislative procedures and new offences over the past 20 to 30 years. It is hardly surprising, in these circumstances, that the short, simple and efficient criminal trial of the 1970s has been replaced by the long, complex and often inefficient criminal trial of the 21st century."

The report took pains to ensure the authors were not criticizing the Charter, the Supreme Court of Canada, or Parliament, citing collective initiatives, accompanied by strong arguments for "entrenched constitutional rights, principles-based evidence law, 'criminal-organization' offences, 'terrorist' offences and 'third-party records' procedures to protect the privacy interests of complainants and witnesses." Lesage and Code were not recommending "turning back the clock" on initiatives they said represented legitimate policy choices, "even though they came with significant costs to trial efficiency."

It wasn't the changes they took issue with, but with their cumulative effect on the system, noting that "the convergence of all three of these major developments ... has placed an enormous burden on the trial courts." They observed that the legal reformers, in both the Supreme Court and Parliament who initiated these "profound changes" never stepped back to ponder whether the justice system could "effectively and efficiently absorb all of these changes at once." The report reasoned that each of the major changes combined to create longer and more complex court proceedings.

"Cumulatively, their impact on trial length, efficiency and delay has been very significant," Lesage and Code concluded. "We are operating today in a very different legal context."

This new context was blamed for exacerbating weaknesses in the justice system in three specific areas involving new Charter remedies, new motions challenging evidence law, and new statutory procedures. All generally impacted on pretrial proceedings, making them more elaborate and therefore more likely to delay trials. The justice system, they noted, had not responded well.

"Indeed," they wrote, "a somewhat complacent culture seems to have developed. There appears to be an attitude within the justice system that motions will inevitably go on for months, cross-examinations and examinations of witnesses and legal arguments will inevitably go on for days and trials will inevitably take years to commence."

Even the slightest new development in a case led either the Crown or defence to "reflexively" seek adjournments, which were routinely granted, "no matter how unfounded or fanciful" it might be. As provincial Legal Aid would pay counsel for arguing any motion in court, regardless of its merits or utility to the case, it offered "a financial incentive for endless motions." That had to change and both lawyers and judges must "aspire to the standards of an earlier era" that did not tolerate such delays. Legal arguments, examinations, and cross-examinations of witnesses must again be "succinct and focused." Adjournments, they reasoned, should only be granted where some truly significant development arises unexpectedly—frivolous motions should be summarily dismissed. (Ontario lawyers were also threatening to boycott Legal Aid, demanding more money, at the time of this writing.)

"The modern culture of delay causes great harm to public confidence in the justice system and it needs to change," they concluded.

Second, Lesage and Code believed the changes had made the court system both "error-prone and fearful of error"—that the "avalanche of new and complex legal procedures," whether from the Charter, the so-called evidence law "revolution," or from continuous statutory amendments, had created a system with too many difficult and "nuanced" decision rationales. No one should be surprised that errors were being made in such an environment, prompting fearful judges and lawyers to become overly cautious and calling excessively marginal evidence, listening to more arguments, disclosing more information, taking too long to rule, and then ruling in the most protective way, out of undue concern for appellate review. Again, the cumulative effect of these trends meant unduly long trials. The authors sought to reverse "this phenomenon of exhaustive and exhausting lawyering and timid judging," believing that the increasing complexity of modern criminal procedure and evidence law has created a need for judges with real expertise who will be able to effectively manage these cases, especially at the pretrial stage.

"We also believe that effective case-management practices can be stated clearly and simply, as rules, and not as infinitely flexible principles," they wrote, adding that the leading members of the bar and the best Crown prosecutors should be assigned to the "most serious and difficult cases" to avoid errors.

Third, they cited the "broad cultural changes" they had identified for creating a "significant increase in animosity and acrimony" between Crown and defence lawyers, noting that many of the recent cases that dragged on for far too long were characterized by "abusive and uncivil conduct" from one side or the other—or both. Noting that the adversarial nature of trials had always created opportunities for conflict, they were alarmed by the apparent rise in incidents—another serious development that had to be stopped.

"When counsel attack each other on a personal level, the adversary system breaks down because nothing gets settled out of court," they admonished. "Every petty dispute is fought out in the courtroom in a hostile and provocative way, and the trial ceases to focus efficiently on the real issues in the case."

Everyone, it seemed, who had explored the issue of prolonged trials had concluded that the system must change, in some cases revert to kinder and simpler days, fully aware that the Charter had changed everything. But, as Professor Martin Friedland asked in his paper to the International Society for the Reform of Criminal Law in June 2007: "Who's in charge of the reform of criminal law?" He concluded that Parliament has much more latitude for broader consultation than the courts, which, in *R v Askov,* freed an accused because his case took too long to be heard, setting off another fifty thousand acquittals across the land. In that case, he noted, the court heard only from the litigants and had no concept of the "potential systemic implications of its decision."

In his *National Post* column, Asper concluded that now that the complexities of criminal trials and the delays they caused had been identified, Parliament had to act, arguing: "Delay in the fix is as bad as delay in the process." That seems logical. But the cautionary question is: How impartial are those who oversee the justice system? That question was debated in 2005.

On June 3, *Hansard* records that Bloc Québécois MP Richard Marceau moved: "That the House denounce the recent remarks made by Mr. Justice Michel Robert stating that it is acceptable to discriminate on the basis of political opinion when appointing candidates to the federal judiciary and that it call on the Standing Committee on Justice, Human Rights, Public Safety and Emergency Preparedness to create a special subcommittee with the mandate to examine the process for appointments to the federal judiciary and make recommendations for reform, with the primary goal of eliminating political partisanship from the process, by October 31, 2005."

Marceau, referring to witnesses who had appeared before the Gomery Commission of Inquiry into the Sponsorship Program and Advertising Activities, which reviewed allegations of wrongdoing as high as former prime minister Jean Chrétien's office and was created by his successor Paul Martin in 2004 and reported in 2005, was talking about revelations made by Benoît Corbeil, the former director general of the Quebec wing of the Liberal Party of Canada, that aspiring judges "needed to have friendly relations with those people"— whom the Bloc identified as "members of the Liberal network who can influence the political machinery." Marceau also cited comments by Michel Robert, the chief justice of the Quebec Court of Appeal and a long-standing Liberal and president of the Liberal Party of Canada from 1986 to 1990, who, on November 29, 2004, had told the Radio-Canada public-affairs program *Maisonneuve en direct* that he did not believe he would have been appointed to the Court of Appeal if he had been a supporter or an elected representative of a sovereignist party, commenting: "I believe the Government of Canada appoints people with federalist sentiments when there are openings in the hierarchy." He stopped short of conceding there was a "political" dimension to his appointment, but conceded there was a "constitutional dimension."

Marceau also cited Robert's comments in a later Radio-Canada interview: "To be nominated to a federal judicial function, I think it's a sort of prerequisite, one must not be sovereignist, I mean, I think this is a generally held opinion among Canadian judges."

The Bloc MP said such comments by the chief justice of the

Quebec Court of Appeal "constitute a serious error in judgment," and that Robert had "crossed the line, which should be and which is extremely clear, separating the political and judicial branches."

Marceau considered it a failure in his duty to refrain from public debate by freely crossing into political debate—a serious breach of judiciary duty.

"There is a fairly serious problem of perception as far as the politicization of the judiciary is concerned," Marceau claimed, later adding: "Unfortunately, people are starting to mistrust the judiciary, which is, as I said, the cornerstone of our legal system in a country where the supremacy of law must be enforced." The allegations sparked vigorous debate in the House of Commons, but the issue was now in the public domain. Can judges who are politically appointed be deemed independent? The answer is probably yes. Everyone who rises to the point where they are considered for a judgeship has probably forged some political connection with any of the major political parties during their career. Being known as a Grit or a Tory, an NDP or Bloc associate should not preclude an agile legal mind any more than for elected judges in the United States who are known Democrats or Republicans. Justices are answerable for their rulings in court, not usually their political alliances, and the politicians who appoint them are also responsible for removing them, requiring a joint resolution of Parliament on the recommendation of the Canadian Judicial Council, comprising twenty-two chief justices and judges—a very rare occurrence. The council has only recommended removing two judges from the bench: Quebec Superior Court justice Jean Bienvenue in 1996, who resigned before the justice minister could make the request to Parliament, and Ontario justice Paul Cosgrove.

In early 2009, the council recommended removing Cosgrove who, during a 1998 murder trial that involved the dismemberment of a man in Kemptville, Ontario, had cited more than 150 breaches of the accused's Charter rights and accused Crown attorneys and police of "deceit and misconduct." The fallout destroyed, or at least badly derailed, the careers of some police and prosecutors. Overturned on appeal in 2003, Cosgrove failed to stop the inquiry into his actions and his belated apology was deemed to be too little, too late to save him as the council ruled: "The judge's misconduct was so serious and so destructive of public confidence that no apology, no matter its sincerity, can restore public confidence in the judge's ability to impartially carry out his duties in future." Meanwhile, the accused Cosgrove had freed had returned to the Barbados. She was later located in Costa Rica and extradited back to Canada where she pleaded guilty to manslaughter and was sentenced to seven years.

But Cosgrove was condemned by his peers for having "no factual basis" for his ruling and allegations and for having "misused his power," not for being a former federal Liberal cabinet minister or mayor of Scarborough, Ontario.

If the miasma infecting the courts were so troublesome and deeply rooted to cause such angst for some of the greatest legal minds in the country, what hope did the police, who numbered few lawyers in their ranks, have to find their way through the maze to distant blind justice?

They were having enough problems just keeping up with the increasingly sophisticated organized crime factions and increasingly violent gangs they were chasing. Even if fixing the courts was actually their battle, which it clearly is not, they just didn't have the time, staff, or resources for such an onerous undertaking. Their first calling—fighting crime and keeping the peace—was already stretching their thin bruised line to the breaking point.

SIX

TAKING CARE OF BUSINESS:
Mobsters and Gangsters

Crime abhors a vacuum.
—true-crime author Julian Sher

On April 15, 2009, police dealt a crushing blow to the Hells Angels in Quebec and New Brunswick, launching co-ordinated raids that they claimed shut down the outlaw motorcycle gang's East Coast operations. While the media estimated that between 123 and 156 people were arrested, all agreed that an overwhelming majority were full-patch members. The rest were associates.

Operation SharQc 2009, which had run for three years, was reportedly the culmination of more than eighty investigations dating back to 1992. In all, the media reported, more than 1,200 officers from the RCMP, Sûreté du Québec (SQ), and nearly twenty municipal police forces executed the arrest and search warrants, seizing $5 million in cash, dozens of kilograms of cocaine, marijuana and hashish, and thousands of pills. Police arrested so many bikers that they had to be arraigned by videoconference at the Gouin Courthouse in Montreal. Most were charged with first-degree murder (twenty-two charges), attempted murder, gangsterism, or drug trafficking. Eleven prosecutors were assigned to the case.

The raids also seized contents from five Hells Angels bunkers, and the timing could not have been better. A day later, the Supreme Court of Canada ruled in favour of provinces being allowed to seize possessions believed to have been procured through proceeds of crime. The potential windfall was staggering. As Kirk Makin reported in the *Globe and Mail*: "Since 2002, Ontario has seized or launched forfeiture proceedings involving almost $16-million in property; 73 per cent of it was from drug-related cases. B.C. has seized $4.5-million under its own provision since 2006."

The three-year Quebec investigation was a resounding success for law enforcement against an organized crime group that operated in such a good businesslike manner that Justice John McMahon of Ontario Superior Court said in 2008 that it "would be the envy of many international corporations." The scope of the raids also drew praise in the media from noted true-crime authors Yves Lavigne and Julian Sher. Lavigne, who confessed to seldom having a kind word to say about anti-biker efforts by the police, dubbed it "probably the most unique and most successful bust ever." He was also one of the few who did not seem concerned about competitors rushing in to take over the Angels' turf, telling the press: "There's nothing to fight about. The street gangs work for the Hell's *(sic)* Angels, the street gangs get their drugs from the Hell's *(sic)* Angels. There's no turf to fight for here. There's no one else, there are no other organizations in Quebec that can come in and fill this void."

Sher was less certain, stating: "Crime abhors a vacuum. Drugs aren't going to disappear off the street. That's certainly not the purpose of these kinds of raids."

The last crippling blow to an outlaw motorcycle club had been delivered more than a decade earlier when the Ontario Provincial Police destroyed the powerful Outlaws. Ironically, that success also removed the last deterrent to the Hells Angels from entering the final province in Canada. Patched members were spotted in Hamilton and Guelph within a very short time and several of the Outlaws' affiliate clubs "patched over" to the new ruthless kids on the block.

These latest successful raids allegedly resulted from information provided by a retired Hells Angel for a reported princely sum of $2.9 million, underscoring the "Two Gets" of good policing: Get off your ass and get an informant. While the police continued looking for the handful who had escaped the net, they assured everyone that they could handle anyone who tried to replace the bikers. As Lavigne observed, the police had shattered the bikers' mythical cloak of invulnerability.

In fact, the police had taken a page from the bikers' playbook. For years, the Hells Angels' catchphrase had been "taking care of business" and now the police, or at least the SQ, were operating as a business and expected to see a handsome return on what they'd invested to nab the outlaw bikers—the largest reward ever paid by the province.

In May 2008, Normand Proulx, director general of the Sûreté du Québec, explained in a media interview that "[L]uck comes to those who are prepared."

As a young patrol officer in St. Eustache, back in 1976, Proulx swapped his evening shifts for weekend duty to allow him to attend night school. He wants others to follow his example and, within ten years, all SQ officers will reportedly be required to have a university degree. The article notes that, in 1997, only 3 per cent of its managers had a university education; by 2005, 20 per cent of the thirty chief inspectors were involved in postgraduate studies, as were 14 per cent of the fifty inspectors, 16 per cent of the masters and 6 per cent of lieutenants.

The SQ certainly seems to have cleaned up its act. The article notes that it has not had a single scandal since 2003; the 175 in 1999 are credited with prompting the reforms. And, Proulx claimed, they're coming in, on, or under budget. And now they've helped beat the bikers at their own game—taking care of business.

The success of Operation SharQc 2009, involving so many police forces, seems to be an admirable example of what can be accomplished when police pool their resources and work together. Police in Ontario had staged their own impressive clampdown on the bikers a short time earlier. But imagine for a moment what might truly have been accomplished.

Clearly, the raids proved that the police were capable of shutting down a major organized crime group. Why then only in Quebec and New Brunswick, and before them, Ontario acting alone? No doubt it's due, at least in part, to the fact that that was where the informant was. But where there's one, there are presumably others. The bad-boy band of brothers will never be able to totally trust one another after this. There's always someone who savours the thought of becoming an instant millionaire, provided witness protection accompanies the cheque. With this template in hand, it would seem logical that the game could be repeated in other provinces by the Mounties working with other police departments.

Prior to this stunning success, the only people putting a dent in the biker gangs were the bikers themselves. The Hells Angels massacred one of their own chapters allegedly because those members were starting to sample the drugs they were selling. Members of the Bandidos Motorcycle Club were convicted (and are appealing the verdict) for killing eight of their members and associates, who were found crammed into vehicle trunks in southern Ontario, in 2006, in what is considered Ontario's worst mass murder. A horde of OPP investigators descended on that crime scene and followed the killers' trail to Winnipeg. The second shoe dropped on the police a short time later when a Native land dispute at Caledonia threatened to erupt into violence. Officers were promptly seconded there from detachments across Ontario, a tactic that was sustained beyond the summer. During that time, the thin blue line was seriously depleted across much of the province.

Lacking an informant may make it difficult to duplicate the success of Operation SharQc 2009, and puts greater emphasis on traditional intelligence gathering. That usually means the CISC and its provincial agencies.

CISC bills itself as the voice of the Canadian criminal intelligence community, whose basic task is to "facilitate the timely and effective production and exchange of criminal intelligence," providing leadership and expertise to help its member agencies to "detect, reduce and prevent organized and serious crime affecting Canada."

The central CISC bureau in Ottawa is primarily a repository for the information gleaned by the provincial and territorial bureaus and is best known for its annual reports. Until recently, they tended to identify the same handful of organized crime groups—bikers, Asian Triads and Yakuza (Japanese), traditional Mafia—adding First Nations Warriors and Eastern European mobsters in later years. Today it claims to have identified 950 organized crime groups in Canada. That's not as shocking as it sounds when you check Section 467.1 of the *Criminal Code*, which defines "Criminal organization" as a group, however organized, that:

a) is composed of three or more persons in or outside of Canada; and,

b) has as one of its main purposes or main activities the facilitation or commission of one or more serious offences that, if committed, would likely result in the direct or indirect receipt of a material benefit, including a financial benefit, by the group or by any of the persons who constitute the group.

The definition excludes groups who form randomly to commit a single crime.

The "2008 CISC Report," widely reported by the media, identified the drug trade, notably marijuana and methamphetamine, as still the largest criminal market in Canada in scope and the degree of involvement by the majority of organized crime groups, concluding: "Canada is also a primary source country of ecstasy for the world's drug trade." It also noted that the war in Afghanistan had done nothing to affect "record-high opium production" and that opium seizures in Canada have increased significantly, but were still low compared to other drugs.

As always when dealing with organized crime, you have to follow the money to determine what the bad guys are up to. While old-school raids clearly still exist, criminals are becoming ever more sophisticated and tech savvy. Technology has simplified crime for everything from mortgage fraud to the market in illegal cigarettes. CISC estimated that mass-marketing fraud operations gross over $500 million a year and that counterfeit or altered cheques and money orders are increasingly being used by organized crime to commit mass-marketing fraud. Technology is abetting debit-card fraud while wireless technology allows information to be relayed from point-of-sale terminals to people in cars stationed nearby. The CISC article notes that the stolen data are transferred almost instantly to "card factories" around the world. And, of course, online access is facilitating money laundering and the sale of illegal goods. Gun smuggling and human trafficking also seemed on the rise, both tying into the United States.

CISC expected the Internet would become increasingly appealing for criminals looking to buy and sell illegal guns. The United States is believed to be the main foreign supplier of guns smuggled into Canada. Organized crime gangs are also actively involved in human-smuggling operations in Canada with a "significant increase" in illegal migration from the United States into Canada.

The Internet has created problems for law enforcement that previous generations never had to face and could never have anticipated. CISC produced "The Organized Crime Marketplace in Canada" summary to help explain what that meant to investigators and citizens. The primary threats fell into two main categories: new crimes committed with and born out of new technology; and traditional crimes committed with new technology (i.e., hacking and "spoofing" websites, identity theft, extortion, and fraud). The problems grew in step with the increased numbers of people surfing the Web and the expansion of global e-commerce. CISC reported that organized crime groups are broadening their targets to tap into online storage of valuable personal, financial, and intellectual-property information. Spam has gone from annoying clutter to a menacing tool for distributing malicious "malware"—viruses, worms, spyware, and Trojan horse software—that can access the recipient's personal or sensitive data. Internet "pharming" allows hackers to exploit vulnerabilities in the domain name system (DNS) server software and then illicitly redirect Internet traffic to targeted websites and redirect unsuspecting users to fake sites for "phishing," threatening the security of online financial transactions. CISC also found that criminals are forming more and larger botnets, or networks of computers with broadband Internet connections that are compromised by malware and are thus "software robots or zombies." These remotely controlled attack networks undertake a variety of crimes: sending spam or phishing emails, hosting spoofed websites for pharming scams, and distributing viruses or Trojan horse software to facilitate online extortion or compromise more home computers for larger botnets. Online "carder networks" illegally buy and sell stolen personal and financial information, many selling blank or bogus credit cards, which leads to identity theft. CISC cites Operation FIREWALL, an eighteen-month operation launched in 2005, after twenty-eight people from eight U.S. states and several countries sold nearly two million credit-card numbers in two years, causing losses of more than US$4 million. An increasingly popular extortion scheme involves either threatening to launch or actually launching denial-of-service (DoS) attacks or directed denial-of-service (DDoS) attacks against businesses. These attacks, often undertaken through botnets, involve overloading computer networks or servers with enormous amounts of data to disrupt or interrupt service to users.

Internationally, some criminal groups, according to the United Kingdom's National High-Tech Crime Unit, are also showing increasing interest in using the Internet for pay-per-view child pornography, its production and distribution facilitated by new technologies and innovations. The report notes that computer software can digitally alter images of child pornography to enhance or change the image, for example sexualizing content by removing clothing. Similarly, in contrast to software that digitally ages missing children, images of child pornography can be created by "de-aging" images of adult pornography. With developments in animation, digitally created child pornography may become widespread as criminals learn innovative ways to conceal information, like child pornography, and distribute it in a secure fashion.

The new technology that provides increasingly secure,

anonymous, and rapid communication, through tools like encryption software, wireless devices, encrypted cellphones and anonymous re-mailers that forward emails without revealing their origins, allow online drug trafficking, eliminating physical interactions, thereby reducing the risks of detection and prosecution. And intimidation, bullying, threatening, and cyber-stalking in chat rooms are but a click away.

Even for the new generation of tech-savvy police officers, it's all combined to make law enforcement much harder. The CISC report admits that even trying to get a handle on its scope and extent is difficult to determine, domestically or globally, largely due to "chronic non- or under-reporting" by victims. As a result, computer crime and its associated financial losses are soaring.

"It is increasingly expensive and difficult to respond to evolving threats from computer-related crime as well as to update protective software continually—firewalls, encryption and anti-virus and anti-spam protection," the report said. "Businesses face increased costs from malware ranging from lost worker productivity, degraded network performance, security risks and waste of technical support resources to expensive, time-consuming repairs and upgrades." CISC cites the Canadian Banking Association's estimate that domestic banks spend more than $100 million annually to prevent, detect, and deter fraud and other crimes against banks, including activity related to identity theft.

"It is essential that law enforcement, the private sector and the public work together to promote awareness of technologically-related crimes, to encourage the reporting of all crimes and to discuss ways to reduce the threats," CISC concluded.

Or, as RCMP National Police Services deputy commissioner Peter Martin observed: "The pervasiveness of organized crime impacts individuals and communities across Canada. People are robbed of their physical safety, their security and their assets. The solution is an integrated approach by law enforcement across Canada, working to keep our citizens and society secure."

Writing about the foundations of the organized crime marketplace in the 2008 CISC report, Vancouver chief constable Jim Chu noted that it affects everyone in the community, calling it a plague that must be stamped out. The first step is to recognize the key aspects of the Canadian organized crime marketplace. Chu identified the British Columbia lower mainland, southern Ontario, and greater Montreal regions as the primary criminal hubs, home to the largest concentrations of criminal groups and the most active markets. Illicit drugs remain the main criminal activity with the broadest scope and the most groups involved. Police successes in dismantling or disrupting the trade usually affect a single group; a short-term victory quickly undermined by creating opportunities for a new group to move in. "In general," Chu confirmed, "criminal markets are highly resistant to long-term disruption as they continue to exist in response to meeting consumer demand."

Jurisdiction was also a problem for police as organized crime groups increasingly exploit international borders and form global linkages with other criminal groups to protect supply and distribution of their illicit products and human trafficking. In the end, crime groups have had success tapping into legitimate businesses to launder their profits while insulating themselves from scrutiny, further frustrating police and undermining public confidence.

Police in the Vancouver area have long accepted that they are in a hub for major criminal groups and have introduced innovative responses over the years, such as the Organized Crime Agency of British Columbia in 1999. But that wasn't their first response; decades earlier they had discovered their first CLEU for battling organized crime.

Created in 1974, the Coordinated Law Enforcement Unit (CLEU) included not only staff, investigative, and operational resources from all the police forces in the region, but it also housed a legal division. This blend of expertise allowed prompt and meaningful action on intelligence, followed up by a team of dedicated prosecutors whose overriding focus was to bring organized crime cases to trial. Justices came to realize that they were seeing many of the same gangsters over and over again, leading to stiffer sentences for repeat offenders.

In its day, CLEU set a new world standard for the most complex, time-consuming and costly criminal investigations in the world. But that meant that in the end, they were rounding up very senior criminals, not just the foot soldiers who could be easily replaced. The unit boasted a permanent force of sixty-six officers. Its legal branch was modelled on the American experience, a unique approach in Canada to help facilitate investigations and expedite prosecutions by assigning dedicated prosecutors who would be appearing before the same judges with the same high-level charges, often against the same people or their associates. A pattern could be shown, one major identifier for "organized" crime. Policy analysis allowed experts from various disciplines to address organized crime from numerous perspectives (numbers varied by funding, caseload, and complexity). Civilian analysts also played a vital role because as investigators transferred in and out of the unit, the analysts were a constant; they fostered and maintained CLEU's early tradition of excellence.

The unit's first operation, Project 29, was named for the number of investigators on the task force to nab a top Mafioso. Successes quickly followed against the Hells Angels, Chinese Triads, and other crime groups, derailing drug-trafficking and money-laundering systems. The courts began issuing harsher sentences.

The payoffs were immediate and clear as CLEU tackled major crime figures, not just the street-level rounders. By 1976, 52 of the 119 major criminals identified two years earlier had been charged, 38 were inactive or had fled the province, and many others had been rendered ineffective without charges being laid. The consistency of CLEU's sustained assault on organized crime proved much more successful than the previous ad hoc joint-force operations that were dismantled after each specific operation.

CLEU's targets were identified by their perceived threat to society, the stature of the criminal, and the suspect's depth of involvement with organized crime. Investigators had to prove that their quarry was involved in multijurisdictional crimes and was living off the proceeds of those crimes. Finally, it came down to the probability of success and the availability of staff and resources. The unit would be as good as their overseers allowed it to be. Political funding and patience were vital to prolonged investigations and long-term successes. It was imperative that the talented people be involved and that funding and other resources would not be withdrawn as soon as CLEU had accumulated enough drugs, weapons, or other contraband for a media photo op.

By 1977, CLEU had racked up an impressive record of arrests that included twenty-one in a bookmaking conspiracy, sixteen in the Robertson cocaine conspiracy, nine in the Sitybell heroin conspiracy, fifty-eight gambling charges, and numerous others against counterfeiters and persons living off the avails of crime.

Significantly, the quality of the charges was as impressive as the quantity. Conspiracy charges, which target the top of a criminal organization, are rarely laid in most investigations, but a successful prosecution of living off the avails of crime meant that the convicted felon's property could be seized and used or auctioned by the respective level of government—long before the practice was challenged in the Supreme Court.

Success, however, came at a price. Each victory in court made other crime groups more wary. They learned how CLEU operated through public court records. And successful investigations and prosecutions were expensive: the cost just to protect and relocate witnesses in one historic cocaine conspiracy sting was estimated to be roughly $350,000. And that was thirty years ago!

In 1995, CLEU began assessing the impact of new forms of organized crime in British Columbia, designing, developing, and implementing aggressive strategies to combat and suppress the activities of emerging crime organizations. They built a special investigative team to monitor the activities of these groups, created training and educational programs to help field officers better cope with the problem, and formed ad hoc task forces to facilitate interagency work throughout the province, raising public awareness and support wherever and whenever they could.

CLEU was strong enough to survive the first "problem children" dumped in its lap by senior RCMP and city-police brass who were looking for an easy way to transfer out officers who, for whatever reason, were not meeting performance expectations in more traditional policing roles. It was essentially an out-of-sight, out-of-mind solution that really benefited no one except the senior officer wanting to shed the responsibility for an officer under his or her command. But CLEU could not survive the accumulative effects of too few staff, too little money, and growing distrust and decreasing information exchanges between member departments. In 1997, it received the coveted Webber Seavey Award for Quality in Law Enforcement, the most prestigious award presented by the International Association of Chiefs of Police (IACP), for "innovative solutions to local and international law enforcement issues." Recognized for its program to assess, monitor, and create new ways to respond to emerging, provincewide trends in organized crime, CLEU was praised by then IACP president Darrell L. Sanders: "These programs dramatically illustrate the commitment of law enforcement agencies around the world to develop and implement creative solutions to some of our most challenging policing and social problems. They also represent a substantial professional contribution which can be used by other agencies as model programs."[1]

No one in the room suspected that Sanders's tribute would be CLEU's eulogy or that the award was virtually a posthumous presentation. Compromised by what former insiders describe as internal distrust, jurisdictional jealousies, political and personal agendas, and intelligence thwarted by ego, the intelligence stream was doomed; its leads to major criminals wither. The next year, a "Blue Ribbon" panel consisting of a politician and former police executives recommended terminating CLEU. What began as a death by a thousand cuts ended in 1999 as an execution. CLEU was disbanded and the Organized Crime Agency of British Columbia rose from its ashes on March 11, 1999.

OCA is an independent policing agency with a mandate to "facilitate the disruption and suppression of organized crime which impacts all British Columbians." Governed by a politically appointed board representing "ethnic diversity, gender balance and expertise from the legal, business, education and other professional sectors" to oversee "highly sophisticated, highly sensitive [organized crime enforcement], requiring strong co-operation among all law enforcement groups provincially, nationally, and internationally," it has a clear mandate to be "an aggressive, professional, and respected team combating organized crime, in partnership with other organizations, through the bold and innovative application of ethical and progressive law-enforcement techniques."[2]

Like CLEU, OCA enjoyed early successes. There was hope that the police were once more engaged in a true battle with organized crime. As former Canadian police officer and security expert Leo Knight observed on his website, Primetimecrime.com: "In the space of two years, OCA was instrumental in taking down a number of criminal operations and seized enough drugs and property to fund themselves for the foreseeable future were they actually able to utilize the fruits of their labours as does the U.S. Drug Enforcement Agency [DEA]. In fact, it's reasonable to say that OCA did more in two short years than the RCMP did in the previous decade." But if the Mounties lacked success, they certainly didn't seem to lack ambition—or a thirst to control the agency. In 2004, Knight warned that senior RCMP officers had "managed to manipulate" the Solicitor General a year earlier, convincing him that the annual OCA budget should be administered through the provincial policing budget. The decision was then made to direct the roughly $14 million annual budget of OCA through the auspices of the RCMP. "The result," Knight wrote, "was OCA needed to go, cap in hand, to the Mounties when they needed anything to do their job."

It seemed that the jurisdictional infighting and internal power plays that had plagued and eventually imploded CLEU were at work again—with predictable results. Knight laid the problem at the feet of the "carpet cops" at RCMP E Division headquarters— senior officers he considered "so far removed from the sharp end of the stick, they think handcuffs are a sexual aid"—who drive the "real cops" crazy. "By design," Knight recapped, "[OCA] was an independent agency not mired in the bureaucratic meanderings, which typically made it next to impossible to actually do anything in the complex, yet fast-paced investigations into organized crime . . . After a couple of years of some limited successes, OCA began to branch out and feel its oats, so to speak. In the interim, the

Mounties, who see themselves as the rightful owner of the organized crime file, became jealous of the attention and wins their independent cousins were getting ... All that served to do was to give the RCMP control over their bastard child, the one they had not been able to keep under their bureaucratic thumb."

Recalling that OCA had been created in 1999 to replace its "moribund" predecessor, CLEU, as "a leaner, meaner, fast moving response to the challenges presented to law enforcement from the likes of the Hells Angels and the Asian organized crime groups like the Big Circle Boys, 14 K and Sun Yee On Triads, all exceptionally active in British Columbia," Knight also touched on what seemed a growing national trend, whereby police seize and destroy drugs but don't lay charges, presumably to save court time and expenses. He accused the Mounties of having "booted a major conspiracy file" when 2.5 tonnes of cocaine were seized in the waters off Washington State and, at the time of his writing, no charges had been laid.

Knight also took issue with B.C. Solicitor General Rich Coleman's recent announcement that OCA—a partnership between federal and municipal policing—would now fall under the "command umbrella" of the RCMP. It seems no one bothered to tell then Vancouver Police Department chief Jamie Graham, who apparently knew nothing about the administrative change when asked at his first management meeting upon his return from out of town.

"Considering Graham is part of the joint management team, the oversight committee of OCA, [the command shift] seems strange indeed," Knight observed, suggesting the change had been "ram-rodded through" while the city chief was "out of town and out of touch."

"Why?" Knight asked. "[The change in command responsibility] is all about control and nothing to do with actually fighting organized crime. It seems the politics of policing has handed organized crime another victory."

That sentiment is echoed by authors Julian Sher and William Marsden, whom Knight cites from their 2003 exposé, *The Road to Hell: How the Biker Gangs Are Conquering Canada*, which notes: "Plagued by rivalries, incompetence, and a general underestimation of the threat posed by the bikers, the police in B.C.—especially the RCMP—did little to take on the Hells Angels until their power made them virtually impregnable."

And that was just the bikers—the most visible and therefore most identifiable threat to Canadians. That might change if we knew more about ethnic crime groups, but that's harder, and who has the staff, time, or budget?

By 2005, there was growing concern that the police couldn't even keep up with domestic marijuana-growing operations, commonly known as grow ops. Headlining the first of the two-part series "Out of control: Criminal justice system 'on the brink of imploding,'" journalist Chad Skelton wrote in the March 11 *Vancouver Sun*: "With more than 4,500 reports last year of illegal indoor pot-growing operations, B.C. police cannot keep up." It had become a numbers game for prosecutors who were finding that anyone with less than nine convictions was unlikely at risk of even 50/50 odds of being sentenced to jail—despite the fact that children were found on site in roughly 20 per cent of the drug raids. "In B.C.'s war against marijuana-growing operations, a groundbreaking new study makes one thing clear: The growers are winning and the situation is out of control," the article said, citing the pending release of the study. "Police are less likely to investigate marijuana growers, prosecutors are less likely to lay charges against them, and judges are less likely to send them to jail than they were in the late 1990s."

The $250,000 study, paid for by the RCMP, was headed by Darryl Plecas, a criminology professor at the University College of the Fraser Valley; he was free to report whatever he found. It wasn't good news for the police: "It seems, no question about it, that the system is increasingly unable or otherwise failing to respond to this problem, despite the fact that we have every indication that the problem is worsening. I think we have a criminal justice system that is very much on the brink of imploding."

The study, which reviewed all reported cases of marijuana growing in British Columbia from 1997 to 2003, was not particularly flattering to its sponsor, the RCMP. One key finding was that the percentage of grow ops reported to police that are "fully investigated," most often by executing a search warrant, had dropped from 91 per cent in 1997 to just 52 per cent in 2003.

"During that same period, the percentage of cases where police only conducted an 'initial investigation'—such as driving by a suspect property for any outward signs of marijuana growing—jumped from just two per cent of all cases to 26 per cent," Skelton reported. "And the share of cases where police did nothing at all has jumped from seven per cent to 22 per cent."

Perhaps most alarming, charges were virtually non-existent: "The percentage of raids that result in 'no-case seizures'—where police seize any plants they find but don't send a report to Crown counsel—has jumped from just over a third of all cases (35 per cent) in 1997 to two-thirds (64 per cent) in 2003."

Plecas believed that many in policing had simply "thrown in the towel" on grow ops, saying: "Some jurisdictions appear to have folded their tent. They seem to have given up."

Inspector Paul Nadeau, head of the RCMP's Co-ordinated Marijuana Enforcement Team, acknowledged being troubled by the findings, conceding: "Nobody in [the study] is looking very good." Citing possible "grow-op fatigue," he said, "I think police are tired, just like everyone else is, in dealing with these things."[3]

Nadeau said the Mounties would study the report and come up with a game plan. But if the police were sending fewer cases to Crown prosecutors, they also seemed less inclined to pursue the ones they were given. The study found that, in 1997, they had laid charges in 96 per cent of such cases they received from police. That fell to 76 per cent by 2003. Similarly, the number of suspects charged plummeted from 2,116 in 2000 to just 798 in 2003, despite that the number of grow ops reported to police had tripled.

The only positive news in the report was that 93 per cent of marijuana-growing cases that do get to trial end with a conviction. And even that good news was tempered by the study's finding that fewer perpetrators were going to jail. Noting that provincial court chief judge Carol Baird Ellan declined a request to comment on the study's findings, reporter Skelton reminded his readers of what Ellan has said in the past: "[J]udges in B.C. are simply responding to changes made to the Criminal Code in 1996 and later rulings by the Supreme Court of Canada that say imprisonment should be a last resort in sentencing and that, where appropriate, offenders should be permitted to serve their sentences at home."[4]

Plecas suggested that such lenient sentences are "partly responsible" for police becoming less aggressive: "It's this sort of throwing up your hands and saying, 'What's the point ... if, at the end of the day, the judge is just going to turn the person loose?'"[5]

While British Columbia Solicitor General Rich Coleman shared the police's frustrations, he told the *Sun* he still expects police to "do their best" to crack down on growers.

"I'm asking law enforcement to go out and perform their function," he said. "Their function is to enforce the law. They don't go out there and decide what laws to enforce. They should go out and do their job."

That was a rather biting indictment considering that the traditional police lament has been to ask politicians and the courts to let them do their jobs. This raises the question Just how well are the police doing their job and what do they need to do it better?

In 2006, Neal Hall had reported in the *Vancouver Sun* that an awful lot of major crimes were going "unprobed" in British Columbia. The Mounties blamed this situation on a shortage of investigators.

"B.C. has not had enough RCMP officers to investigate some of the province's most serious crimes for at least a decade, according to a confidential 2005 provincial government document," Hall wrote, citing a briefing note by the Ministry of Public Safety and Solicitor General, and obtained by the *Sun* through freedom of information legislation, which said: "There are insufficient resources to address the many serious crime investigations, including homicides, abductions, armed robberies, [marijuana] grow operations, home invasions, sexual predators, child pornography, exploitation of children on the Internet, white-collar crime and high-level organized crime." Nor had there been any substantive increases to the authorized strength of the RCMP for provincial or First Nations policing since the mid-1990s, months after Premier Gordon Campbell had announced on January 24, 2005, that the province would add 215 RCMP officers in communities as part of a crime-fighting strategy that would invest $122 million in policing, corrections. and courts over the next three years. Instead, despite that cash infusion and aggressive recruiting aimed at adding up to 1,700 new RCMP officers to the Force across Canada that year, British Columbia was still almost 400 officers short of being fully staffed—a gap that continued to widen due largely to retirements.

Quite simply, the article noted, the 5,426 regular members in the province numbered well below the 5,804 positions for which there is funding. The result? Insufficient resources to address many serious crime investigations, despite the premier's comments in January 2005 that the police are doing "the best they can every day to fight crime and keep us safe. But more resources are needed."

"The federal Conservative government also pledged in its recent budget to spend $37 million to expand the RCMP training depot in Regina, and $161 million for more police officers and federal prosecutors," Hall wrote. "But the RCMP now faces the problem of finding enough recruits to fill the new positions."

That has created a growing backlog of unfilled, but funded, positions, and vacancies created by attrition, including early retirement, which Vancouver RCMP corporal Tom Seaman described as "a short-term problem that is in the process of being addressed by aggressive recruiting." Hall persisted, asking: Does the shortfall mean some crime will not get attention until the current backlog of positions is filled? Seaman explained that investigations are prioritized. Topping the list were homicides, abductions, armed robberies, home invasions, sexual predators, child pornography, and exploitation of children on the Internet. Admitting that some long-term projects may be put "on the back burner," he said the Mounties would continue to investigate organized crime.

Hall then reminded his readers that earlier that same month, then commissioner Zaccardelli had testified to the Senate Standing Committee on National Security and Defence that his investigators could tackle only "about one-third" of known organized crime cases due to limited resources.

From a political perspective, it all seemed like a numbers game.

The article quoted Kevin Begg, assistant deputy minister of B.C.'s Ministry of Public Safety and Solicitor General, at length: The province had provided $57 million in new funding to create 400 new positions since the previous January, including $30 million for the 215 new RCMP positions, $10 million for 76 positions in the new integrated Indo-Canadian crime unit, plus another $17 million for 110 positions in the integrated traffic safety unit. Insisting that this "significant investment" in policing would help enable the police to pursue "more serious crime," Begg suggested the perceived shortfall was "misleading" as a vacancy can exist even though an officer exists, but has been seconded to an integrated joint-forces unit that includes both RCMP and municipal police. Other vacancies stem from vacations, maternity, or sick leave. How that made it better was unclear: those positions were not filled by a body in the office or a car on the road. Finally, Begg offered that, as the province only funds 2,025 Mounties who work as provincial contract officers in rural detachments and communities with fewer than 5,000 residents, the shortfall for those positions is only 121, concluding: "The overall rate of vacancies is not out of proportion." That sentiment may have provided small comfort to officers scanning the vacant horizon for backup. But staffing numbers was not the only concern. Nor was organized crime.

In 2006, the Mounties listed organized crime and terrorism among their top five strategic priorities. Gangs, which we'll read more about later, weren't even on the radar, it seemed then. But who was watching the terrorists and how good a job were the police doing in that regard? The answer led to some pretty murky waters.

There was a time that the RCMP were entrusted with that task. But then consecutive public inquiries—the Keable Commission in Quebec and the federally appointed McDonald Commission—both determined that the police were breaking the law to preserve the peace in the late 1970s. Accused of, among other things, warrantless mail opening, destroying evidence, covert thefts and break-ins, disinformation campaigns, and, perhaps most memorable, arson, including burning down an empty barn where alleged FLQ (Front de Libération du Québec) terrorists were expected to meet.

McDonald urged the government to replace the Mounties with a civilian agency responsible for domestic security but without powers of arrest. In 1984, the passage of Bill C-9 created the Canadian Security Intelligence Service, mentioned earlier, headed by a civilian commissioner, but essentially run by senior Mounties who had survived the inquiry unsullied. The question would seem to beg, why, if there were pure-hearted talents in the RCMP, did they not just put them in charge there and save the many millions necessary to create a new agency?

The problem with reporting on the shadowy world of espionage is that only agents' failures tend to get exposed. While police operations eventually come to light in court, spies don't work that way. Just as the police worked behind the scenes for years setting up major raids against biker gangs, those working in intelligence and counter-intelligence capacities are not known for telling people what they're doing. And award-winning investigative journalist Andrew Mitrovica claims in his 2002 CSIS exposé, *Covert Entry*, that silence extends to telling their civilian overseer, the Security Intelligence Review Committee, whatever they feel like and cloaking the rest under claims of "national security."

Mitrovica described CSIS as "riddled by waste, extravagance, laziness, nepotism, incompetence, corruption and law breaking" virtually from its moment of conception, leaving him "shaken and very worried" and public safety "in jeopardy." In essence, they seem to have become what they were supposed to replace: civilian shadows that the author claims have powers unmatched in government to "invade the lives of Canadians." And this, it should be remembered, is an agency that was created with no powers of arrest.

For our purposes and passing reference, we can probably best sum up CSIS in two words: Air India.

In March 2007, Henry Jensen, the former deputy commissioner who had headed RCMP criminal operations for most of the 1980s, told the inquiry into the June 1985 terror bombing, which killed 331 men, women and children, that stripping the RCMP of responsibility for intelligence-gathering and handing the job to CSIS had made Canada a "riskier place." The worst mass murder in

Canadian history, Jensen claimed, was the result of "the biggest and most disastrous civil intelligence failure" in Canadian history.

While others made the point that then RCMP commissioner Robert Simmonds had never accepted losing the anti-terrorism intelligence turf war to CSIS, his successors seem not more kindly disposed to the civvy spooks. Departing commissioner Giuliano Zaccardelli fired his own broadside at CSIS (and the administration of U.S. president George W. Bush), as he resigned his career over two more words: Mahar Arar.

In September 2008, nearly two years after leaving the Mounties, Zaccardelli told *CBC News* that while the RCMP had been watching Arar, who was suspected of having ties to al Qaeda, they had told the Americans, who had detained the Syrian-born Canadian citizen, that they lacked evidence to arrest or detain him. He blamed CSIS in part for allegedly telling U.S. authorities not to share any information with the Mounties that would help their investigation. That might help explain why the RCMP surveillance team ready to watch Arar never found him; the Americans flew him to Syria where Arar was detained for a year, and claims to have been tortured repeatedly. An ensuing inquiry found Arar had no terrorist connection, the Americans kept him on their watch list, and the Canadian government paid him $10 million compensation.

All of which may explain why the police seem to focus more on organized crime.

In November 2008, Rob Linke reported in the Saint John, New Brunswick, *Telegraph-Journal* that the police and courts needed more resources to keep pace with organized crime, telling the federal Department of Public Safety that they were "short on training, money and technology."

The Strategic Counsel, a private polling and research firm in Toronto, released a report based on 124 in-depth one-on-one interviews with staff of police forces and Crown prosecutor's offices involved in the fight against organized crime in Canada at the federal, provincial and municipal levels. The report presented Public Safety with a simple message: Fighting crime is expensive and governments have to commit the necessary resources if the battle is to be won or, at a minimum, significant gains are to be made. Their look at current strains on policing across the country presented the feds with "a rather dire picture of the present capacity and future ability of authorities to combat organized crime."

Atlantic Canada's law enforcement needs are the same as those being experienced by police across the country—more money to hire more people and buy newer technology to catch more bad guys who are increasingly hiding behind "legitimate" business fronts. Police officials stressed the need for a "significant boost" and expressed their frustration that they are not closely linked to other government branches such as the Canada Revenue Agency, border services, and the prison system. The report also noted the desire of police in Atlantic Canada for a co-ordinated effort to help law enforcement keep pace with organized crime, which is growing in sophistication and forging links with other groups outside traditional regions or typical criminal activities, requiring the police to move, as one interviewee said, "from a culture of 'need to know' to one of an 'obligation to share.'"

And with current organized crime experts set to retire, the police worry about the pending "brain drain," fearing that "the loss of continuity on some cases, as well as the weakening of corporate memory, combined with recruiting challenges, could leave police agencies vulnerable." And, if those we arm to protect us are vulnerable, what about the women and children who are most often at greatest risk from predators? If the police are strained putting people away for drug trafficking, what hope is there for stopping the apparent growth in human trafficking? It is not a happy prognosis.

In August 2005, Jacqueline Oxman-Martinez, Marie Lacroix, and Jill Hanley—all PhDs writing for the Research and Statistics Division of Justice Canada, issued their report on "Victims of Trafficking in Persons: Perspectives from the Canadian Community Sector." They concluded:

"Trafficking in persons constitutes a serious human rights violation. Trafficked persons, predominantly women and children, are forced into degrading situations and conditions of suffering. Victims are controlled by fear of exposure and deportation, violence, and the threat of violence to themselves and their families. The United Nations Office for Drug Control and Crime Prevention (UNODCCP) estimates that trafficking by criminal organizations amount to $5–7 billion annually. . . . A recent report by the US Department of Justice increases this estimate to $10 billion. Since trafficking is a lucrative business that can complement activities in the drug and sex industries, it has attracted international organized crime rings. Trafficking in persons also occurs on a smaller scale where individuals, small 'businessmen,' acquaintances of victims and even family members can be involved."

While the authors found it extremely difficult to calculate the number of victims each year, given its clandestine nature and the relative lack of research, they note that, based on a survey of available sources, the RCMP estimates that "between 700,000 and four million people are trafficked every year worldwide," a number which they say roughly coincides with the UN estimate of two million persons.

"The RCMP has also made a conservative estimate that approximately 600 women and children are trafficked into Canada each year for sexual exploitation alone," they write, "and at least 800 for all domestic markets (involvement in drug trade, domestic work, labour for garment or other industries, etc.)."

Citing an unpublished 2005 RCMP report, which estimates that between 1,500 and 2,200 people are trafficked from Canada into the United States each year, the authors suggest that Canada is a source, transit, and destination country—a criminal trifecta of human misery.

Noting that global trafficking involves the flow of people from poor, less-developed countries to Western industrialized nations, they cite the May 2005 International Labour Organization (ILO) estimate that, at any given time, there are "a minimum of 2.45 million people in forced labour as a result of trafficking in persons, of which 270,000 are trafficked into industrialized countries."

While victims of trafficking arrive in Canada come from "a wide variety" of source countries, the 2005 unpublished report identified Asia and the former Soviet Union as the primary sources.

Police leaders may regret the political decision to end an

operation early, may lament the lost opportunity to strike higher and harder, may even resent realizing, as if they'd ever forgot, how easily their civilian overseers can control their operations through budgets, not legislation, and diminish their impact and efforts to make the streets and communities safer for the public and their own officers, but they tend not to speak out. They do nothing to publicly convey how the ultimate long-term cost and threat to society, and to their own officers, is raised by short-sighted expediency. Too few stand up to say what has to be said. No senior officer with any force has resigned in protest in decades, and that includes the relatively recent departures of the RCMP and OPP commissioners.

If they cannot depend on their superiors to speak up, how well prepared are the front-line officers—through numbers, training, and equipment—to confront the historic perils of the job? Consider this. The raids on the bikers in Quebec and New Brunswick would be armed entries led by elite tactical squads bearing heavy firepower. No matter how many times they have practiced this scenario, there seems little doubt that at the moment of truth, mental preparation may be as important—perhaps more important—than physical stamina or well-rehearsed marksmanship. We can assume that as the "pucker factor" (i.e., extreme nervous tension) peaks in the final moments before the doors are shattered by rams or explosives, mouths are dry, hands are clenched around weapons or protective shields, hearts race, and more than a few helmets are lined with sweat.

At this moment, our police are transformed into men and women on the front lines of a war. A war on drugs. A war on terror. A war on crime. All of them wars of nerves. This is not a place for the faint-hearted, the inadequately trained, or poorly led. It has been this way since the rise of SWAT units, by whatever name, since the 1970s. But the front-line officers today face a new challenge never faced by earlier thin blue lines. Gangs and guns have become a daily threat across Canada. And the best defences for front-line officers when the gunfire and violence erupt are their wits and instincts.

Policing is statistically not the most dangerous occupation. In fact, according to the 2005 Workers Compensation Board online winter newsletter, the profession does not crack the top ten most lethal occupations (loggers and aircraft pilots top the list). But policing is the only one, aside from military service, where the potential exists, no matter how remote, that you may be killed. That, thankfully, is a rare event, but it's getting more common as more guns reach the hands of more people willing to use them. The streets of Toronto and Vancouver have erupted into war zones, with lethal consequences. And when the flashpoint occurs on the streets or at a roadside stop, there is no time or opportunity to summon tactical support. You are on your own. And the lurking peril is not limited to city streets.

In February 2009, RCMP constable Michelle Knopp testified in the first-degree-murder trial of accused cop killer Curtis Dagenais that as she instinctively ducked down in her truck cab and drew her pistol from its holster after the first bullet smashed through her windshield and grazed her, she thought: "I'm not going to die here tonight ... my boy needs me."[6]

Despite all the noise around her—the sound of the second shot fired at her, the flashing lights, and blaring sirens on the two police vehicles at the scene—Knopp recalled everything being eerily silent at the end of a vehicle pursuit, reported by the press in July 2006 as ending violently and tragically on a hilly, muddy trail in rural Saskatchewan.

Knopp became the face of all police officers in the courtroom, a reminder of the human being behind the badge. Transcripts of the radio communication between the pursuing officers and dispatch confirm that they did not have Tasers and had been advised that their quarry was known to be armed and a reputed cop hater. Dispatch told the police that it was imperative he be prevented from reaching the family farmhouse he was racing towards. All the officers involved felt the adrenaline pounding as those in the chase cars reported that the suspect was speeding "all over the road" at an estimated 120 kilometres per hour on spraying gravel after he had attempted to ram them.

Tensions eased briefly as Knopp radioed: "We have him ... we have ..." In the time it took the dispatcher to ask for their location, Knopp was back on the air, reporting: "... shot, I'm shot." Asked to repeat her last transmission, she replied: "Shots fired. Shots fired. I'm shot. Rob, I'm shot."

The scene had become a killing ground. Exiting her vehicle to find her two colleagues shot, one still buckled in the car, the other lying on the ground beside their vehicle, Knopp managed to get off a shot but missed. Now it was a nightmare; she was alone with an armed suspect and had no idea where he was. As dispatch summoned an ambulance and redirected every police vehicle to the scene of the shooting, it suddenly dawned on Knopp that she wasn't sure of her location. All she could do was to drive south, the direction she had come, in the hope that she would encounter those rushing north to her aid.

Dagenais testified at his trial that he never meant to kill the police officers, but was convicted of first-degree murder in the shooting deaths of RCMP constables Marc Bourdages and Robin Cameron, as well as the attempted murder of Knopp, and sentenced to three life sentences.

The trial in Saskatchewan was a reminder of the murder of four Mounties in Mayerthorpe, Alberta, just one year earlier. There had been no survivors to tell the tale of what exactly had happened that black day in 2005 when another cop-hating, gun-toting fugitive opened fire on the four unsuspecting officers guarding his property, awaiting a search warrant for the house—a routine duty carried out by police across Canada every day. Those tragedies sounded the alarm that the historic peace in the valley between the police and the rural population had been infected by what Alberta criminologist Bill Pitt termed "nasty little cauldrons" of "ticking time bombs," of "socially marginalized" people increasingly willing to act on their hatred of the police. The former Mountie, who teaches at the University of Alberta, cautioned that rural tranquility can create a false sense of security; that living in a small town where everyone knows you by name does not remove the numbers of guns nor the potential threat posed by "marginalized" people willing to use them.

"When you start peeling back the layers, [small towns] can be as dangerous, if not more dangerous, than urban areas," Pitt said, adding that the number of centres where police resist being posted to is more common than many would think. "It's like these little pockets of anomalies that gain reputations of having bad relations with police, that have people [who] are openly cop haters."[7]

His sentiments were only partly echoed by Chief Superintendent Mike Woods, who oversees community policing for the RCMP. Woods told the Canadian Press, "The notion that there are ticking time bombs living in our communities is real. There are people who have problems, issues, concerns with authority. But I think those kinds of problems exist as much in rural as urban communities."

But social problems and victimization can be amplified by isolation, distance, and the lack of timely backup in rural areas. Hirsch Greenberg, a Saskatchewan social worker with thirty years' experience who teaches justice studies at the University of Regina, said social agencies and crisis centres that can intervene at an early stage in cities usually don't exist in rural areas. That, he said, makes domestic situations, potentially the highest risk situations for police, more dangerous.

"What's different in a rural setting is that police don't have the backup, they become the last resort, they become the net," Greenberg told the Canadian Press. "The critical point ... the crisis ... tends to fester longer, and when something does happen, it explodes in a much more violent way because there's no way to catch the buildup. Emotions that could be tempered earlier tend to fester."

Pitt believed that gunning for cops has just grown too easy: "Going after police officers has become much more of an option. People don't think they will be punished."

Having conceded after the Mayerthorpe tragedy that they were outgunned, the police also found themselves staring down more guns in younger hands than ever before in history. As organized crime receded into the background, swapping greasy dungarees for designer suits and more often riding first-class in airliners than straddling their chopped motorcycles, it opened the door for street gangs to launch new terrors in Canada's towns and cities. None of the old rules seemed to apply.

It's not that gangs are a new phenomenon in Canada. In his 2008 overview for the Canadian Points of View Reference Centre database, Lee Tunstall traced their history to the postwar outlaw motorcycle gangs. The original bikers comprised disgruntled hell-raising bomber pilots in the United States whose impact spread north of the border; again, in no small part due to their Hollywood portrayals by Marlon Brando and others. Audiences found them cruel, yet somehow cool. The founders began allying themselves with associates and hanger-on wannabes, inevitably diluting the gene pool. Police intelligence agencies long suspected that the bikers were tasked with the menial jobs of larger organized crime groups, and while they were a problem—a social scourge the politicians never seemed to want to tackle—they were at least relatively identifiable by their club patch. And they were overwhelmingly white. That's no longer the case with the rise of ethnic gangs.

Tunstall identifies a range of gangs in his report. Beyond the bikers, the sole "gangs" historically lumped into the long-held concept of "organized crime" with imported clandestine clans, brotherhoods, and secret societies, there are now youth gangs, prison gangs, and street gangs, which he further divides along ethnic lines that suggest the world's entire criminal underbelly—personified by vicious Aboriginal, Asian, Indo-Canadian, Eastern European, Caribbean, and White Supremacist thugs—now stalks Canadian streets. The gangs are often in competition, but have also been known, like organized crime groups, to co-operate when crime pays so well that there is lots to go around for everyone. Crime has morphed into pure capitalism where profits trump turf wars, religious and cultural differences, and race.

The emergence of street gangs in Canadian cities is generally traced to the 1980s. The early warnings that something was amiss may have been ignored because the ethnic gangs in particular seemed to focus on their own communities, terrorizing minority populations with threats and violence. What happened in closed ethnic communities who may have born a distrust of police dating to their experiences in their native lands tended to stay in those communities. The police were rarely, almost never, contacted by victims who presumably feared either violent retaliation by their tormentors or distrusted the police intensely based on the corrupt police who had operated as a malevolent arm of the state in their homelands. Gangs were also shown to be dispersed into specific geographic areas. Aboriginal gangs were found in Alberta, Saskatchewan, and Manitoba; Asian, South Asian, and Indo-Canadian gangs in British Columbia; and Caribbean gangs in Ontario and Quebec. Like the bikers, these street gangs are believed to be somehow connected to larger organized crime groups, providing the muscle that allows organized crime to remain at arm's length from any violence while they rake in the huge profits from gang-run drug trafficking, prostitution, theft, and fraud.

The gangs rely heavily on social alienation for their recruits and there seems no shortage of young people, traditionally male but increasingly female, willing to endure a violent hazing to find a sense of belonging they apparently could not find at home, school, or work. And if they had a job, it doubtless paid less than the proceeds of crime. As youths, none feared long jail terms if caught; the courts rarely tried them as adults. Even if the police and courts get them off the streets, gang life and association continues in prison where Tunstall estimates 5 per cent of the incarcerated population are involved in gang-related activities—most of them Native gangs, given the disproportionate number of Aboriginals behind bars.

By the mid-1990s, gang violence had pushed government to respond. A year after the National Forum on Organized Crime in September 1996, Parliament passed its first anti-gang legislation, Bill C-95, intended to better equip the police to combat the violence. There were successes against the bikers, but ethnic gang violence continued to escalate. In 2002, Ottawa passed Bill C-24 and threw $200 million and greater powers to the police who, again, were told to fix the problem.

Tunstall also notes provincial efforts to address the gang scourge. In 2004, British Columbia enacted civil liability for members, allowing an avenue for civil, if not criminal, trials, and outlawed all types of gang identification, such as logos, backing their new laws with a new Integrated Gang Task Force to allow greater co-operation across several police jurisdictions. As details of CSIS's role became public during the Air India inquiry, it may have been missed that Tunstall identified another hundred Indo-Canadian men who had been killed in drug-related gang violence over the preceding decade.

The tipping point came in 2005, which, as mentioned earlier, was proclaimed "The Year of the Gun" in Toronto, where fifty-two of the seventy-eight homicides that year were listed as gang-related, culminating with the Boxing Day murder of Jane Creba, an innocent bystander gunned down in a crossfire on Yonge Street. The youth found guilty for her death was sentenced as an adult in 2009. Eight others were charged and are awaiting trial. (Several manslaughter charges were withdrawn by the Crown in November 2009, citing low expectation for a conviction, but the murder charges remain in effect.)

In 2006, Toronto police arrested seventy-eight members of the Jamestown Crew, but there are still an estimated 180 youth gangs active in the Greater Toronto Area. Western Canada has its own share of gang violence. In 2007, nineteen people were killed in metropolitan Vancouver in a rash of gang-style murders, six of them killed in a Surrey apartment that included two victims with no known gang affiliation. That November, the provincial government added a Violence Suppression Team to its Integrated Gang Task Force to target known gang hangouts. The police were still charging people in 2009 in connection with the Surrey murders, begging the question, had these new specialty units actually helped the police or simply created more bureaucratic red tape? As journalist Ian Bailey asked in the March 14, 2009, *Globe and Mail*: Are the police spread too thin? By contrast there were so many government bureaus involved from three levels of government that it was easy to lose count. Worse, Bailey wrote, it was making it impossible to fight crime in British Columbia.

Asked just how many agencies, units, and task forces were active in the policing war on gangs, a Vancouver officer started to count. He stopped at eleven.

"The list includes the Combined Forces Special Enforcement Unit, the B.C. Integrated Gang Task Force and the Uniform Gang Task Force," Bailey wrote. "There are federal agencies such as the Canadian Border Services Agency and the Integrated National Security Enforcement Team. Then there's the Integrated Homicide Investigation Team, which looks at homicides outside Vancouver, Delta and West Vancouver, and has lately been very busy with gang-related cases. And gang units within Vancouver's municipal forces such as the Vancouver Gang Crime Unit."

The list went on from there. To no one's surprise, critics considered this approach ineffectual, arguing for a single enforcement approach, beginning with the creation of a regional police force to co-ordinate the eleven municipal forces and 126 RCMP detachments with more than a dozen police forces in metropolitan Vancouver alone. Instead, the proponents of "strength in numbers" have created a host of combined forces identified in Bailey's article:

Special Enforcement Unit, formerly the Organized Crime Agency of B.C., is comprised of [*sic*] RCMP officers and seconded officers from all municipal police forces in the province to "facilitate the disruption and suppression of organized crime which affects British Columbians."

The B.C. Integrated Gang Task Force, created in October 2004, to address gang violence within the Lower Mainland, Fraser Valley and the province, using resources from Vancouver Police, RCMP, Abbotsford Police, Delta Police, New Westminster Police, Port Moody Police and West Vancouver Police.

Integrated Border Enforcement Team (IBET), developed by authorities in British Columbia and Washington State in the mid-1990s has since expanded to include 15 locations across the country. Comprised of [*sic*] both U.S. and Canadian law enforcement to nab drug smugglers, illegal immigrants, organized criminal members and terrorists, its five core agencies are the RCMP, Canadian Border Services Agency, U.S. Customs and Border Protection/

Office of Border Patrol, U.S. Bureau of Immigration and Customs Enforcement and U.S. Coast Guard.

Integrated National Security Enforcement Team (INSET), led by the RCMP and federal partners including the Canada Border Services Agency and the Canadian Security Intelligence Service, has offices in Vancouver, Toronto and Montreal to "detect, prevent, disrupt and investigate terrorist targets and ultimately bring terrorists to justice prior to serious, violent, criminal acts being perpetrated in Canada and/or abroad."

Integrated Proceeds of Crime Unit is a federal interdepartmental initiative dedicated to the "disruption, dismantling and incapacitation of target organized criminals and crime groups." Public Safety and Emergency Preparedness Canada regularly evaluates the initiatives and provides policy co-ordination. Partners include Canada Border Services Agency, Canada Revenue Agency, Department of Justice, provincial and municipal police forces, Public Safety and Emergency Preparedness Canada, Public Works and Government Services: Forensic Accounting Management Group—Seized Property Management Directorate, and the RCMP.

The B.C. Civil Forfeiture Office was created to penalize those who profit from crime. The Civil Forfeiture Act was brought into force on April 20, 2006.

Canadian Border Services Agency, a frontline response and defence against the import of drugs and weapons, which could be used by gangs, also gathers intelligence on groups in Canada exporting drugs to the United States.

Gang Crime Unit, part of the Vancouver Police, develops intelligence and conducts investigations on criminal street gangs.

Uniform Gang Task Force, created in late 2007, is a joint effort of the RCMP and Vancouver-area police departments to try and cut down on gang activity in the Lower Mainland.

Integrated Homicide Investigation Team probes homicides, police-involved shootings and in-custody deaths outside

Vancouver in the Lower Mainland. It is policed by the RCMP, Abbotsford, New Westminster and Port Moody police departments.

Vancouver Major Crime Section, part of the Vancouver Police department, includes the homicide, robbery/assault and missing-persons squads.[8]

Each unit has its own bureaucratic hurdles to overcome. No wonder, just more than a week earlier, that Vancouver mayor Gregor Robertson, a proponent of regional policing, had dubbed local anti-gang efforts "a losing battle," insisting more would have to be done to turn the tide.

But the police can't win this, or any, war without outside support. While youth gangs remain a notorious scourge upon public peace and order, Tunstall reminds us they are more than just a criminal concern. "Gangs remain a complex social issue throughout Canada. Recent research has shown that the reasons given for joining a youth gang include a desire for power, respect, money, protection, social support and companionship, social alienation and defiance."[9]

Just one more "social" issue handed off to the police for fixing.

In his 2000 study of gangs and related crime in British Columbia, Robert Gordon, of the School of Criminology at Simon Fraser University in Burnaby, reported that there are actually three distinct groups in play: criminal business organizations, street gangs, and "wannabes" who were more like social cliques who did not consider themselves a "gang" and whose common interest just happened to be crimes like armed bank robberies. Gordon concluded, based on extensive interviews with mostly visible minorities and earlier research by others, that joining a gang seemed voluntary and gradual, often a case of running away from a dismal family life more than rushing to join an outlaw group. Many, lacking job and language skills, simply told him they could never hope to make as much money with a legitimate job. He also made the important distinction that most gangsters were "young adults" not "young offenders," with a median age of nineteen. These findings were consistent with Tunstall's results.

Gordon found that while the police play an important role in deterrence, they cannot fight this street fight alone, and that the most successful efforts had been to deter possible recruits than to persuade gang members to leave their group.

Tunstall, in his later report, noted that of the lucky few who escaped the violent lifestyle, most left their gangs in response to family pressure, fear, and arrest. Some simply grew up; a few expressed feelings of remorse or redemption. They were quickly replaced, often by young women joining Aboriginal gangs across the prairies and Asian gangs in British Columbia.

While the gang problem in Canada seems less severe than in the United States, the government responses here—passing new legislation, giving the police greater power, and throwing money at them to create various rapid-response teams and guns-and-gangs units—have enjoyed mixed results. The latest attempt was announced in February 2009 when the federal government unveiled its "new measures to combat gangs and other forms of organized crime." These new amendments to the *Criminal Code* were touted as enhanced tools to better equip the police and the courts to act against organized crime and particularly "gang murders and drive-by shootings," which the government claimed accounted for 20 per cent of all homicides (117 out of 594) in Canada. The government release claimed that its new bill would strengthen the *Criminal Code* by:

- Specifying that murder is automatically first-degree when it is committed in connection with a criminal organization. First-degree murder is subject to a mandatory sentence of life imprisonment without eligibility for parole for 25 years.
- Creating a new broad-based offence to target drive-by and other intentional shootings involving reckless disregard for the life or safety of others. This offence would include a mandatory minimum sentence of four years in prison with a maximum period of imprisonment of 14 years. The minimum sentence would increase to five years if the offence was committed for the benefit of, at the direction of, or in association with a

criminal organization or with a restricted or prohibited firearm such as a handgun or automatic weapon.

- Creating two new offences of assault against a peace officer that causes bodily harm and aggravated assault against a peace officer. These new offences would be punishable by a maximum of 10 and 14 years' imprisonment respectively.
- Clarifying that when courts impose sentences for certain offences against justice system participants, including peace officers, they must give primary consideration to the objectives of denunciation and deterrence.
- Strengthening and lengthening "gang peace bonds" (preventive court orders requiring an individual to agree to specific conditions to govern their behaviour). The peace bond could be issued for up to 24 months (as opposed to the usual 12 months) against a defendant who has been previously convicted of intimidating justice system participants, or of committing an organized crime or terrorist offence. This reform to the *Criminal Code* would make it clear that a judge has broad discretion to impose any reasonable condition necessary to protect the public in that particular case.

There seemed no doubt the government had to do something. The media had been writing about the scourge of gang violence since the early 1990s, often finding themselves accused of sensationalizing and inflaming the issue to near hysteria. Yet in 2009, *Maclean's* magazine was reporting that gang-related crime had hit epidemic proportions, citing figures from Statistics Canada to illustrate its "Blood on the Streets" chart showing that gang-related deaths had risen to 117 in 2007 from a mere 28 in 1997. "In February alone, there were some 19 shootings in the [B.C.] Lower Mainland, eight deaths and a mounting fear that authorities were powerless to stop the anarchy. And with good reason," Ken McQueen wrote. "One of every five people killed in Canada is now the victim of a gang hit. While B.C. has the current political spotlight, it accounted for just 20 per cent of gang murders in 2007. One of every four gang killings, in fact, happened in Ontario.

Where there is progress, even that is a mixed blessing. Twelve years ago, Quebec accounted for a staggering 61 per cent of the nation's gang murders. By 2007 its share was down to 19 per cent, not because Quebec is more peaceful, but because gangs in other provinces are more violent."

With files from six correspondents, McQueen chronicled the rising terror, complete with proposed solutions from experts. Noting that the national crime rate had dropped to its lowest point in thirty years in 2007, he wrote: "That good news is tempered by the intractable problem of violent youth crime—on the rise since the mid-1980s, and a troubling entry point into gang life. Although the level is unchanged from 2006, it is double the rate of twenty years ago. The homicide rate by minors dropped, but it remains the second-highest since 1961."

Experts suggested several steps to help stem the violence. They urged choosing policy over politics, noting that research showed harsher penalties such as those proposed by the Stephen Harper Conservatives did not deter crime. Instead, the government should try to get on top of the problem using "an intelligent, coherent strategy." Lawmakers need to think strategically, like chasing the money, filling loopholes for gun importers, and providing better protection for witnesses who come forward to protect them from intimidation or worse, possibly by simply toughening existing contempt-of-court and obstruction-of-justice laws. Prevention is another key step, offering better alternatives to gang life before the person joins. The police have a role to play in all of these initiatives, but there was another more clearly defined role for them: the politicians were urged to "unfetter" their peace officers.

"Gang investigations—with fearful witnesses and a gang code of silence and retribution—are a policing challenge," McQueen wrote, citing a federal study that showed the average gang-related murder in Canada takes more than six months to investigate compared to about a week for many domestic or other homicides. Police superintendent John Robin, head of the B.C. Lower Mainland's Integrated Homicide Investigation Team (IHIT), explained that at least eight officers are assigned to each murder, at least partly to "document the required high legal standard of Charter and privacy rights."

"It's unlikely serious crime investigation in any other jurisdiction in the Western world consumes as many resources," he told *Maclean's*. "And that's because of court rulings. That's because of disclosure rulings. That's because of just the complexity of the cases we're addressing."

Superintendent Doug Kiloh, head of the Combined Special Forces Enforcement unit in B.C., added that, "In real terms the system is backed up and lack of prosecutors, as well as the urgency of other matters, influence charge approval and prosecution."

McQueen reported on a system so flawed that delays seem understandable and perhaps unavoidable. "The case required police to draft 371 documents and warrants for judicial authorization, totalling 8,154 pages and 4,800 hours of officer time," he wrote. "Seventeen reports to Crown counsel were drafted: 3,948 hours of police time, and a further 4,568 hours for bail briefs. Documents disclosing the case to the defence total almost 60,000 pages and 53 hours of videotaped evidence. Thousands more hours of police time will be spent meeting disclosure needs in the months and years ahead as the cases crawl toward trial."

As Kiloh concluded: "In my view, disclosure law has evolved as a weapon for defence counsel, not an assistance to providing a fair trial. It has paralyzed the system."

This problem extends beyond the courts. And it's not just too few police in the thin bruised line. There is also the problem that perception is reality—which puts a lot of power in the hands of the media.

In 2001, the Nathanson Centre for the Study of Organized Crime and Corruption, in Toronto, released its "Exploratory Review of Media Coverage," based on articles published in nineteen major and daily newspapers and national magazines across Canada between 1995 and 2000. Co-authors Margaret Beare and Juan Ronderos pored over thousands of articles to produce a CD-ROM with 27,893 article references and coded analysis on 1,237 full-text articles, which just represented the year 2000.

They reported that, while extensive, media coverage in no way paralleled any rise or fall in organized criminal activity and was often limited to traditional topics like bikers, illegal immigration smuggling, drugs—not large "organized" financial frauds and scams. "The term 'organized crime' was often used when in fact no specific criminal activity was the subject of the coverage," they wrote. "This was particularly true in the case of 'bikers' where in the majority of the cases, the articles were about 'bikers' themselves rather than specific criminal activities." They also found that reporting priorities seemed to reflect geographic regions, with Ontario more interested in illegal gaming and British Columbia more focused on marijuana grow ops. But Canadians everywhere seemed ambivalent towards organized crime "either as consumers or in providing a near-celebrity status to high profile notorious organized criminals."

The study accused the media of "playing into this" by "on one hand acknowledging that groups such as the bikers wanted a high profile, and then providing the criminals with this profile by writing long articles about them."

The institute and the study's authors are known for their interest in "transnational" crime—global enterprises that extend beyond national borders—and reported that the media is also becoming more interested in national and international crimes and government, and also, one suspects, police responses. Topics in the study included: drug manufacturing/trafficking; environmental crime; smuggling and cigarettes; contraband; economic crime; telemarketing fraud; illegal migration/immigration; document fraud; human trafficking and smuggling; counterfeit and fraud; vehicular theft; money laundering; bikers and crime; corruption and public officials; high-tech/computer crimes; intimidation and officials and crime; gambling and crime; forfeiture; diamond mining and crime; surveys and organized crime; proceeds of crime; and, criminal association.

"While one must not make the claim that an increase in media coverage relates directly to an increase in organized crime activity, it may be correct to assume that the focus on certain types of criminal activity has affected the public's perception of the amount and seriousness of these criminal activities," they concluded.

Biker stories dominated the reporting, with less attention given to Colombians, South Americans, Jamaicans, Italians/Mafia, Nigerians, Russians/East Europeans, Americans, Asians, Chinese/ Triads, Vietnamese, street gangs, First Nations gangs, government, and other multiple groupings of unknown origin/ethnicity.

"In some cases, the 'tone' was clearly of a 'situation totally out of control' as words such as danger, fear, threat were woven though the articles," the study found. "Other articles, often presenting the details of the same incident were strictly presenting the 'facts.'"

While there seemed to be themes of fear and alarm, there wasn't always much substance: "In many cases no evidence was offered; this was often true with the articles that spoke along the lines of threats to democracy and the infiltration of civil society. After these dire warnings, the reader was often given no supporting evidence for these claims."

In the end, the study selected four specific themes for discussion: media coverage/criminal incidents; bikers; public ambivalence; and, legitimacy of the laws. Coverage appeared to spawn more coverage: "Hence, a biker incident in one part of Canada can result in other regions producing biker articles that may be historical or 'predictive' of the future ... When there is a controversy or a high profile criminal incident, politicians have to respond. This 'incident-response' cycle alone appears to generate increased coverage." In other words, the media could create the incident then milk the response.

The bikers were by far the most reported organized crime group. Ignoring the fact that the bikers—white, often easily identifiable, and versed in at least one of the two official languages—are the easiest stories for the media, the study identified three specific catalysts that prompted a frenzy of reporting, ironically all of them involving Quebec: the accidental death of eleven-year-old Daniel Desrochers in August 1995 when a bomb exploded outside a biker hangout; federal-provincial politics (Quebec was demanding that the federal government take action to address the biker problem); and, the shooting of crime journalist Michel Auger on September 13, 2000.

"An analysis of the media around the 'biker' issue reveals an interesting pattern," the study found. "The police will comment that the bikers want to become high profile in order to indicate their supremacy and then the police facilitate this profile building by providing a large amount of media coverage. During the early months of the year, the police were repeatedly seen predicting further violence coming from the bikers both in terms of more physical violence and in terms of the expansion of their territories."

Although the police were apparently working behind the scenes, it would take eight years before they swooped in, effectively crushing the Hells Angels in Quebec with Operation SharQc 2009. But who knew if even that success would shake public ambivalence to organized crime.

"Even with the incredible amount of media attention, both in the form of careful, thorough analysis as well as the more hysterical 'panic' rhetoric aimed at organized-crime activity, the media articles revealed a continuing ambivalence on the part of the public to the 'danger' of, or tolerance for, various organized-crime activities and specific organized criminal groups," Beare and Ronderos wrote, noting there had been a "major flurry" of articles when celebrities Ginette Reno and Jean-Pierre Ferland sang, apparently gratis, at the wedding of a biker friend of Hells Angels head honcho Maurice "Mom" Boucher. But even then, they noted that the photos of that event indicated "a festive, 'elite' gathering."

But the biker impact wasn't limited to Quebec: "The community of Port Dover, Ontario, seemed to see the biker rally into their town as an occasion that was 'good for business' and advertised 'Biker breakfast specials'. This support, or at least tolerance of biker gangs is of course in addition to the public's continuing demand for drugs of all types as well as the other illicit commodities that fuel the biker economy as well as the economies of many other organized-crime operations."

The study conceded that "questions of the legitimacy of the laws" may contribute to the public ambivalence specifically to the bikers, but said their media analysis revealed two other areas where the public appeared to question the prevailing laws: hydroponic marijuana growing in British Columbia; and illegal "house" card gambling in Ontario. Both were viewed by police as "significant" problems that warranted "crackdowns." The media had no problem finding elected officials like the Nanaimo city councillor who was quoted in the *Globe and Mail*, April 5, 2000, saying: "People are just not that concerned about marijuana. It's not really clear that they see this as a very serious issue." But there was also another side to the reporting, "a scenario involving Asian gangs, bikers, violence and children at risk," which described police initiatives that included, for the first time, claims that they had "saved" children, with the assistance of child-care authorities, from dangerous fire-prone homes and menacing fiery-tempered parents.

In 2002, Judith Dubois, a professor at the Université du Québec à Montréal, unveiled her study on the impact of the media on public attitudes towards organized crime, written for the Research and Evaluation Branch, Community, Contract and Aboriginal Policing Services Directorate of the Royal Canadian Mounted Police. She reported that Canadians are exposed to "extensive media coverage of events related to organized crime" daily—what Dubois terms "an impressive array of stories" appearing in both print and broadcast media. Citing a 2001 study, which estimated that more than 27,000 articles referred to organized crime in fifteen Canadian dailies and magazines over a six-year period, she concluded: "This massive exposure is significant, as the media are among the sources of information people count on to mould their opinion of the world around them. And with respect to crime, surveys have shown that up to 95 per cent of people say they rely on the media as their primary source of information in this regard . . ."

Noting such extensive coverage and its role as a possible source of public information on organized crime for Canadians, Dubois deemed it "imperative" to ask: Does media coverage of OC-related events influence public opinion, and, if so, how?

While she could find no scientific study dealing with the topic, she was able to conclude, based on "topic-related" studies, that "the criminal events that the media decide to report on are not necessarily always those, in actual fact, that are the most significant in terms of frequency, trends or range of offenders involved."

In other words, human nature kicks in, finds the path of least resistance and journalists report what's easy and can be written in time to meet deadlines and keep their editors happy. But if the story has sensational overtones, well, that's a consideration, too.

"The little research we were able to find indicates that the media seem to give precedence to crimes that are extreme or involve vulnerable victims," Dubois wrote. "Other studies suggest that the commission of violent crimes against the public may affect how it perceives crime-related risk. There is also believed to be a connection between how crimes are presented by the media, society's sense of fear and the public's crime-policy preferences."

That finding ties in nicely for those, inside and outside of journalism, who have maintained over the years, "If it bleeds, it leads." Dubois found little to contradict that unflattering assessment.

"Little has been written about the impact of OC media coverage on public opinion in editorials and opinion articles in Canada," she notes. "However, problem-related analyses published in the media clearly show that the deaths of innocent victims at the hands of bikers, and especially the shooting of crime reporter Michel Auger, have led to extensive media coverage of the issue, in the process awakening public opinion and leading to the implementation of harsher crime-fighting policies. In-depth interviews with news, court house and investigative reporters confirm this hypothesis."

It's not clear what exactly those "harsher" crime-fighting policies are, but there certainly seems little room to dispute the core finding that the press is drawn to violent crime. And that, in turn, probably influences Canadians. The journalists seem to agree.

"In fact," Dubois wrote, "the reporters we interviewed all agreed that OC media coverage most certainly does influence public opinion. They felt that providing information on OC-related events makes people aware of what is happening and lets them then develop an opinion. Individuals who are well informed have a better grasp of reality."

But while appearing to concede their impact, the journalists seem to dispute that the media are the message.

"However," Dubois continued, "these same reporters did not believe that media handling *per se* influences public opinion. They felt that incidents are reported in a fair and balanced fashion. But they confirmed that some OC-related events receive more media coverage and often make headlines in newspapers and news bulletins, compared to other less 'appealing' crimes."

These journalists, Dubois states, claim to be merely responding to the demands of public interest.

"The information compiled in the course of this study leads us to believe that in some circumstances, media coverage of OC-related events can influence public opinion," she concluded, citing the Auger shooting. "Various other hypotheses may help us explain public reaction. But this example may also be a mere exception to the rule. Do the media have an impact on public opinion in matters not involving crimes against the person? And can it be said that media handling *per se* in no way influences public opinion?"

Dubois, citing the absence of scientific studies dealing specifically with OC media coverage—and "considering the high-ranking position of OC in the information media"—is unsure. She suggested further research should be done.

A year later, Dubois was back with a "Police Managers Survey on Media Coverage of Organized Crime," written for the same RCMP branch and directorate. Her detailed approach explored the perception of media coverage of organized crime, ranging from in-depth articles, to editorials and investigative reporting. In addition to exploring the violence and socially accepted events linked to crime groups, she also touched on political interventions and criminal activities "overlooked" by the media.

In summary, she found: "Police managers feel that the media tend to focus too much on organized-crime activities that involve violence. Because of this emphasis on violence and sensationalism, the media often underplay organized crime activities with no apparent violence. The activities downplayed the most by the media, in terms of impact, are money laundering and economic crimes.

Police managers also stated that the media give too much exposure to positive or socially acceptable events linked to organized crime. They consider, however, that police operations, trials and political interventions related to organized crime receive adequate and relatively proper coverage. Police managers are concerned about a lack of in-depth articles, editorials and feature stories that could provide an in-depth look at issues related to organized crime. According to some managers, the biggest shortcoming is that the media never provide a comprehensive view of the actual causes and overall impact of organized crime in Canada."

As for the impact the media play, she concluded: "Almost all interviewed police managers stated emphatically that public opinion regarding organized crime is definitely influenced by the media. This situation is said to have a negative impact. In fact, several managers argue that the media give citizens the impression that organized crime generates much more violence than it actually does. The way organized crime–related events are covered by the media heightens the sense of insecurity in the community and causes citizens to call on the police more often to deal with violent criminal activities. On the other hand, it is felt that the public is unaware of the adverse effects of non-violent organized crime activities."

What then, Dubois asked, is the likely impact of community concerns on police management?

"About two thirds of respondents said they have to take public opinion into account in their decisions and actions. Most interviewed police managers agreed that law enforcement's role is, first and foremost, to serve the community and to listen and remain accountable to them. However, several stated that public opinion could sway their decisions, providing it was warranted by circumstances."

And how heavily did media coverage influence this?

"Respondents were qualified in their opinions regarding the influence that media coverage of organized crime activities might have on their decisions and actions. Police managers generally contend that police priorities and procedures are not affected by the media. However, several respondents stated that they take into account what is disseminated in the media, because they are accountable to the community and are concerned about what is perceived by the public through the media. Many respondents also stressed that the information on organized crime disseminated through the media has an impact on their communication and fact-checking procedures. A few managers explained that, even though they are not generally affected by the media, there may be exceptions for special, unavoidable cases such as the bomb death of Daniel Desrochers and the shooting of crime reporter Michel Auger."

There were, however, a few police purists who insisted they would not be told by the media how to do their job. But they had other concerns.

"Lastly," Dubois concluded, "some respondents stated that they are not influenced by the media, but they sometimes have to take into account the positions taken by elected officials, who obviously can be influenced."

And there you had it. You would think that the announced Toronto-based operational centre in 2003 to house investigators from eleven municipal, provincial, and federal agencies to coordinate efforts in fighting and preventing organized crime and terrorist activity might influence political will. You might wish that revelations produced by the Jack and Mae Nathanson Centre on Transnational Human Rights, Crime and Security based at York University in Toronto (successor to the Jack and Mae Nathanson Centre for the Study of Organized Crime and Corruption, established in 1997) might influence policy and laws. But in a world where perception is reality, it is more likely that the most influential impact on elected officials and their staffs may well be the latest public-opinion polls and media reports and broadcasts. It often seems that the "facts" are less important than how they can be spun favourably by the politicians and their staff. Ironically, that may open a window of opportunity for the police.

The media impact on politicians and other government decision-makers is fully appreciated by Major General (ret'd) Lewis Mackenzie whose book *Generalship and the Art of the Admiral* includes a chapter entitled "The Media as a Tool of the Military

Commander." Edited by Lieutenant Colonel Bernd Horn, a history instructor at the Royal Military College of Canada, in Kingston, Ontario, and Stephen J. Harris, chief historian at the Department of National Defence Directorate of History and Heritage, in Ottawa, the book features a who's who of the Canadian military and military historians writing on a variety of topics tied to the book's subtitle, *Perspectives on Canadian Senior Military Leadership.*

As a military commander in charge of United Nations forces in Bosnia in the early 1990s, Mackenzie was exposed to some of the best, brightest, and bravest journalists on the planet. He studied them as they studied him and grasped not only what makes reporters tick, but also how best to use them to get out your message. He views the media as a tool and even a weapon, which is only as good as the person wielding it. That does not require overt or subtle manipulation; it means explaining your story simply, highlighting what matters and hope that that prompts some intelligent questions. His later career as a media commentator and pundit underscored the power of the press in his mind, giving him a forum to make his points to his desired audience in a way that he never could as a soldier. While in uniform, even as a general, he was subject to civilian political oversight that could border on whim, but on the working end of a microphone he was a force to be reckoned with—and heeded.

That was a lesson for police leaders to learn as technology and terrorism further complicated an already complex world for crime fighters. For politicians to simply expect the police to fix these new problems associated with gang violence by rounding up the usual suspects was unrealistic without the political will and social policies and budgets to address the root causes of poverty, ethnic marginalization, and social and family dysfunction.

The unspoken truth was that tackling ethnic gangs raised the spectre of racial profiling, first levelled years ago against the Toronto police by the *Toronto Star.* Those allegations have been hotly contested by many far removed from policing or journalism, but no matter how you interpret the evidence, it has been a hard label for the police to shake. To an extent, it was the latest in what seems to be an ongoing love-hate relationship between the police and the media, which dates to at least 1970 when Justice Campbell Grant was appointed to head the provincial inquiry into "alleged improper relationships between personnel of the Ontario Provincial Police and persons of known criminal activity." Eric Silk, the OPP civilian commissioner, was among those caught in the allegations raised in the Ontario Legislature that June by High Park MPP and renowned crusading coroner Morton Shulman that some in the provincial police were a little too cozy with reputed "Mafia" figures. As inquiry commissioner, Grant determined no wrongdoing by the police in his report that December. And while he did underscore the need to include ethics in police training, especially for senior officers, he was more concerned with the role of the media, specifically the head of the Burlington news bureau of the *Hamilton Spectator*, who was identified as the source for Shulman's allegations, writing:

"[The reporter] could have written a very interesting story if only he had kept to the facts of the case. . . . He would have been quite justified and performed a commendable duty as a newspaper reporter commenting on the facts of the case and the evidence adduced thereat giving full details of the court proceedings but he continued to state as facts matters which he must have known were if not untruthful at least clothed with very considerable doubt."

There would be no provincial inquiry to investigate the allegations of racial profiling, but the police protests that they were being unfairly painted as racists found some support from several academics who publicly questioned the methodology, and therefore the legitimacy, of the accusations. But you didn't read or hear much of that in the media.

SEVEN

LIES, DAMN LIES, AND STATISTICS:
The Media and Racial Profiling

There are three kinds of lies: Lies, damn lies and statistics.
—Benjamin Disraeli and Mark Twain

American humorist Mark Twain popularized those words, first spoken by British statesman and future prime minister Benjamin Disraeli to note that anyone can use any data to make any point. The meaning of statistics is in the eye of the beholder—and the spinner.

Media critics in all walks of life accuse many reporters of being "spoonfed" by their sources and government and corporate spin, lamenting that too many take dictation rather than report or investigate their subjects. The almost daily media scrums, typified by a herd of screaming reporters plunging a wall of microphones into the face of the hapless *victim du jour* who tries to remain composed and not sweat under the glare of the television lights, but often looks like a deer caught in headlights, may be the best example of how spontaneous today's pack "gotcha" journalism has displaced reasoned questioning and critical thought.

Happily, however, there are exceptions.

In the latter months of 2008, two western newspapers questioned the gathering and veracity of crime statistics that they were being fed to pass along to the public.

On September 12, *Regina Leader-Post* journalist Heather Polischuk asked, in response to readers' online comments to the paper's Sound Off section, whether the numbers, usually coming from Statistics Canada based on data submitted to them by the police, meant there was less crime or that there were fewer victims reporting it.

The overriding sense seemed to be why bother calling the police because nothing ever happened. People began to believe that no officer would respond, and if one did, they would have little time to conduct any sort of meaningful investigation before racing off to their next call. Thus, the statistics showing a 26 per cent drop for the first six months of 2008 compared to the same time frame for 1999 were suspect at best and "deceptive" at worst.

Noting the apparent discrepancy between the 2004 national General Social Survey (GSS), which found only 34 per cent reported potentially criminal incidents in Saskatchewan and Regina's 2007 Omnibus Survey, which found 73 per cent of crime victims reported the crimes to police (a decline from previous years), the response from Regina Police Service (RPS) spokesperson Elizabeth Popowich was that the two surveys couldn't be accurately compared due to differing content and sample sizes to determine the provincial and municipal statistics.

That still left the following lingering questions: How do you prove a negative? How do you count the number of people who do not do something, like call the police after a crime?

Popowich confirmed that the police were aware that a lot of crimes were not being reported, and suggested: "It's possible that the larger or more urbanized a centre becomes, the less likely people may be to report crime, especially minor property offences, and it just seems to follow that the larger the pool of possible suspects, the more difficult it is to solve the crime and sometimes that can contribute to someone's feeling of hopelessness or cynicism."

Switching to a glass-half-full perspective, Popowich suggested that the drop in crime stats could also be attributed to "better crime prevention practices, community partnerships and police resources." Popowich encouraged those who distrusted the police to learn more about their local servers and protectors by visiting the police website, attending an open house or participating in the Citizens' Police Academy, an eleven-week program run every spring and fall to give residents better insight into police work through lectures, demonstrations, and ride-alongs. The program has reputedly built a strong bridge between the public and the police. Graduates can advance to join the Citizens On Patrol Program which uses volunteers to patrol their neighbourhoods as another set of eyes and ears for the police. Popowich also urged citizens to continue reporting crimes, even if they felt it would be a waste of time.

"The citizens out there play a very, very important role," she said. "Police can't be everywhere all the time and we rely on citizens who first of all choose to abide by the law and secondly report any crime they see or anything that happens to them. And we can't investigate it unless we know about it. So for the people who are cynical, I will stubbornly encourage them to come forward and report crimes to the police simply because if something is unreported then it's guaranteed the outcome won't be a successful one."[1]

A month later, *Vancouver Sun* reporter Peter McKnight questioned the statistics, but reported their value despite their flaws. Observing that any discussion of a crime "epidemic" usually meant there was an election under way, he suggested that "stoking" public fears is a proven way to get their votes, as demonstrated by the federal Conservatives' rise to power in 2006. Two years later, he reported that the strategy was proving more difficult: "Amid the lies and damned lies about crime, some pesky statistics keep threatening to derail politicians' efforts to send the public running for cover."

Fear mongering, if true, was undermined by police numbers released by Statistics Canada that suggested the national crime rate had fallen yet again—and that crime in British Columbia had hit a thirty-year low, which prompted Justice Minister Rob Nicholson to mutter: "We are not governing by statistics."

McKnight noted a key distinction between statistics that

suggest people are safer and people who claim they don't feel safer. He also observed that the Vancouver Board of Trade had been arguing that very point for some time, citing its chief economist, Bernie Magnan, who had argued that while the StatsCan data revealed a 7 per cent drop in violent and property crimes between 1999 and 2004, the "rates for these crimes actually went up by 19.5 per cent over the same period."

Magnan had found a way to prove a negative, stating that 66 per cent of violent and property crimes during the relevant period were never reported to police, by citing Statistics Canada's Canadian Centre for Justice Statistics' 2004 Criminal Victimization Survey, which documents Canadians' experiences, beliefs, and attitudes toward crime.

"So, what Magnan is doing is simply comparing the police statistics with the self-reports of a sample of Canadians, and concluding that any discrepancy between the two is the result of inaccuracy in the police stats," McKnight explained. "In effect, then, while accusing StatsCan and the media of taking the police stats as gospel, Magnan treats the victimization survey as exactly that. But of course we shouldn't treat any measure of crime as gospel. And we must be especially careful when comparing two measures that have different objectives, use different methodologies and survey different populations."

The article refers to the Uniform Crime Reporting Survey (UCR), the police statistics that have been compiled as an annual census of all criminal incidents reported to or discovered by police across Canada since 1962, and notes that victims who don't know a crime has occurred or don't bother to report it won't be reflected in the data.

"Similarly," McKnight added, "an incident might not make it into the official statistics if the police decide that they have insufficient evidence to conclude a crime has occurred.

"Consequently, far from treating the UCR as gospel, StatsCan freely admits that 'Any measure of criminal activity based on officially recorded crime statistics will be an underestimate.' This is especially likely in cases of relatively minor property crimes, since people are less likely to report such events."

McKnight also alludes to challenges facing victimization surveys, which can lead to both the "over- and underreporting" of crime. He cites StatsCan's victimization survey, part of the broader General Social Survey, which has been conducted approximately every five years since 1988 to assess public perceptions of crime and the justice system and risk factors associated with victimization. The GSS also tracks experiences with eight specific offences. (The UCR considers more than a hundred categories of crime.)

The problem, identified by Clayton Mosher, Terance Miethe, and Dretha Phillips in *The Mismeasure of Crime*, comes when people fabricate crimes, presumably to please the interviewer or to effect policy change. That phenomenon, they claim, is more likely to occur when politicians and the media sensationalize crime. Or the respondents may simply be confused, believing a lost item has been stolen.

"In this respect," McKnight reports, "police stats may be more accurate because when police are presented with a complaint, they can determine if there's sufficient evidence, while the GSS must simply rely on people's own reports ... [and it is] only as good as the memories of people it surveys."

Quite simply, he explains, if people forget being victimized, it can lead to under-reporting. Conversely, "telescoping" incidents into the wrong time frame can skew results for that year, leading to over-reporting. Even Stats Can acknowledges that its GSS doesn't know "whether the reported offence rates are above or below actual rates."

"That," wrote McKnight, "should caution us against assuming that the GSS provides the true crime rate, from which we can judge the accuracy of the UCR." He suggests regarding both systems as "valuable, if flawed, measures of crime."

"The UCR is particularly valuable given its breadth of coverage of types of crime and the volume of data it contains," he concluded, "while the GSS is unmatched in its ability to provide us with an assessment of the impact of crime. Consequently, rather than setting these two measures off against each other, as Magnan does, or worse, dismissing statistics altogether as the Conservatives do, we ought to use them both, to discern the level of crime, to understand what crime does to us, and what can be done to stop it."

Yet for all our doubts, we remain a society obsessed with statistics, whether it's the stumbling stock markets, our bumbling millionaire professional athletes—or crime stats. Problems of accuracy associated with that last category, McKnight noted in his 2008 *Vancouver Sun* article, can be magnified "when one considers that definitions of crime vary substantially across cultures and groups based on gender, age, race and social class." He cited American studies that found "Caucasians and people in rural areas tend to overestimate victimization compared to city-dwellers and members of minority groups. And one study discovered that college-educated subjects recalled three times as many assaults as those with an elementary school education."

But we rely on the media to report what's happening and what it means. Sadly, journalism, like policing, has fallen on hard times in the first decade of the twenty-first century. Newspaper and broadcasting newsrooms have been gutted by voluntary departures and layoffs, century-old paid-circulation community newspapers have been killed or folded into new free publications staffed by too few reporters and often no on-site editor. While advances in technology have made it easier to find news online, content has suffered and many view the vaunted fourth estate as a shadow of its former glories. While the media remains healthier in Canada than in the United States, where major daily newspapers have or are threatening to close their doors at the time of this writing, there is a widespread notion that media convergence and concentrated ownership by a new corporate breed have weakened the flow of information and crippled the public's right to know.

There are great similarities between police officers and journalists. The best in both worlds consider their chosen path a calling rather than just a career; they believe passionately in what they are doing and seek to help others and, in general, make the world a better place by identifying wrongdoing, be it crime or political intrigue alternately championing criminal and social justice, and any other assignment they are handed. Both make their living taking notes and interviewing people to find the evidence or facts to make their case, in court, in print, or on the air. Both professions are rather insular, at times linked to the world by phone, radio, and Internet, where their best leads can come from Facebook and YouTube because young people who hesitate to tell the police or the press anything can't shut up online.

The police are aware that the media can be a powerful ally and there have been valuable collaborations. Many journalists instinctively recoil from any possibility of being seen to be co-opted as an "agent of the state," but in the end, reporters working their sources for information simply need to clarify at what point they cease being a neutral observer and ensure they don't cross it. That leaves lots of common ground for both sides to co-operate for the greater good, especially when it touches on officer and public safety.

On July 21, 1992, CHCH News, then an independent television station in Hamilton, Ontario, produced and aired an innovative interactive crime re-enactment: *The Abduction of Kristen French.* The broadcast was a combined effort by the police, the media. and the community to help find a fifteen-year-old girl who was abducted from a city street in broad daylight while walking home from school on April 16, 1992, the day before Good Friday. It was also a case of no good deed goes unpunished as a Camaro prop used during the broadcast seemed to deafen the eyewitness voice-over accounts, which reported the car they had seen could have been a cream or light brown Camaro or "similar to a Camaro or Firebird." Police across southern Ontario, from Toronto, west to London and south to the Niagara Frontier, were soon stopping Camaros while predator Paul Bernardo drove around freely in his gold Nissan with his wife and accomplice, Karla Homolka. News blackouts were imposed prior to their later trials, underscoring that nature—and the media—abhor a vacuum. Denied material by the courts, journalists simply looked elsewhere for anything they could report. In the end, the media were tipped off, presumably by a disgruntled investigator, and nearly arrived at Bernardo's home before the police showed up to arrest him.

Other cases were less adversarial.

A decade earlier, RCMP sergeant Michael Eastham participated in a re-enactment by Global TV of the 1982 mass murder of pensioners George and Edith Bentley, their daughter and son-in-law, Jackie and Bob Johnson, and granddaughters Janet and Karen. Police needed an airplane to locate the Johnsons' burned vehicle, containing the charred remains of all six family members, in the dense foliage near Well's Grey Park, in British Columbia. But there was no sign of the Bentleys' missing 1981 Ford F250 Camper Special. Global provided a look-alike, which the Mounties later took on the road, driving east across Canada, prepared to follow the trail of tips they had received, wherever they led, hoping to twig the public's memory of seeing the missing vehicle, believed to have been driven by two French-speaking men. Despite those credible tips, the Johnson car was located about 30 miles from the murder scene. Despite the misdirection, Eastham praises the press in his book, *The Seventh Shadow*, which recounts the manhunt and eventual apprehension and conviction of the killer.

More recently, retired RCMP staff sergeant Ron Lewis, who chronicled his long battle over the Mountie pension and insurance scandal in his 2009 memoir, *This Is Not the RCMP I Joined*, commends the quality of reporting on that story and the public hearings, which led in part to the Brown Commission. An internal police issue had become a very public national debacle, attracting enthusiastic coverage from veteran political reporters in the National Press Gallery, bringing a distinctly broader approach to typical crime reporting.

Recent budget and personnel cutbacks, caused primarily by shrinking advertising dollars, have forced newsrooms to stretch their now-limited resources. In other words, there are fewer reporters and editors than in previous years to actually find and publish the information the public needs to know in order to give its informed consent on any issue. The result? Rewrite press releases, stick on a byline and push it through. Press obsessions with getting quotes and balanced reporting leaves little time and perhaps less inclination for today's journalists to think about *what* they're reporting to apply any critical thinking to what the story actually means.

That perceived need to take shortcuts, perhaps more than anything, is what sometimes annoys the police about the media. Journalistic reporting, police note-taking, and report writing essentially share the same mantra: get it right, write it tight, and never screw with your editor or staff sergeant, depending on which applies. If the police notes are incomplete or incorrect, the guilty may walk free or, even worse, the innocent may go to prison. The entire justice system depends on the police's ability with a pen and a keyboard. The reporters at least have an editor to review, if not their notes, then certainly their reportage. A constable is expected to document what he or she saw, heard, and experienced on a call, if not in isolation, then certainly with no hint of collusion or "help" in writing their notes. It can be a lonely feeling; indeed, as Ottawa police sergeant Ralph Heyerhoff told aspiring constables as a guest lecturer at Algonquin College's Police Foundations program in 2008: "Every time your pen touches paper, you have the potential to have your notebook appear before the Supreme Court of Canada."

With the onus on police to "get it right," they grow anxious, angry, or at least frustrated when they believe the media got it wrong. Police want journalists to be held to the same high standard they must meet to ensure accuracy and fairness. That seems reasonable. So why does it seem that the most strongly fortified section of the Blue Wall—an invisible barrier that seems to be cracking under the strain in so many places—exists between the police and the press? How did it go so horribly wrong?

Both parties can shoulder some of the blame. It isn't likely a deliberate attempt to err or irk. The reality is that police recruits are probably taught no more about dealing with the media than the reporters are given insights to the true demands of policing from their journalism school instructors. The police beat is often an entry-level position at larger news organizations. That means that the police may, for the short term, at least, be dealing with rather inexperienced reporters. But those journalists generally tend to be crime reporters as opposed to actual police reporters, reporting on investigations, not issues. Their contacts and sources are often the media-relations officer and perhaps the cops they meet at the scene. The police are slow to trust, wary that anything they say—a simple one-liner to ease the tension at a crime or accident scene—may come back to haunt them. No one, they insist, will ever remember the name of a reporter who "burned" them; they will only recall the cop who "screwed up."

Conventional wisdom has always been that you don't pick a fight with someone who buys ink by the barrel or computer toner by the truckload, virtually ensuring they will always have the last word in any debate. But the irony is that policing and journalism are very similar. Each is an active participant at what can be exhilarating, even life-and-death, events. They are also observers, not mere spectators, bearing witness to the best and worst of the human condition on a daily basis. Both groups ask questions and pry for information. They interview, interrogate, and cajole their informants or sources, the police supported by the power of the state while the power of the press enjoys the leverage of being able to offer inducements for access. It becomes an issue of integrity. Journalists are expected, if not actually necessary, to protect their sources, even go to prison for contempt of court if required. But it is a very slender line between preserving integrity at all costs and simply giving spin doctors free rein to advance an agenda. The police are often much better at processing the information they are given with an open eye to catch an inconsistency or questionable evidence. They're certainly not perfect—few ever truly master that skill—but they are better at it than the media, which often simply takes dictation in a rush to meet deadlines. For example, nothing could be easier than a cut-and-paste story like this gift from Statistics Canada:

- In 2007, police services saw the second largest annual increase in the number of police officers in the past 30 years in Canada. There were over 64,000 police officers in Canada in 2007, a 2.7% increase from the previous year.
- The increase in the number of officers nationally (+1,673) was mainly due to increases in Ontario (+691) and British Columbia (+397).
- The largest percentage increases in police strength between 2006 and 2007 were seen in Newfoundland and Labrador and

Nova Scotia, each up 6%. Over the past decade, Newfoundland and Labrador (+15%) and Saskatchewan (+12%) have seen the biggest gains in police strength.

- Despite recent increases, police officer strength has remained relatively stable over the past 30 years. In 2007, the rate of 195 officers per 100,000 population was 5% lower than the peak of 206 reached in 1975.
- Saskatchewan continued to report the highest rate of officers per capita (207 per 100,000 population), followed by Manitoba (204) and Quebec (198). The lowest rates were reported in Prince Edward Island (164), Newfoundland and Labrador and Alberta (both 165).
- Among the census metropolitan areas, Thunder Bay reported the most officers per 100,000 population (212), followed by Saint John (201) and Winnipeg (188). The lowest rates were seen in Saguenay (123), Québec (140) and Kingston (143).
- Police clearance rates, one measure of police performance, have increased in each of the past two years. In 2006, police cleared (solved) 36% of all *Criminal Code* incidents, up from 32% in 2004. Similarly, clearance rates for violent crime have increased from 69% in 2004 to 72% in 2006. However, clearance rates for violent crimes had generally been declining since peaking (76%) in the mid-1990s.
- The number of female officers continued to rise (+6%) in 2007 at a faster pace than the number of male officers (+2%). Females now account for almost one in five officers in Canada, compared to approximately one in ten a decade ago.
- In 2006, expenditures on policing totalled $9.9 billion, a 4.4% increase over 2005 after adjusting for inflation, resulting in a cost of $303 per Canadian. This was the tenth consecutive constant dollar increase in policing costs, increasing an average of 3% annually.
- Ontario ($268) and Quebec ($246) reported the highest per capita costs for municipal and provincial policing, while Prince Edward Island ($149) and Newfoundland and Labrador ($165) had the lowest.

At least some journalists have made the effort to show why such stats should not go unchallenged. As *Vancouver Sun* columnist Peter McKnight observed in 2008, the ploy of using the fear of a crime epidemic was proving harder that year than when the Conservatives rode it to victory in 2006, writing: "Amid the lies and damned lies about crime, some pesky statistics keep threatening to derail politicians' efforts to send the public running for cover."

His *Sun* colleague, columnist Barbara Yaffe, showed similar insight when she reported on what appeared to be a very important concession by Guiliano Zaccardelli, Mike Boyd, and Julian Fantino to the Senate committee cited earlier that a "thinning Blue Line" of police investigators stood between the public and crime, writing: "Today, police deal with Internet crime; terrorism threats; national health emergencies; marijuana grow-ops; international crime syndicates; human trafficking and youth and street gangs." The fact that story received so little play suggests that a growing number of journalists have simply become human wire services. It's certainly not a case—for the print media at least—that they are suppressed by government oversight. But that may change with the corporate convergence that has print media owned by private broadcasters. Freedom of the press belongs to those who own the presses—and that's a smaller group than ever before.

Former *Ottawa Citizen* publisher Russell Mills raised that caution in his convocation address to graduating Carleton University students in 2002, saying: "A relatively new development is that companies involved in broadcasting have become owners of newspapers; the Southam papers in the case of CanWest and the *Globe and Mail* in the case of BCE, which also owns the CTV network. This is being driven by convergence, the idea that companies need different types of media in order to serve the evolving needs of readers, viewers and advertisers. From a press freedom perspective, the main potential issue is that broadcasters operate under licences granted by government while the print media in western democracies are unlicensed and unregulated by government. In a democracy, a newspaper should not require a licence any more than you should require a licence to write a letter or send an e-mail message. The fact that many of Canada's newspapers are now owned by companies that require licences from government to operate their broadcasting services creates at least the potential for government interference."

Mills, who was being presented with an honorary Doctor of Laws degree that day, must have also raised some eyebrows among the graduating journalism students when he told them that Canadian journalists, unlike their American counterparts, enjoy no special rights—nor should they.

"The freedom of expression that is guaranteed in our Charter of Rights and Freedoms applies to everyone, not just the news media," Mills explained. "When we publish a critical editorial about government, we are using exactly the same right that you have to complain about some government action in an e-mail message or letter to a friend. We have no more freedom than you do and should have no less. The most important element in freedom of expression is freedom from control or influence by government. If government controls the news media, either directly or indirectly, democracy cannot work properly."

Days later, Mills was fired by his employer, the staunchly Liberal Asper family, for running an editorial that had criticized then prime minister Jean Chrétien's role in the "Shawinagate" golf-course scandal for allegedly intervening on behalf of a constituent who was seeking a loan from the federal business bank. Response was immediate and dramatic—everywhere outside his own paper where a few reporters withheld their bylines in protest, but no journalist or editor resigned to preserve their journalistic integrity.

The public and journalists writing for papers not owned by the Aspers and CanWest were more blatant in their disapproval, such as Jeffrey Simpson, writing in the *Globe and Mail*:

> Freedom of the press has just suffered a terrible blow in Canada from a combination of Prime Minister Jean Chrétien's personal furies and the lickspittle owners of CanWest Global Communications Corp. That blow illustrates the potential perils of media concentration and a de

facto one-party state, both of which are so evident in this country. [Simpson cites Mills as the latest CanWest victim] ... Then, yesterday morning, they marched into the offices of Scott Anderson, the newspaper's editor, and reamed him out for the same reason they fired Mr. Mills— for being too tough on their hero, Mr. Chrétien, whose recent fundraising dinner in Winnipeg was partly organized by a member of the Asper family.

So much for the Aspers' declarations of their newspapers' editorial independence and journalistic integrity. Their promises in those areas are as worthless as some of the ones they give the Canadian Radio-television and Telecommunications Commission for their television licences. The publicly given reason for Mr. Mills' downfall was a form of corporate insubordination; the real reason was the Aspers' craven attitude toward Mr. Chrétien. They had already fired *Southam* columnist Lawrence Martin for reporting about Chrétien's alleged attempts to get government money to bail out a hotel next to a golf course in which he had an interest. They dumped the publisher of the Montreal *Gazette*, Michael Goldbloom, for allowing tiny bits of criticism of Israel in his paper. Then they imposed badly written and drearily argued "national" editorials on their Southam papers, including one that showered praise on the beleaguered Prime Minister ... Little did any of us expect when the Aspers bought Southam from Conrad Black how creepy would be their journalistic standards. It almost makes you pine for Lord Black, although he didn't exactly give his editors free rein, either.

Black was later convicted and imprisoned in the United States for some of his financial dealings, adding newspapers to the list of corrupt business elites like the heads of Enron. But his deal with the Aspers, while the biggest media sale in Canadian history, was certainly not unique in the realm of concentrated media ownership and convergence. Heritage Canada produced the following chronology of events in the decade between 1990 and 2000:

1992
- Hollinger acquires Torstar Corp.'s 22.6 per cent share in Southam.

1993
- Power Corp. acquires 18.7 per cent of Southam shares.

1994
- Rogers Communications acquires control of Toronto Sun Publishing through Maclean-Hunter Ltd. acquisition.

1995
- Hollinger acquires 12 dailies and 7 community papers in Ontario and Saskatchewan from Thomson Newspapers Ltd.
- Hollinger acquires 2 dailies in Saskatchewan from Armadale Co. Ltd.: the *Leader-Post*, in Regina, and the *StarPhoenix*, in Saskatoon. These acquisitions result in the loss of 170 jobs.

1996

May
- The Burgoyne family of St. Catharines, Ontario, sells its newspapers, including 3 dailies, to Southam.
- Hollinger acquires 6 dailies and 1 community newspaper in the Atlantic provinces from Thomson Newspapers Ltd. Thomson announces its intention to sell all its daily newspapers in Eastern and Central Canada, with the exception of the *Globe and Mail* and the *Chronicle-Journal* of Thunder Bay.
- Hollinger acquires six Ontario dailies from Thomson Newspapers Ltd.
- Hollinger acquires control of Southam by buying Power Corp.'s shares. With a 41 per cent interest in Southam, Hollinger now controls 59 Canadian dailies, 20 of which belong to Southam.

- In July, a coalition of organizations, including the Council of Canadians, demands an independent public inquiry into the acquisition. In September, the Council files an application for leave to appeal the Competition Tribunal's decision to approve the transaction. The request is eventually denied because it was filed after the deadline.

Conrad Black's arrival as the head of Southam prompts some resignations. In August, the editor-in-chief of the daily *The Gazette*, Joan Fraser, leaves, stating that her decision is due to the major changes taking place at Southam. In October, the editor-in-chief of the *Ottawa Citizen*, John Travers, resigns.

August
- Ted Rogers sells his controlling shares in Toronto Sun Publishing to a group of managers of the chain. The company is given a new name: Sun Media Corp. Quebecor was interested too, but decided not to outbid the group of managers. The transaction results in the loss of 100 jobs.

1997
- Southam acquires two British Columbia dailies belonging to Thomson Newspapers Ltd.

1998
- The Thomson and Southam chains exchange three dailies: Thomson acquires the *Medicine Hat News* and hands over two U.S. dailies to Hollinger International.
- Southam acquires six Vancouver Island newspapers owned by Thomson Corp., including the two dailies.
- Sun Media Corp. transfers ownership of the *Financial Post* to Southam, and in return it acquires four southern Ontario dailies.
- Southam's new daily, the *National Post*, is launched on October 27.
- In December, Quebecor acquires the Sun Media chain. Torstar

had already made an unsolicited offer for Sun Media, but Quebecor made a higher offer that was deemed more attractive. However, the four southern Ontario dailies acquired by Sun Media from Southam in exchange for the *Financial Post* are resold to Torstar. The new Quebecor/Sun Media empire goes through a new round of cuts, with 180 jobs being eliminated.

1999

- Southam becomes a private company after Hollinger buys up the interests of minority shareholders.
- Hollinger sells the Lloydminster *Daily Times*, a small Saskatchewan daily, to Bowes (subsidiary of Sun Media).
- Hollinger buys the *Record*, a small Quebec daily, from Quebecor.
- Hollinger creates a new company: Hollinger Canadian Newspapers, Limited Partnership. The company encompasses most of the newspapers in smaller Canadian markets in which Hollinger is active. The dailies in the Vancouver, Edmonton, Calgary, Ottawa and Montreal markets, along with the *National Post* and the *Halifax Daily News* in particular, remain under Southam ownership.

2000

- In February, Thomson puts all its newspapers except the *Globe and Mail* up for sale. Thomson's other five remaining Canadian dailies are the *Chronicle-Journal*, in Thunder Bay, Ontario, the *Brandon News* and the *Winnipeg Free Press* in Manitoba, and the *Lethbridge Herald* and the *Medicine Hat News* in Alberta.
- In April, Hollinger puts about 350 of its North American news-papers, most of its community newspapers and a number of small dailies, up for sale. The Canadian assets offered for sale (April 5) are all part of the new company, Hollinger Canadian Newspapers, Limited Partnership.

Heritage Canada also explored the impact of concentrated ownership of community newspapers, noting: "The impact on public opinion of an increasingly concentrated weekly newspaper industry is seldom raised as an issue, because newspapers of this type do not have a reputation for broaching controversial subjects or even for being opinion-makers. The weeklies owned by the big chains reserve a great deal of space for advertising and in many cases do not have an editorial page."[2]

But even local papers that had, in fact, been speaking out for more than a century, weren't faring well under the thumb of their new owners. In February 2008, columnists for both the *Ottawa Sun* and *Ottawa Citizen* chronicled the demise of historic community newspapers in the Ottawa Valley under Metroland Media Group ownership, a subsidiary of Torstar, which also owns the *Toronto Star*.

Tom Van Dusen fired the first salvo in the *Sun*, writing: "Two of the Ottawa Valley's most venerable paid-circulation weekly newspapers will be blended this week, replaced by a free combined publication . . . Each paper served its community for more than a century." Former long-time weekly newspaper reporter and editor Gerry Huddleston, now executive director of the Almonte General Hospital/Fairview Manor Foundation, spoke for many employees and subscribers when he said, "These newspapers had a tremendous history in Almonte and Carleton Place and this feeble way of folding them shows no respect." Metroland, through its local arm, the Ottawa Region Media Group, put a more positive spin on its move, but the only person who seemed happy was the local mayor. He thought it made economic sense. Coincidently, fewer reporters meant less scrutiny of local government.

Kelly Egan offered a more impassioned eulogy for the newspapers in the *Citizen* ten days later, writing: "These are bad times for newspapers, big and small. In particular, it is sad to witness the changes at some of the oldest publications in Eastern Ontario, little papers that ran on sweat and shoe-string at the best of times.

"The *Carleton Place Canadian* was founded 133 years ago. As of this month, it is no longer.

"The *Almonte Gazette*, meanwhile, is even older, founded in 1867. As a stand-alone, paid product, it's gone.

"The titles have been combined into a free, merged newspaper called the *Carleton Place Almonte Canadian Gazette*—a title twice as long, a paper half as good? We shall see."

Egan was equally cautious about the Metroland's "bold assurance" that the merge would not mean less news—apparently produced by just two full-time reporters.

"Pretty distressing news, really," he wrote, noting that another Metroland paper, the *Perth Courier*, founded in 1834, was losing its long-time editor with no replacement listed on the masthead.

"It doesn't end there," Egan continued. "*The Arnprior Chronicle-Guide*, as a paid publication, is no longer, but it was merely a junior paper—founded only about 130 years ago. It, too, is now a free publication.

"Does it matter to anyone that a small town no longer has its own paid newspaper, or its own editorial control? I hope so. Newspapers, surely, reflect the place. The editorial voice, hopefully, is home-grown, for good reason. The proprietor wants to see the town prosper because he wants his newspaper to prosper. He wants good governance and a watchful eye on crime and corruption . . . Without a rooted newspaper, who is going to get on the mayor's case, when the mayor's case needs getting on? Who is going to catalogue the police chief's bungling?"

After noting that almost all small towns have lost their police chiefs, too, Egan concluded: "The paid paper is there to muckrake, blow whistles, rock the boat, annoy. Knowing things, after all, is a fundamental part of living in a democracy . . . Strange times we live in, this so-called information age. Pete Hamill, the New York newspaper man, once got to the heart of it in a couple of words—information is static; news is a verb."

The columnists might also have included the *Kemptville Advance*, just south of Ottawa, which had, over the previous year, been turned around and won back former subscribers with a new aggressive approach to newsgathering. By January 2009, only one of the nine people who staged that miraculous turnaround remained at the paper they had saved without any support from senior management.

Metroland had taken earlier hits in larger centres. Writing in the March 2005 edition of the *Ryerson Review of Journalism*, Angela Boyd headlined her story, "Elephant in the Room: Metroland rolls over Toronto with bland community newspapers, but the independents fight on." Her article summed up the situation: "Metroland has a reputation for being a category killer—gobbling up independent papers, scooping up ad revenue, and replacing independent editorial voices with its own bland, feel-good copy." That business plan was symptomatic of why so many people, including the mainstream media, show little respect for the community newspapers that can report aggressively, break major stories, and give voice to people no one else writes about when given adequate guidance, support, and funding.

If the result of newspaper mergers, depleted newsrooms, and concentrated media ownership has not been to actually mute voices of dissent, it has unarguably limited and homogenized what passes for news today, blurring the line between information and entertainment to produce and publish an *infotainment* hybrid.

The reality for the police is that they know from their own studies that media reporting influences public perception of crime fighting. Crime fighting has become a war of words.

In her 2003 report, "Media Coverage of Organized Crime—Police Managers Survey," for the Research and Evaluation Branch of the RCMP Community, Contract and Aboriginal Policing Services Directorate, Judith Dubois, of the Université du Québec à Montréal, noted that many police complained of superficial reporting: "Police managers are concerned about a lack of in-depth articles, editorials and feature stories that could provide an in-depth look at issues related to organized crime. According to some managers, the biggest shortcoming is that the media never provide a comprehensive view of the actual causes and overall impact of organized crime in Canada." In other cases, the police insisted the media just plain got it wrong. The flash point was the *Toronto Star* accusing that city's police of racial profiling. In July 2003, Julian V.

Roberts, editor of the Canadian Justice Association's *Canadian Journal of Criminology and Criminal Justice*, took the rare step of devoting an entire edition to racial profiling, an issue so volatile and potentially damning to the police and the Canadian justice system the CJA editor felt that an academic review was required.

At the centre of the storm were Toronto police chief Julian Fantino and his department. Controversy was nothing new to Fantino. There were times he seemed like a magnet for discord. But this was different. The racial-profiling allegations questioned his moral compass as much as his professional attributes. The allegations greeted him shortly after he returned to Toronto as chief on March 6, 2000, possibly residue from earlier racial allegations that appeared to prompt him to leave Canada's largest city to become chief elsewhere.

As editor of a prestigious publication, Roberts waded directly into a no man's land between the police and the press, writing:

> From time to time, this journal examines in greater detail issues of particular importance to criminology and criminal justice in Canada. One such issue is clearly the implications of a series of articles published by the *Toronto Star* in 2002 and available on the *Star*'s Web site. For example, on 20 October 2002, a headline in the newspaper proclaimed that "Police Target Black Drivers." The actual story told a somewhat different tale, using much more equivocal language: "Star analysis ... suggests *racial profiling*" (emphasis added). An article published on 1 March also takes a more tentative posture. Speaking of the series, the article notes that "What we didn't do is draw any firm conclusions." But if "Police Target Black Drivers" isn't a firm conclusion, what is?
>
> The *Star*'s conclusions have, not surprisingly, been hotly contested by police representatives in Toronto. In 2003, the Toronto Police Service[s] [Board] released a review of the *Star*'s research that concluded that "the results do not provide evidence of systemic racial profiling being

practised by the Toronto Police Service." (The author, Professor Edward Harvey, declined an invitation to participate in this colloquy.) The reaction is understandable; if these allegations are founded, public confidence in the police, and indeed, the justice system, will be dealt an irreparable blow. This is one reason why it is vital that the research on which such allegations rests must be impeccable. Documenting the existence of discrimination is a very tricky business. In addition to the complex statistical challenges, it is important that the research be conducted by individuals (Harvey) who have considerable experience in the area and by individuals (police) who have taken no a priori position with respect to the issue.

The public must be understandably confused by the wealth of claims and counter-claims with respect to this issue. One way of clarifying matters would be through the use of a judicial inquiry, drawing upon a select group of researchers who are clearly impartial. Such a panel could examine the data, collect additional information if necessary, and draw some scientifically valid conclusions. We owe this to the public in general, to the specific community allegedly affected, and of course, to the police. In the context of the current controversy, some quite intemperate language has been directed at social science researchers, the implication being that the research can establish anything (or nothing). But careful, systematic, multivariate studies will provide scientific answers to questions pertaining to the conduct of police officers, or any other criminal justice professional.

This special section of the journal contains three contributions on the issue. Scot Wortley and Julian Tanner, two of Canada's leading researchers into race and criminal justice, provide a commentary on the issues raised by the *Star*'s analysis. Ron Melchers, a specialist in methodology and policing, offers his own interpretation of the *Toronto Star*'s research and places it in the context of research on this issue.

The third article is a commentary by Alan Gold, one of Canada's most distinguished criminal law practitioners.

But let's start at the beginning. As Fantino recalls in his memoir, *DUTY: The Life of a Cop*, he was the superintendent in charge of 31 Division in 1989, which included what the media routinely dubbed the "Jane-Finch Corridor" in the Borough of North York. He condemns this moniker as a slight to the 75,000 people living in that community northwest of Toronto who coped with the socioeconomic stressors of rampant public housing and inadequate infrastructure and support for residents and newcomers. A consequence, he notes, was "considerable" crime, "much of it violent." There were tensions between the police and what Fantino terms "elements" of the community. In late 1988, then a staff inspector in 31 Division, he and his old homicide partner, District 3 staff superintendent Wally Tyrell, met with the North York Committee on Community, Race and Ethnic Relations to discuss the negative relations between the police and local black youth. They asked Fantino to compile information about the state of crime in the community and show how it related to police contacts. Fantino collected the data and was immediately concerned because of the prevalence of negative interaction between local black youth and the police. He was, he recalls, encouraged to "tell it like it is." Tyrell, his boss, assured him he would be speaking to a closed, in-camera session.

On February 16, 1989, Fantino presented statistics which confirmed that a great deal of crime was being committed by black youths, but hastened to note that many of the victims were also black. The next logical step would have been to determine how the committee and the police could work together to address the issues. And maybe that was the plan. We'll never know, because the next thing Fantino knew, he was being questioned by a *Toronto Star* reporter who had apparently also been invited to attend the meeting. No one, apparently, thought to tell Fantino or Tyrell that a member of the media would be present. There is nothing to suggest that Fantino manufactured the statistics—compiled from official police records—or that he would have withdrawn anything he said. But he had already expressed his concern that the information he had been asked to compile could be volatile if taken out of context. The key point is that he had done what he had been asked to do—nothing more; nothing less. He presented his findings directly to the committee that had requested the information, but he might have simply presented his findings to them without comment had he known the press had been invited. Or at least one newspaper.

The ensuing *Star* headlines, which Fantino recalls made him feel that he and his police department were being accused of racism, prompted him to seriously consider resigning. Tyrell talked him out of that, but Fantino left Toronto a short time later to become police chief in London, in southwestern Ontario. When he returned to Toronto as chief in 2002, it was déjà vu all over again. This time the *Star* had created a new phrase that would haunt police across Canada for some time: racial profiling.

Which brings us back to the *Canadian Journal of Criminology and Criminal Justice*.

Scot Wortley, a criminologist, and Julian Tanner, a sociologist, both at the University of Toronto, described by Roberts, the CJA editor, as two of Canada's leading researchers into race and criminal justice, commented on the issues raised by the *Star*'s analysis. Their article, entitled "Data, Denials and Confusion: The Racial Profiling Debate in Toronto," was a review of University of Toronto sociology professor Edward Harvey's conclusion that racial profiling does not exist in the Toronto area.

Defining racial profiling as "racial disparity in police stop and search practices, racial differences in customs searches at airports and border-crossings, increased police patrols in racial minority neighborhoods and undercover activities, or sting operations that selectively target particular ethnic groups," Wortley and Tanner associated it further with "racial bias in police treatment after arrest."

In painstaking detail, the authors review the issue over words, including charts and extensive footnotes. "It is clear," they write, "that the debate concerning racial bias in police treatment after arrest cannot be resolved with the current data provided by either the *Toronto Star* or Professor Harvey. What is required is a properly reported multivariate analysis—perhaps a series of logistic regression models— that would investigate whether race is a significant predictor of both the release and the bail decision, after other relevant legal factors have been taken into statistical account. Such a procedure would simultaneously control for variables like criminal record and current charges, without eliminating multiple offenders and artificially reducing the size of the data set. Such an approach would also permit us to examine whether blacks with a criminal record are treated differently than whites with a similar criminal history. To our knowledge, such standard analyses have not yet been conducted."

In further discussion, the authors challenge Professor Harvey's re-analysis of the Criminal Information Processing System (CIPS) database over what it has identified as methodological issues and problems of interpretation. They lament that critics of his (Harvey's) report had not yet had a full opportunity to discuss these issues in the public arena, noting: "[Critics] were supposed to be given that opportunity at a special meeting of Toronto's Police Services Board on 28 April 2003—more than two months after Harvey originally presented his findings. However, a coalition of minority organizations actually walked out of this meeting after learning that the Board would only give them five minutes to respond to Harvey's report and his conclusion that the police do not engage in racial profiling . . . Harvey and his colleagues, incidentally, were given over two hours to present their results to the very same Police Services Board."

The authors further noted that this issue has generated unhappy times for more than the police and the press, writing that "social science in general—and the discipline of criminology in particular—has taken a beating" over its role in the racial-profiling debate.

"Most damaging," Wortley and Tanner note, "are accusations that social scientists can be hired to provide support for any side of an argument. This sentiment was perhaps best expressed by Councillor Gloria Luby—the vice-chair of the Toronto Police Services Board. In response to the *Star*'s analysis, Luby claimed that statistics can be used to prove anything.... We obviously disagree with this argument. However, we strongly believe that, under ideal circumstances, statistical analyses of sensitive issues should be subject to intensive review by academic experts before the figures are released to the public. This is why academic journals usually adopt a strict peer review process that ensures the basic integrity of published research. Clearly, such a system of quality control has not been applied to media discussions of racial profiling.

"Almost as damaging to the reputation of criminology are accusations that research can actually cause social problems. Chief Fantino expressed this opinion when he was initially asked to comment on the *Star*'s investigation: 'It seems that . . . no matter what honest efforts people make, there are always those who are intent on causing trouble. Obviously this is going to do exactly that.' Consistent with this view, Fantino recently dismissed community attempts to further discuss the racial-profiling issue as 'mischief-making.' Councillor Luby expanded on this theme when she stated that 'we've been getting along quite well. Police discrimination has not been an issue. So why should it suddenly become one? Because the *Star* did this research?

"The argument seems to be that studies that document racism within the justice system do more harm than good. That public discussion of evidence of racism creates distrust, damages relationships with specific minority communities, and lowers morale among criminal justice personnel. We could not disagree more. Good, objective social research does not create social problems—it merely documents them. Research has not caused the apparent problems that exist between certain racial minority groups and the police. It has only documented a situation that already exists. The discomfort of having to talk about racism—and deal with it in the policy arena—should not be used as an excuse to prevent further research in this area."[3]

From the authors' perspective, this was the beginning, not the end, of the issue.

"In conclusion," they wrote, "it is clear that the controversy over the issue of racial profiling is far from over. It is also clear that the criminological community must take a much more active role in this debate. We must provide more detailed commentary on the research than has already been conducted—and demand that research funds be set aside to conduct more thorough investigations of this phenomenon. Most importantly, we must vigorously defend our right to examine sensitive topics and conduct research that may not coincide with the interests of major players within the criminal justice system."

Ronald Melchers, a criminologist at the University of Ottawa and considered a specialist in methodology and policing, offers his own interpretation of the *Toronto Star*'s analysis and places it in the context of research on this issue. Defining racial profiling as "a significant threat to the ability of the police to maintain order, ensure public safety and prosecute those accused of criminal offences," Melcher analyzes their "possible engagement" by asking, "Do Toronto Police Engage in Racial Profiling?"

He begins by reviewing the evidence for claims of racial profiling, based on the *Star*'s own analysis of arrest data from the Toronto police's CIPS database, obtained under a freedom of information request, using data recorded between late 1996 (when CIPS was first implemented on a trial basis) and early 2002. The *Toronto Star*'s investigative team, under the supervision of Dr. Michael Friendly, professor of psychology and director of consulting services at York University's Institute for Social Research, worked with a database consisting of 483,614 incidents in which someone had been arrested, charged, or ticketed. These incidents resulted in more than 800,000 charges being laid under criminal and other statutes or bylaws. Of these charges, 301,551 were for *Criminal Code* or drug offences. No individual identifying information was included in the information obtained by the *Star* under the freedom of information request and offences were aggregated into broad categories to preserve an individual's privacy. As well as incident, charge, and police disposition detail, information was also provided about the age, gender, skin colour (white, black, brown, other), immigration and residency status in Canada, employment information, and country of birth of those arrested, charged, or ticketed. The data also provided information on the criminal histories of individuals arrested: previous convictions, bail status, probation orders, or conditional release status. Complete information, the *Star* reported, was not available in every instance, and the analysis excluded those cases where specific information was missing. As with all police-recorded data, the more serious offences would tend to be overrepresented among completed records and the least serious offences underrepresented. This was all preamble to the crucial question Does racial profiling actually exist?

"Polls and some studies consistently show that a majority of the public, and yet a larger majority of some visible minority groups (notably "Blacks"), believe that police are racially biased," Melchers wrote. He notes that the term "profiling" has grown in popular usage throughout the last decade to describe more or less formal practices of police and other public officials for singling out individuals by specific traits for investigation, while crediting the "popular media and the entertainment industry" for the initial success of the expression and for its entry onto the political stage. But, he argued, "racial profiling" is an expression "for rhetorical value alone."

"It attempts," he writes, "to redefine racial discrimination as more than individual bias, or even as improperly tolerated individual wrongdoing in an organization, but rather as the official policy and sanctioned practice of organizations. Drawing upon myths of the news and entertainment media, the term ... dramatizes public discourse on the issue of racial bias and discrimination. In June 1999 U.S. president Clinton officially consecrated the expression, calling it a 'morally indefensible, deeply corrosive practice' and further stating that 'racial profiling is in fact the opposite of good police work, where actions are based on hard facts, not stereotypes. It is wrong, it is destructive, and it must stop.'"

In our post 9/11 world, Melchers notes that many police and other public service organizations now routinely monitor the skin colour and ethnic backgrounds of persons stopped, questioned, or investigated to determine whether their personnel are acting in a discriminatory manner, noting: "Racial Profiling Data Collection systems have become a common feature of public administration, to respond to widespread public belief that such practices exist and to attempt to maintain or restore public confidence." But whether police and other enforcement agencies actually engage in racial or other sorts of offender profiling is, he warns, rarely as simple to assess on the available evidence as many might initially think. He illustrates his point with the example of a hit-and-run collision involving a taxicab, which an eyewitness describes as green.

"Only 25 per cent of the 4,000 licensed taxicabs in the city are green, so this narrows the investigation considerably," Melchers observes. Noting that any eyewitness account is prone to error, he allows for 20 per cent—which he considers a small error rate—and asks: What is the likelihood that any single green cab pulled over by police in the course of the investigation was the one seen fleeing the scene of the accident? Should police devote their investigative efforts to checking the logs of every green cab in the city?

"The answer to the first question is one in 1,250," Melchers writes. "There are 1,000 green cabs to be pulled over, but the probability that the cab was actually green is only 0.8, because of the possibility of witness error. The answer to the second question should be obvious: it would not be a good use of police effort to investigate all green cabs. If the error factor were higher than 50 per cent, as witness reliability often is, such profiling would more often steer police in wrong than in right directions. The point of this illustration is to point out that error rates multiply when additional factors are brought into any prediction. Statistical likelihood would be a very poor alternative policing strategy to traditional evidence gathering, as many police investigators have discovered at their expense."

Quite by accident, Melchers was underscoring a real event. When the Green Ribbon Task Force was first formed, it expended scarce resources searching for the wrong type of car based on eyewitness accounts, which described a Camaro "or like a Camaro or Firebird" driving from the scene where fifteen-year-old schoolgirl Kristen French was abducted by Paul Bernardo and Karla Homolka—driving, it turned out, a gold Nissan.

"It is simply implausible that actual profiling policies or practices on any basis, be it psychological or racial, would ever be officially adopted by any rationally behaving organization as an alternative to traditional, evidence-gathering, investigative practices," Melchers insisted. "How is it, then, that so many observers are confident that police and other investigative organizations have adopted official policies and practices of racial profiling? First, this may be because so many organizations have indeed done so, despite overwhelming indications of the folly of such approaches. One need only think of current U.S. border controls that target all travellers of Middle East and Central Asian origin."

Melchers also suggested alternatives to racial profiling to account for seeming overrepresentation of certain groups in crime statistics that he says are "systematically and seemingly intractably integrated into the functioning of all social institutions and behaviours"—poverty, deprivation, isolation from broader social values, lack of community social cohesion, and so on. In the end, he concluded that while it is "highly plausible" that, once all legally relevant factors have been accounted for, differences in the treatment of groups according to race will remain, even this in and of itself may not be evidence of actual discriminatory practices, as opposed to any number of equally valid explanations of these differences.

"The best research can conclude in such cases is the modest statement that the possibility of discrimination cannot be excluded," Melchers concluded. "In the absence of compelling evidence, to make any more ambitious statement goes against the scientific ethic."

Alan Gold, one of Canada's most distinguished criminal lawyers and author of *Expert Evidence in Criminal Law: The Scientific Approach*, reviewed the issue from three perspectives: media hype, racial profiling, and good science. He had been retained by Chief Fantino on behalf of the Toronto Police Services to make submissions relating to the merits of the *Toronto Star*'s newspaper articles claiming statistical proof of "racial profiling." Gold said he was writing this commentary "purely in my private capacity and reflects no one's views other than my own." He defined racial profiling as using race to decide whom to suspect as criminal, associated with racial bias in police investigation, not racial bias in arrest decisions or racial bias in police treatment after arrest. His goal was to discuss the concept as an empirical phenomenon that is supposed to exist at the Toronto Police Services, and the claims that the phenomenon has been proved by evidence, which had been offered by the *Toronto Star* in a series of newspaper articles.

"The requirements for good science are basically simple," Gold began. "They comprise a clear understanding of what is being investigated; objective and reliable collection and recording of observations, findings, or data; and rational analysis of those observations, findings, or data in order to draw sound conclusions. The requirements for articles that sell large numbers of newspapers are clearly different, comprising good stories or anecdotes, generally told by sympathetic victims of some injustice or other, accompanied by sweeping generalizations couched in emotional or provocative language. The latter masquerading as the former is what is found in the *Toronto Star's* articles claiming to have statistically proved racial profiling on the part of the Toronto Police Services."

Not surprising for a lawyer, Gold's focus was "evidence."

"Anecdotal evidence of racial profiling and the fact that there is, in many quarters, a belief in racial profiling are significant and important social realities," he conceded. "But as evidence of the reality of some objective phenomenon to which that label is being attached, such anecdotal evidence is unacceptable. Anecdotal evidence speaks more to beliefs than facts, especially when the anecdotes and beliefs are themselves being widely publicized in the media. There is more than a real possibility of a vicious circle or self-fulfilling prophecy regarding racial profiling, which begins with claims, is fuelled by publicity, and leads to stronger belief and more claims. An even greater possibility of self-generating smoke without real fire exists where the beliefs have spawned a multi-million-, if not billion-dollar industry devoted to the problem."

Gold begins detailing how such a major issue as racial profiling has become south of the border, leading to new laws, lawsuits, new government agencies, megaconferences, instant "experts" and best-selling authors. But, he notes, that's America, not Canada.

"Without any recognition of historical or other differences between the United States and Canada, on the topic of racial profiling our 'longest undefended border' is truly undefended; the American literature and experience has been simply imported in its entirety and assumed holus bolus to be applicable to Canada," he wrote, cautioning that the community must appreciate the "potential for self-serving claims that are either intentionally or even unwittingly false" to help a "guilty accused" escape punishment and deeming it unfair to demand that every claim of "professional impropriety" against the police be presumed valid.

His goal was to deal with racial profiling as "an empirical phenomenon that is supposed to exist at the Toronto Police Services" and to review claims that the phenomenon has been proved by evidence which has been offered by the *Toronto Star* in a series of newspaper articles. He too began by asking, "What is racial profiling?"

Conceding that a handful of police may "unfortunately and illegally be bigots," he wrote that the Toronto Police Services, along with every other contemporary government institution, does not tolerate racial profiling and does its best to root it out. Citing the variety of "profiles" in criminal law literature—the drug courier, the sex offender, the smuggler, the child batterer, the power rapist, even the fleeing driver, not to mention the ad hoc profile generated by the FBI and other police profilers (who, he claimed, have been so demonstrably wrong in recent years)—he concluded: "Profiles can be characterized in blunt terms as 'junk science,' for the simple reasons that first, they generally involve vague and non-specific characteristics that can be manipulated in particular cases, raising great dangers of examiner bias and precluding reliability, and second, the profiles are never successfully diagnostic and generate substantial and overwhelming numbers of false positives. So if the issue is the scientific merit of profiles and profiling, the answer is obvious: there is none. If racial profiling is simply another subspecies of this junk science, the police should not use it. But trying to show whether the police use it, recognizing it as a subspecies of profiling, raises perplexing issues. Because all the other forms of profiling are quite overt, their proponents put them forth as productive and seek to defend them. Racial profiling stands as a unique kind of profiling that is not described in the same fashion. This immediately signals caution regarding the phenomenon."

To Gold, it appeared that reviewing profiling in general meant that racial profiling is one-dimensional "where race or ethnicity replaces all other characteristics." He cautioned that it is already viewed as unique, saying that "it is not an overt creation and it is not defended by anyone but rather is admitted by all concerned to be junk science and indefensible."

He viewed using racial profiling to target a suspect on that one characteristic to be an attempt to identify previously undetected criminals based solely on race.

"At this point, the confusion with racism becomes apparent, because racism is logically irrelevant," he wrote. "Deciding that driving an old car is part of the drug-courier profile does not depend on a hatred of old cars. In theory, a profile is just an attempt at empiricism: predicting the success of future attempts at identification of offenders from previous data. There is a difference between believing in racial profiling in drug offences because one believes that a disproportionately high number of blacks have been found with drugs in the past, or believing the stereotype that blacks generally use drugs, or being a racist towards blacks and attributing excessive drug use accordingly. The last situation involves a bigot, who can be identified, as any bigot will be. The first two cases involve the same erroneous reasoning as is implicated in profiles generally and are simply instances of the same junk science as drug-courier profiling and battering-spouse profiling. They do not involve racism (although the second example does involve false, stereotypical reasoning) and it is difficult to see why they cannot be dealt with as ordinary matters requiring countervailing education. The two important factors that come out of this analysis of racial profiling are that the phenomenon must involve police decision making based upon race and that the police activity involved is aimed at identifying criminals."

When it comes to collecting data, Gold states that racial profiling has no relevance to situations where an offender has already been identified as belonging to a particular race, noting: "To state the obvious, if the police stop only black males because the perpetrator of a homicide has been described by witnesses as a black male, this practice is absolutely irrelevant to any claim of racial profiling."

The onus falls on those making racial-profiling claims to distinguish between proactive and reactive policing: "For example, statistics on police stops must obviously exclude stops involving the police looking for a racially identified perpetrator. Yet this obvious fact is not acknowledged in the profiling literature. But there can be other, less obvious, inherent causal factors that innocently bring the police into greater than random contact with visible minorities. If police activity is stepped up in response to community concerns about local drug pushers or local speeders and that community (unsurprisingly) is economically disadvantaged and (equally unsurprisingly) is more heavily populated with visible minorities, the statistics will be skewed towards more police-minority interactions. But the police are only giving greater attention to that area to reflect community concerns. It is simply not police-initiated activity that is occasioning the greater attention to the particular minority."

Conceding that police work is surprisingly reactive, Gold insists that "good science demands that researchers carefully distinguish between situations in which the police are 'using' race and where they are 'finding' race." He says the *Star* articles contain "not the slightest recognition" of such issues.

"The principal defect in the *Star*'s approach is that it assumed the validity of the data collection and the appropriateness of the data's use for its purposes," Gold wrote, dismissing them as completely arbitrary and unwarranted assumptions. "Viewing the data as a sample of the large universe of police-citizen interactions during the relevant time periods, there is absolutely no basis to conclude that the data constitute a random or representative sample."

Gold challenged perceived assumptions by the media, noting: "The *Star* assumes that crime is randomly distributed throughout the general population and thus occurs within subgroups in the same proportion as their proportion of the total population. This basic and fundamental assumption is not just unwarranted, but simply wrong. Different groups commit different crimes at different rates and that unpalatable reality dooms all conclusions based upon statistical disparities. Males are grossly overrepresented in prison populations and women grossly underrepresented, but no one suggests it is for any other reason than that males commit a higher percentage of the offences."

Citing the *Star's* own data, which showed that blacks accounted for 8 per cent of the population but 27 per cent of arrests for violent crimes, Gold opined: "Such crimes almost invariably involve reactive police conduct with little discretion. Blacks are overrepresented compared to census population in homicide arrests where allegations of racial profiling would be preposterous." Using statistics for drinking-and-driving charges, Gold said, showed "blacks strongly underrepresented and whites significantly overrepresented" and asked if that is evidence of white racial profiling in drinking and driving cases?

"The point is," he wrote, "that statistical disparity—even if it truly existed—is relatively meaningless and in no way justifies the leap to claims of racial profiling against a police force expressly committed to intolerance of any racial bigotry."

Citing the Beltway Sniper (American serial killer John Allen Muhammad [formerly John Allen Williams], forty-two, and his accomplice Lee Boyd Malvo, eighteen, who killed or wounded more than a dozen people in Washington, D.C., Maryland, and Virginia) as an example of criminals benefiting from erroneous profiles, Gold concluded: "Racial profiling is all about using race to decide whom to suspect as a criminal. If it is as undoubtedly an erroneous basis as we believe then its very failure will give it away. If the police are wrongly relying on race then that will be reflected in an increase in unsuccessful outcomes. The acquittal and withdrawal rate for black defendants should be significantly higher than for white accused."

In other words, the alleged profile would be judged by the same criterion as the accused on the result of the trial. In his summation, Gold stated: "The *Star*'s research violated the most basic rules of scientific investigation and, therefore, in no way provides a foundation for the conclusions so loudly trumpeted."[4]

The *Canadian Journal of Criminology and Criminal Justice* revisited the topic in 2004 and 2005. In October 2006, Aaron Doyle, of the Department of Sociology and Anthropology at Carleton University, in Ottawa, waded in on the issue of the media in general with "How Not to Think About Crime in the Media." Essentially, Doyle argued that while existing research literature generally acknowledge the direct political and institutional effects of crime and the media, it should be supplemented by more interpretive research on the impact for particular audience members, and suggests the need for a sustained analysis of the interplay between crime news and crime fiction. If there are, in fact, lines being drawn in the sand between politicians, the police and the press, the media may not win every battle, but it does appear to be winning the war.

"Recent research offers extensive empirical illustrations of how institutions both within and outside the criminal-justice system are increasingly devoting massive resources and shaping their activities to achieve favourable media coverage," Doyle wrote. "The criminal-justice system and, particularly, the police are becoming 'mediatized.'"

But the police weren't the only ones questioning the racial allegations being fired at them by the press. The *Toronto Star* prides itself on crusading journalism, but at least one "issue" left even the paper's ombudsman shaking his head in disbelief.

In the March 2004 edition of the *Ryerson Journalism Review*, Keri Schram reported Don Sellar's stunned reaction at his cottage on the 2003 Canada Day weekend to the headline in his Saturday paper: "The White Jays? In a city of so many multicultural faces, Toronto's baseball team is the whitest in the league. Why?"

"When I saw it, I just about fell over," Sellar recalled a month later in his fifth-floor office near the *Toronto Star* newsroom. He was less distraught with the "jarring headline" than the twenty-five mug shots, mostly white, that accompanied the text.

"Many readers took the headline to mean the paper had uncovered evidence of racism in the Blue Jays front office ... I for one drew that inference," he had written in his July 5 ombudsman column amid the flurry of more than 2,000 angry emails and irate phone calls to the *Star*.

"'The White Jays incident produced more negative [reaction] than anything I had seen in 10 years,'" Sellar told Schram, "shaking his head in disbelief."

The ombudsman had braced for exactly this type of mass protest following the *Star*'s earlier investigative series on domestic abuse and racial profiling, but those outcries had paled alongside this one-time sports story, described by one irate reader as a "baseless, inflammatory article." Others, Schram noted, cited the "lack of diversity in the *Star*'s own newsroom and the paper's 'well-known obsessive fantasies about race.'"

Crusading journalism always comes at a price, but this incident seemed to underline that in all callings, it can be a very fine line separating champ from chump.

So who do you trust more: the police or the media? In poll after poll, Angus Reid routinely scores high marks from Canadians for the police as a "most trusted" profession. While firefighters and nurses consistently top the charts in the mid to high 90s, farmers are close behind. Police ranked seventh from 2003 to 2006, with an approval rating in the low 80s, edging out judges, notaries, and bankers, and blowing senior public servants, journalists, and lawyers out of the water. All of those latter groups are trusted by less than half the population; politicians finish dead last, rising only once in those years above a rating of 14.

The low ranking for journalists may not be so surprising given recent events. On July 17, 2009, legendary CBS television news anchor Walter Cronkite, in his prime voted "The Most Trusted Man in America," died. Exactly one week later, in a *Time* magazine online poll, Jon Stewart was named the current "Most Trusted News Source in America," with 44 per cent of the votes, easily enough to beat out mainstream network news anchors Brian Williams (29 per cent), Charlie Gibson (19 per cent), and Katie Couric (7 per cent).

Walter Cronkite was a career journalist, flying missions in bombers and visiting the front lines as a newspaper reporter, then pioneering TV news and becoming *the* source for news, whether wrestling with his emotions while providing updates on the JFK assassination, smiling like a kid when Neil Armstrong stepped onto the lunar surface, or simply droning deeply that America was not winning the war in Vietnam, marking the beginning of the end of that ill-fated U.S. incursion into Southeast Asian conflict and prompting then president Lyndon Johnson not to seek re-election.

Jon Stewart is a comedian, albeit brilliant, who hosts *The Daily Show* on the Comedy Channel and delivers what he admits is fake news. Yet four months earlier, on March 19, 2009, even the stately *Globe and Mail* gave him a nod in a column by Lawrence Martin, headlined, "To save journalism, bring that Jon Stewart outrage." But it seemed less that Stewart was the hero of modern journalism than that the new breed of owners were the villains of the demise of the media and newspapers in particular.

"As media ownership became concentrated in the hands of a few corporate giants, journalists too often came to reflect the ethos of those corporate giants," Martin wrote. "Counterculture voices of the left, traditional sources of opposition to corporate rule and war, were marginalized. In the Watergate era, they held prime place. But the boomers got old and tired and, in the past decade or so, the neo-cons blew them off the map."

To return to journalism's roots of reporting the news "without fear or favour," as was first promised by *New York Times* publisher Adolph Ochs in 1898, requires, Martin wrote: "More courage and daring and Jon Stewart–type outrage is in order—new rogues of journalism to set us straight. From those corporate owners who sought to impose their bias, the media need regain its independence."

Until that happens, Martin sees no point in looking far and wide for the source of problems assailing journalism today, concluding: "[It] isn't CanWest or Quebecor. It isn't satellite television or the Internet. It isn't the shift of advertising money away from newspapers and network TV to video games and social media. It isn't spin doctoring or public relations. It isn't conservatism or liberalism or capitalism or socialism. It isn't even the recession. It's us—the people who call ourselves journalists."

In the meantime, the media will remain selective in their reporting. One story few people likely ever read or heard was the 2006 Standing Senate Committee on Transport and Communications final report on the Canadian news media, which found troubling shortfalls in ethnic diversity in newsrooms across the land that had so recently taken the police to task for their lack of diversity and alleged racial profiling.

"Several representatives of racial and ethnic minorities told the committee that they were concerned about how they are represented by the mainstream media and the roles that they play in Canada's newsrooms," the study found, recommending that news and information organizations alter their hiring decisions to create a demographic balance reflective of the larger society. That need was underscored by Professor John Miller, of the School of Journalism at Ryerson University, in Toronto, who studied ninety-six mainstream newspapers and reported that roughly 59 per cent of the papers that responded to his survey have "entirely white staffs." Miller found that Aboriginal journalists were the least represented— there was only one among the 2,000 employees at the papers surveyed.

It seemed a case of the pot calling the kettle white. The police were already taking steps toward realizing the goals suggested for the media, and had been for some time, with outreach programs to attract visible minorities and women. In fact, they were doing it so publicly that some joked that the only time the police were ever truly guilty of profiling by race or gender was at the recruitment and promotion stages. Canadian society was changing and the police were working hard to change with it.

EIGHT

RECRUITMENT:
Who Ya Gonna Call?

The perfect policeman was defined by restraint, anonymity, an absence of emotion. A hot temper would not do nor any vanity which would open a man to the arts of flirtation; nor too innocent good nature; nor a hesitating temper or manner; nor any weakness for drink; nor any degree of stupidity.
—London Metropolitan Police Force, 1829

The ideal police constable described above by the London Metropolitan Police Force in 1829 was also adopted by Scotland Yard in 1842. There was no mention of race or gender. It was assumed the applicants would be overwhelmingly white men, probably from the middle class. So where are we today? Conventional wisdom has always dictated that the police represent the society and its values, which they are sworn to serve and protect. Add to that equation the changing times, mindsets, and population demographics, which comprise a far more diverse racial pattern, and priorities change. Toss in media allegations of racial insensitivity, and police recruiting has given rise to various "outreach" programs to attract more visible minorities, Aboriginals, and women into the

traditionally white-male preserve. Even with fewer candidates applying to police forces, the programs haven't stopped the traditional recruits from volunteering for pubic service with the police.

"If we wanted to hire 25 white guys, we don't need any outreach, we can do that tomorrow," Ottawa police chief Vern White
told the *Citizen* in mid-November 2007. "We need to hire more
women and more people from Somalia and Afghanistan and those
types of communities."

In 2007, White's department twice won international honours:
the Webber Seavey Award for Quality in Law Enforcement in
recognition of its Strategic Staffing Initiative, and the Civil Rights
Award from the International Association of Chiefs of Police for its
accomplishments in civil and human rights, specifically its Outreach
Recruitment Project. Despite these prestigious distinctions, the
chief and his staff were not spared from infighting among their
own recruiters.

That same year, Syd Gravel (discussed in an earlier chapter), a
converted champion for women in policing and a staff sergeant
overseeing recruitment, was assigned by White to review and report
back his findings on internal concerns that had been raised concerning the outreach recruitment program they had launched in
2006. The media was already asking if there was a "quota" to limit
the number of white male candidates. Gravel denied that was ever
the case, citing outreach efforts in 2002. But there were "targets" for
more visible minority, Aboriginal, female, gay, lesbian, and transgendered recruits—33 per cent women, 33 per cent visible minorities, and 33 per cent or less for white males.[1] Gravel's internal review
was sparked by what seemed a miscommunication that fewer white
males could be hired if there were excessive candidates in the other
two categories. Conceding that outreach recruiters were feeling the
pressure to meet their one-year deadline, he told the media that
was the root cause of what had become "an intense internal battle"
over diversity hiring.

Quite simply, the Outreach Recruiting Unit claimed its efforts
were being frustrated by the Resourcing Unit, which was responsible
for processing job applications. The latter, Gravel reported, accused

the former of "cheating, manipulating, bullying, threatening, even stealing information to get their candidates through," and of acting as the "gatekeepers" to control hiring. Consequently, the review determined, the Resourcing Unit did not give priority to the candidates submitted by the outreach team, instead placing them as they were received, which often meant behind several white male candidates who were submitted earlier for processing. Giving priority to the target groups was deemed to be jumping the queue. The media reported that an ensuing intervention by an inspector to fast-track the target recruits led to allegations that "files were being manipulated and candidates were not being treated equally ..." Gravel had determined that both units involved in the hiring process "closed ranks ... and failed to work together effectively." This was more than a slippery slope; Gravel termed this a dangerous road that was never intended.

"If you intentionally say white males can be minimized to nothing, we're saying you're eliminating the traditional white male, but also the potential diversity that the traditional white male might bring," he said. "That was not the agreement. The agreement was not about eliminating anybody, it was about including everybody, but making sure we included everybody where we might not have included women and visible minorities before. You have to include them from now on, but not at the expense of anybody else."[2]

So there it was, out in the open. The issue everyone was speculating about on both sides of the Blue Wall was finally taken into the public domain by the media. Anyone aware of Gravel's statements at the 1997 Women in Policing workshop could at least believe that if he was the lead guy on this hot-button topic, at least they'd be getting the truth about what was really happening. A veteran officer who had so publicly confessed to being on the wrong side of the debate when women were first hired as constables would seem to have no reason to fudge the facts when race and ethnicity seemed to add new fuel to a simmering fire. But the significance of his comments, specifically one phrase—"traditional white male"—could have opened another line of questioning.

Police across Canada have made no secret that they are facing a recruitment shortage bordering on a crisis. With estimates as high as 70 per cent of senior officers set to retire before the end of this decade, as well as a host of departures from the rank and file on the front lines, had the police turned their backs on their "traditional" recruiting base of white men? If they were so desperate for warm bodies and boots on the ground, if they were scrambling to hire constables now so that they would have at least some experienced officers when the retirement wave hit, why would they even contemplate closing the door on the one group who had always filled the gaps? They certainly still seemed to be there, ready and willing to serve and protect.

The consequence in Ottawa, and perhaps elsewhere, no matter how good the intentions of everyone involved and despite insistence that "white male applicants did not suffer," even the potential for that happening had, according to media reports, created deep divisions between recruiters and the resourcing officers who screened and interviewed candidates. The explanation given was that the quotas agreed to in preliminary discussions on March 8, 2007, were never approved at an April 30 meeting of police executives. Gravel said he saw nothing wrong with the recruitment process except that it wasn't followed.

But the initial complaint from Acting Sergeant Patricia Ferguson (reported by the media to have been a constable when she complained), which had prompted Chief White to order the review in late September, was that a candidate seemed "overly prepared" for interviews by the recruitment team, possibly "coached" on the answers.

Ottawa Police Association president Charles Momy (now president of the Canadian Police Association) told the *Citizen* that the review raised "serious concerns" with the outreach recruitment program and the quality of the candidates, causing him to worry about the potential risk to public and officer safety by passing over more qualified candidates for the sake of diversity.

"Are they lowering the standards without openly saying they are lowering the standards?" he asked. "I don't care who gets on, as long as they are competent and qualified."

Just a day earlier, Momy had been quoted in the press over an unrelated incident which he had said proved that the outreach recruitment program was in trouble: "[Their] credibility ... is zero right now. Something significant will have to occur to bring back the credibility."[3]

Then deputy chief Larry Hill, co-chair of the oversight committee for the outreach recruitment program, reportedly found Momy's take on the issue "astonishing" considering the association had a representative on the steering committee that helped create it.

"[The Outreach Recruitment program is] about raising people's ability to meet the standards, not changing the standards," Hill said, adding that it was "impossible" for the recruits to be provided with the answers to interview question, since the questions are based on past experience, not hypothetical situations, so there could be no right or wrong answers: "There is no such thing as a perfect answer in a competency-based interview."[4]

Momy seemed to be questioning the local program, not the need for diversity. As early as 2004, he had stated publicly that while he believed attracting the best and brightest candidates should be the overriding priority for police recruiters, that did not preclude the practical merits of a diversified force: "From a police perspective—as a former investigator myself—it's the issue of languages. When our members delve into different communities, and we can't get into those diverse communities, that's when you really do realize there's a problem."

Gravel's internal review recommended that the mandate, roles, and responsibilities of the two units be spelled out in definitive terms; that the two units work out of the same office and operate as a single team. Chief White accepted his recommendation to streamline the recruitment command structure and reassigned Inspector Kai Liu who had headed the outreach program since its inception in 2006. Liu had proven his worth as a translator in his first month on the job. Ottawa firefighters summoned him to the scene of a blaze on an elderly Chinese man's front lawn. The officer's command of Mandarin calmed the clearly agitated senior who had been burning incense and paper on an altar to honour his ancestors. That isolated incident was just the beginning. In May 2007, Liu was the inaugural recipient of the Senator Vivienne Poy Asian of the Year Award for being a role model, balancing community service with his successful career. The first Asian-Canadian recruit with the Ottawa police, Liu had become its highest-ranking visible minority and youngest inspector. He had headed such specialized units as gun registration, high-tech crime, partner assault, and diversity and race relations for the Ottawa police, had worked undercover with the RCMP's organized crime unit, and was invited by the United Nations to lecture on the topic of domestic violence and violence against women.

As head of the outreach recruiting unit, Liu explained that it was designed to "level the playing field" by mentoring candidates with no friends or relatives on the force they can ask for advice, telling the *Citizen*: "Mentoring is not 'here is the answer,' it is 'we believe you can do it.' It is concerning that we have members that may not understand the process." In the summer of 2008, Liu left Ottawa to become police chief in Gananoque, just east of Kingston, Ontario. In the aftermath, the media interviewed "stunned" city councillors who wondered how such a "good news" program had become "a red flag" that could thwart future recruitment efforts.

There was no doubt that Gravel remained a champion of the program to make policing attractive to non-traditional candidates. But he also knew it wasn't enough to recruit from target groups; the police had to retain them. Gravel had come a long way from his Syd Vicious days, when his no-nonsense street demeanor stopped even his wife from crossing the street to say hi. The turning point may well have been when he admitted he had lined up on the wrong side of welcoming women into policing. He still had occasions as the head of recruiting for the Ottawa police when long-time colleagues would wince and ask him why he was hiring such small candidates, arguing that they looked nothing like police officers. "Exactly," Gravel would reply, and move on, leaving another mystified old friend shaking his head as he tried to figure out the logic.

Perhaps Gravel's greatest contribution was to realize that not every recruit would have the same family and community support on graduation day. He devised a formula to explain why sometimes extra steps needed to be taken to keep good potential officers on board and in the front lines. He wasn't talking about special treatment, he was talking about equal footing on a level playing field. He explained it all in an article he wrote for the October 10, 2005, edition of the *Canadian HR Reporter*.

"Police services have a crisis to address; a lack of potential candidates to fill increasing vacant positions," he wrote, suggesting that police organizations had to anticipate candidates' lack of knowledge in three key areas: job knowledge, understanding the competitive process for a job, and awareness of what happens when they're hired. He rated most candidates at "zero to minus five" before the process even begins. Using zero as his baseline, applicable to most Canadian-born candidates who have a basic knowledge of what policing entails, those born elsewhere may lag five points behind at the outset just based on that person's social, cultural, and familial environments. He views that as the recruiter's job to overcome.

The gap widens when the candidates enter the recruitment process, possibly dropping to minus 10. A candidate with a friend or relative on the force has some deeper awareness of the job and can get a ride-along without much effort. Again, it falls to the recruiter to bridge the gap for those lacking such insights and connections. That usually means one-to-one discussion, not just a presentation to a group of thirty.

"I would not suggest that we have to convince people to become police officers," Gravel wrote. "Candidates must already possess the desire to wear the badge; otherwise the spirit isn't there to enable them to do a good job."

But he did suggest that recruiters learn how to nurture the "policing spirit" wherever they find it, then help bring about organizational change to support it. And if the candidate is unsuccessful, Gravel believes the police have to get better at explaining why the candidate missed the cut, writing: "It is not up to individuals with no support, with conflicting traditions or with misconceptions to step up to the plate and figure things out for themselves and fix things for us."

Nor is the effort over for recruiters, and the organization, once the candidate becomes a sworn officer. The gap, Gravel says, is at its widest then—what he calls the Minus 15 Factor. The baseline candidate will be surrounded by supportive and proud family and friends. That's not the case for others.

"Minus 15 candidates may find very little pride exhibited by the family, and understandably so," Gravel continued. "Friends and relatives may not celebrate or even attend the graduation ceremony." At this point, training officers, coach officers (who will work one-on-one with the new constable until he or she is judged to be ready to work independently), supervisors, and platoon peers must move beyond the typical rhetoric about wanting to reflect the diversity of the community.

"It's time to bring such statements into reality," he concluded.[5]

There seemed no doubt, these are interesting times to be a police recruiter. There are three basic approaches to attracting new peace officers: recruit, poach, or absorb them. The latter two likely skew the numbers for those seeking a higher proportion of targeted officers. Simple math and tradition suggest that most sworn officers who are lured from another department will be white males. They are, quite simply, the overwhelming majority when you look at the total picture. Allowing that women account for roughly 20 per cent of sworn officers today[6] (national figures usually peg their number closer to 17 per cent), most of whom are also white, it would probably require a near ban on recruiting white male officers and no one is even considering that.

Poaching experienced officers from other forces, known formally as "direct entries," can provide the double benefit of getting well-trained officers, plus the savings of not having to pay to train your own officers. That's a short-sighted philosophy and a source of frustration for an awful lot of front-line cops with five years or more on the job who are still waiting for their first substantial investigative course. Hiring an experienced officer from another force may make sense financially, but you're effectively telling your own people, who considered your organization to be their first choice, that loyalty has its limits and will not always be rewarded. It just seems short-sighted to bypass the chance to improve your own people for expediency. Instead, not even a strong recommendation from a sergeant will always sway a reluctant staff sergeant or inspector. And training opportunities affect promotional and specialty-unit opportunities. In one absurd example, a constable realized that jumping to another police force, then applying to be seconded back to his current force, would be a faster route to a specialty unit than applying through channels with his own force.

Absorption normally involves the RCMP or provincial police contracting with smaller urban or rural centres to provide policing services, routinely promising more resources for less cost. These so-called "mergers and acquisitions" almost always meant absorbing smaller existing police departments, potentially, some feared, diluting the talent pool of the host service. Traditionally, the Mounties gave them several months to meet their standards; if they did, they stayed, if not, they were cast off. The provincial police seemed more inclined to absorb and keep them unconditionally. In some cases, if they found they had inherited an incompetent, some found it easier to simply promote them out of harm's way than try to resolve the problem by getting rid of them.

The numbers are intriguing. The Mounties have contracts with 200 municipalities, 172 communities through provincial/territorial agreements, 8 provinces (Ontario and Quebec have their own provincial forces, but the Mounties are more active in Newfoundland and Labrador despite the presence of the Royal Newfoundland Constabulary), 3 territories, and 79 First Nations communities, all of which account for nearly half (47 per cent) of their uniformed personnel. Nearly all are twenty-year agreements set to expire in 2012. The RCMP contract partners are spared the portion of the cost that is estimated to still be spent on their real job—enforcing federal statutes.

At the provincial level, the OPP combined its First Nations Programs and Contract Policing Bureau on April 1, 2005, to provide policing services to 299 Ontario municipalities and has 103 municipal policing contracts serving 117 municipalities. It has, since 1985, amalgamated 51 municipal police services and has 129 specialized and support service agreements contracts plus 50 framework agreements. In 2002, there was a massive integration of municipal police forces into the Sûreté du Québec, which now polices nearly 1,200 communities. The greatest advantage to the provincial forces assuming municipal contracts is budgetary; not only are they assured funding from their community partners, but they now qualify for provincial funding that is reserved for municipal policing. The downside for the communities may be that contracts may be priced based on the wages of a first-class constable, even if they aren't always getting first-class constables, "their" police now report to Ottawa or Orillia or Quebec City, and the number of officers that exist on paper may not always equal the number actually in service at any given time due to a wide range of authorized leave—vacation, training, illness, injury stress, or paternity/maternity.

The whole process seems to be folded neatly into the blanket of "community policing."

Since its inception in the mid-1980s, the sacred cow and holy mantra of police forces everywhere has been community policing—an apparent attempt to revive closer ties between the police and those they are sworn to serve and protect. Under the new business models (the RCMP model had been recognized by the Harvard School of Business), citizens had become clients and everyone stakeholders. Everyone (police, politicians, and the media) tells the public their framework has made the world a better, safer place. Well, almost everyone. Community policing was the theme of the 2006 annual meeting of the Canadian Association of Police Boards (CAPB) held in Edmonton. Host chief Mike Boyd opened the plenary session by trying to define the concept. Speaking for its advocates, who insist this is not about "touchy feely, soft policing," Boyd noted: "There is nothing soft about dealing with guns and gangs." He described community policing as "problem-solving through collaboration."

In an ensuing panel discussion, Dave Griffin, executive officer of the Canadian Professional Police Association (CPPA), squared off against Chris Braiden, a retired Edmonton police superintendent generally considered by many as the "father of community policing," in what was generally viewed by the crowd as a "lively, informative, and entertaining exchange."

Conceding that the CPPA and CAPB share numerous common goals, Griffin confirmed there is a lot of cynicism within police associations. He explained that while many of his colleagues believe the principles and concepts of the approach have merit and looks good at the "fly-by" level, community policing has been a "colossal failure" at the grassroots level. Braiden responded by defining community policing as "peace in the hood." Citing statistics on conventional, traditional policing methods and crime-clearance rates in Canada and the United States to show that conventional, traditional policing is a failure, acknowledging that community policing has become a buzzword—"a wagon that many have jumped on"—Griffen insisted that there's considerable difference between communities and how the community-policing model is applied, stripping resources from "the real job" of addressing crime and spreading the front line too thin to accommodate specialty units. Nor did he believe the statistics were a true depiction of policing realities, saying the number of unreported crimes has increased, which accounts for the drop in the crime rate based on the community-policing model. His concern was that credit was being taken for a reduction in crime that hasn't really occurred.

The true downside of all this for local politicians was that once they contracted with outside police, it was very hard to revive their own force if they were unhappy. It wasn't just that all of their personnel and equipment were gone, they sometimes found that the number of officers they had been promised existed only on paper. Sick days, training, maternity leave, and injuries were facts of life; some detachments were better than others at trying to backfill the vacancies, but as the thin blue line got thinner, there weren't always available bodies. Local politicians were also probably dismayed to learn that "their" police no longer reported to them, as RCMP and provincial detachments ultimately took their marching orders from their respective headquarters in Ottawa and Orillia and Quebec City. That was the case when the OPP were ordered to stand down despite pleas from local politicians to arrest Native protesters who broke the law with impunity during the Caledonia standoff.

The takeovers also presumably skewed police demographics. Regardless, all of those who were absorbed from anywhere across Canada by either level of policing seemed to have two things in common: their new police service wasn't their first choice, or their earlier application was rejected, perhaps for failing physical or psychological testing. That is not to say that all those absorbed were deficient. Many proved to be very, very good at policing. But there were also overwhelmingly white, mostly males, and that skewed the new enlightened inclusive approach to recruitment, which meant more aggressive recruiting to attract "underrepresented" minorities, and women, despite having proven themselves over the previous thirty-five years.

Still, from the absorbing police force's perspective, the contracts were a lucrative enticement, especially when the bulk of the work would be traffic enforcement, collaring drunk drivers and speeders, as opposed to investigating organized crime or conducting federal policing. But any benefits realized from what some termed "cash cows" did not always trickle down to the front-line constables working the roads and municipal streets of their new jurisdictions. Even with the influx of staff, the corresponding increase in territory and responsibilities could cause shortfalls. The constables did their best to ensure they weren't sending out their shift partners alone and many worked while ill or bruised. The real problem was the handful of managers who simply refused to call in officers on overtime to save money; those who came in under budget typically were paid some type of performance bonus at year's end, but sending constables out on patrol alone, with no hope of backup, seemed a ruthless way to line their pockets. Transfer requests were notoriously high in such places—and routinely blocked by these same managers who probably knew that anyone so dedicated that they would work alone was worth keeping. If constables were successful in getting a transfer, the manager would appeal to their sense of loyalty to stay, often offering them training courses the constables should have had months or years earlier. A constable who agreed could still be denied the course, citing "operational" needs or priorities.

In Ontario, at least, the "poaching" seems to have started on the new recruits' first days at the provincial police college, the first stage for all forces regardless of size or stature. Recruits were told by their departments to keep an eye out for talent or any sign that a constable might be willing to jump to their force—ideally after their current department paid for their training. In fact, while the RCMP and other forces across Canada were debating whether to pay their recruits or charge them for the training, Ontario recruits, who once paid nothing, now pay thousands of dollars (close to $10,000) for the privilege of becoming peace officers and the opportunity to serve and protect the rest of us. Many recruits have no choice but to tack this cost onto what may already be staggering student loans of tens of thousands of dollars.

Police departments are also interested in attracting experienced officers from other departments and provinces because their training has been paid for—a win-win scenario for police and government bean-counters who control the purse strings. While the poaching was officially denied in the past, it is so blatant now that few bother to conceal it. There have been glaring headlines across the country of rather creative approaches taken by Edmonton to find "direct entries" and raw recruits in Ottawa and elsewhere; they in turn were miffed when Vancouver police reputedly flew an airplane over Edmonton and Calgary towing a recruitment banner that essentially said: "Come work for us." The problem with luring experienced, veteran officers was that their pensionable time was not always honoured by their new department due to government policies—a strong deterrent to anyone with many years of service.

Recruiting had become so cutthroat that a municipal force eyeing a candidate would often call the provincial or federal recruiters to see if they knew anything about the candidate. If they confirmed their interest in hiring the person, the city force recruiter, less encumbered with red tape, could simply call the recruit, offer them a job and sign them up before another force knew they had been robbed. If the recruit happened to be a member of a target group, well, that was a bonus, an ambassador and a role model to a community that may have been long closed to the police.

But how many minority officers were anxious to be automatically assigned to police their own ethnic communities? How many white cops joined large city, provincial, or federal forces to police their own backyards? How many even listed themselves in the phone book? Not one of the thousands of officers with the Los Angeles Police Department is reported to live in that city. Minority officers had traditionally faced unique perils. It was not that long ago that the rules of the streets were that you did not target a white police officer; non-whites were, however, not so secure. The story was often told, even among white officers on a major city force, of the Asian cop who was attending a social event, off duty and out of uniform, when the venue was raided by armed Asian thieves who collected all the guests' wallets and purses. Realizing there was a cop in the crowd, the gunmen identified him, forced a gun in his mouth, and pulled the trigger. The gun misfired and the officer survived with a beating.

For generations, there has been an acceptance that some recent newcomers to Canada fled homelands where the police were corrupt and violent private armies for the ruling despot. They were distrusted and feared and often hated. That, it was reasoned, helped explain why minority communities were so insular and closed off to police. But if you distrusted and hated the police, did race or gender really matter? The rise of armed street gangs suggested that any resentment toward the police more closely represented a larger resentment toward society at large by a marginalized group. If the issue was simply a matter of language, then the police could hire civilian translators who could presumably be contacted by radio or cellphone at headquarters at far less cost than sworn officers. The difference, perhaps ironically, was that a person in uniform might more readily be viewed as a role model for unhappy youths who had not yet slipped to the dark side.

Any internal friction Liu may have left behind had been simmering for a while, confirmed by staff focus groups at least as early as 2004 when Vince Bevan was chief and the *Citizen* obtained two internal studies conducted by Carleton University's Eric Sprott School of Business, headlining its article "Women, minorities face harassment on city police force."

"Female and minority police officers face on-the-job harassment and are far less likely than their white male colleagues to be satisfied with their working conditions," the article began, before listing specifics from the 116 respondents:

- Only 38 per cent of women say they are happy in their jobs, compared to two-thirds of men.
- All of the women interviewed have considered leaving the police, a few for family reasons, but mostly because of frustration over harassment and limited opportunities.
- Minorities and women adhere to a "code of silence," failing to complain about harassment for fear of repercussions.
- Most white officers [men and women] surveyed disagree with the goal of making the police's composition more closely reflect the community's.

One officer was quoted as saying: "My personal opinion of this is that people having different cultures on the force doesn't make it a better police force. The person that's going to back me up on a call may not be the best candidate and shouldn't have been hired at the time, but was because the person was a minority."

A minority officer said: "They have the fundamental belief that policing is still a white man's job. Fundamentally, they don't think that we can do the job because traditionally we have not had those jobs. To them, a police officer is this six-foot-two white male coming through the door and taking charge of the situation."

The report described the police culture as "unchanging, unwelcome and unitary," concluding: "Visible minorities, women and, to some extent, gay, lesbian, bisexual and transgendered members, experience discrimination and harassment."

Chief Bevan was stung, saying: "I was surprised to see the frequency of those kinds of comments. I thought we were past that."

Bevan and Momy both agreed that retaining quality officers was as important as recruiting them.

"It can't be an exercise to get them in, have them unhappy and then see them leave," the chief said, noting that in the wake of a double shooting of Chinese students at Algonquin College, and his determination to recruit more officers from that community, there were still only two on the Ottawa force. "They're not knocking our door down to apply for jobs," he said. "We need to change that."

Momy agreed the plan wasn't working: "There's certainly a sense out there from minority members who are leaving that they weren't supported by their police association or by the police service."

Their pessimism was shared by Carl Nicholson, executive director of the Catholic Immigration Centre and co-chair of the outreach program. "We're going to have a rough time persuading young people from racial minorities to join the police force. Young people will do their own research and find out people aren't happy there."

Gravel admitted he found the employee feedback sobering: "I remember being very uncomfortable reading all those reports. I was losing my enthusiasm about recruiting. Issues of harassment, discrimination, abuse of power in promotions—we have to continue looking at all those things. Recruiting is putting the cart before the horse. You have to have a welcoming organization in order for recruitment to work."

In response to the study, the police launched a harassment-prevention campaign for the workplace and a three-year push to attract more women and minorities, both co-ordinated by Gravel, who sounded philosophical about finding community "champions" for policing: "What we've been doing for 160 years is nothing more than processing the applications of people already attracted to policing. If you come from communities where policing is not viewed as attractive or productive, you won't apply." He vowed the hiring standards would remain the same with a goal of having a much larger selection of candidates.

It was the latest in a rash of police recruitment initiatives across Canada, all seeking the same candidates, most meeting with the same results and sentiments that were identified in Ottawa by the Carleton study. Sometimes the messages were just mixed. For example, in March 1988, the RCMP made headlines by launching their campaign to recruit more women and minorities. In October, then commissioner of the RCMP Norm Inkster told the media that the Mounties were dropping their policy of preferred hiring while insisting the RCMP still wanted more minorities. As the *Toronto Star* reported, Inkster said that the policy adopted five years earlier by his predecessor, Robert Simmonds, meant "bilingual people, women, native Canadians and applicants with university degrees were hired ahead of other applicants." Inkster proclaimed those attributes "helpful but not mandatory." The issue then really seemed to be bilingualism as the *Star* quoted Inkster as saying that "the public's perception of anti-anglophone hiring practices was fuelled by media reports in 1984 that said 64 per cent of the recruits that year were francophones."

To be fair, the alleged resentment against francophone Mounties was less because they were French speaking than because language skills suddenly seemed to trump the traditional virtue in the RCMP: experience. When francophones with less experience were viewed as being fast-tracked into national headquarters in Ottawa, resentment reputedly deepened, culminating with the incident where incoming commissioner Phil Murray and his entourage were chanted off the stage by an angry crowd of Mounties in British Columbia.

While their superior officers were publicly calling through the media for more women and minority candidates, police associations were actively planning or staging public-information sessions to get out their own message—that there were too few cops to do the jobs they were being assigned, and that it had an impact on officer and public safety.

In 1988, the *Star* cited police shortages in the rise of traffic deaths, quoting Staff Inspector Elwood Lowe, head of Metro Toronto Police's traffic support services: "There aren't enough police officers to enforce traffic laws and that's the main reason for the big increase in Metro traffic deaths this year. It's hard to believe, but the Metro force now has 100 fewer police officers than it had 10 years ago."

Four years later, in 1992, the *Saskatoon StarPhoenix* was reporting that the local police association was planning to follow Edmonton's lead and launch their own public-information campaign to sound the same alarm—that too few cops meant an increased threat to public safety. City council had agreed to hire twelve new constables but insisted that ten of them were to be community liaison officers for crime-prevention measures and community contact. Those jobs, argued association president Stan Goertzen, had nothing to do with core police services: responding to emergencies and investigating crimes. He noted there were only as many of those front-line officers as there had been in the mid-1980s when the city was much smaller and likely more law abiding. The association had recently complained to the Board of Police Commissioners that inadequate staffing levels at the 911 emergency call centre meant callers were waiting up to three minutes just to get through to a call taker, noting that "thirteen per cent of incoming calls were abandoned before they were answered." The situation improved when two special constables were transferred to the call centre from the front desk at police headquarters, but that translated into two fewer officers on the streets to replace the departed officers.

"You can only move people around so much to cover off critical areas," Goertzen warned, expressing his concern that his members lack the resources to respond to a major incident or sustain a long-term investigation. Noting the numerous "very serious offenders" at large in the city, he claimed they potentially posed a greater threat because the police lacked the people and resources to target them adequately, possibly miss patterns and links that could stop these predators and prevent multiple attacks because they were just too busy. As a result of all of this, overtime costs had gone "through the roof."

The media reported that Mayor Jim Maddin, who also sits on the Board of Police Commissioners, was "disappointed but not surprised" that Goertzen had raised the issue. Council, he claimed, had never been more supportive and staffing needs were being studied. "We're not ready to go to the people or go to council as a police commission right now and argue convincingly for increased resources, because we're still collecting our information and getting ourselves positioned properly to adequately address the issue of police staffing," he said.

So, which was it to be? Accelerated recruitment to fill the gaps in the front lines or targeted outreach for a more diverse and representative workplace? The two options needn't be mutually exclusive, but would almost certainly complicate recruiting efforts working, as seen in the Ottawa example, at cross-purposes. And Ottawa was certainly not unique: it was just the force that had the good luck—or misfortune—to have the media obtain internal studies and go public with their findings.

The issues were pretty much studied to death over the next fifteen years. All reports up to 2007 seemed to conclude pretty much the same things: there were too few police and especially too few women and visible minorities. In 2003, the Canadian Association of Chiefs of Police pledged to renew its efforts to "better reflect the multicultural population."[7] They claimed their goal for inclusion again in 2008, admitting attracting minority officers was a "major challenge." And during this time, the Police Sector Council continued issuing dire warnings that police recruiting was falling to potentially dangerous levels. In between, the Mounties announced they had their own plan for dealing with officer shortages in 2005: centralizing highway patrols and assigning additional detachments under the command of one supervisor so officers could be sent wherever they were needed most. They also hoped to recall some retired veterans. They were Band-Aid solutions on an open wound that refused to heal.

The focus for everyone seemed to be, at least in public, whether or not the "target" strategy was working. The better question might have been, Was it even necessary? There were two schools of thought. Gravel had clearly made the point with his Minus 15 concept that sometimes candidates who genuinely wanted to become police officers needed extra effort, not to pamper or favour them, but to give them equal footing on a level playing field. But there were also those who wondered how giving women special consideration was not a slap in the face to the first generation who had survived and thrived abuse and harassment? They hadn't needed special consideration; they were expected to make their way and carve their mark in a men's world by men's standards. Overwhelmingly, they did, despite blatant, excessive, and sustained abuse by far too many peers and superiors who condoned or did nothing to stop the almost systemic verbal, physical, psychological, and sexual harassment that cannot be imagined today. They applied to special units, and for promotion, if they were interested, the same as their male counterparts. We have learned that the seeming lack of women writing for promotion likely had more to do with them enjoying the job they were doing rather than wanting to sit at a desk tackling stressful amounts of paperwork, which getting a promotion would mean. As a group, the surveys confirmed that female officers valued family and a balance between work and social life more highly than most men. They did all this on their own, with no female role models to guide them and too few enlightened male colleagues and supervisors. Most, like Gravel, the man in charge of recruiting for the Ottawa police, realized only by observation and personal experience over the passage of time just how valuable were the unique skills women brought to the job. So, again, why was an outreach program necessary for the next generation of women who had seen and heard what their predecessors had accomplished? How were special considerations now not essentially a backhander to the women who made their way with little help and less hope?

If military recruiters have an outreach plan or program, it's less visible. Instead, they opt for fast-paced, dramatic television ads with no dialogue, just a sonorous beating soundtrack. Their message is "Come fight everything from terrorism to fear. We are liberators, not conquerors or occupiers." They don't chase white males or females or visible minorities—they pursue a generation that has claimed in multiple business and academic surveys and studies that they value making a difference and feeling appreciated over making a buck with no input or idea of what the plan is and where they fit in. And it seems to be working.

The differences in approach between the police and the Canadian Forces are evident. Visit the military-recruitment website at www.forces.ca and you'll find they too are interested in recruiting women and visible minorities, attracting them by highlighting the accomplishments of earlier generations of women, blacks, Asians, and Natives. They substitute "determination" for "diversity" to note that blacks fought in the War of 1812 and against the Fenian invaders in 1866, earning their rewards only after winning more personal battles against "discrimination and rejection" on grounds of colour, and 1,200 Asians that fought for this country before Canada would let them vote. They also hightlight the contributions of women, from the nurses who accompanied the troops in 1885, to Major Wendy Clay who earned her wings as a pilot in 1974, six years before that classification was opened to all women, to Corporal Gail Toupin who became the first female member of the Sky Hawks aerial-precision demonstration team in 1976. All of them are praised as role models for this generation.

The military seeks to inspire recruits to want to join them. They challenge them to step up and be all they can be. Their message is simple: Are you good enough to join us? It's all part of what has been called "radical recruiting" that came into fashion under Chief of Defence Staff General Rick Hillier. Gone are the ads of the 1970s of a young officer stepping off an aircraft carrying a briefcase, about which Hillier was widely reported as saying: "That ain't us."[8] The recruitment ads aired on television these days are dramatic black-and-white re-creations of rescuing a hostage, intercepting a drug ship, or rescuing freezing civilians on a downed airliner. There is no dialogue, just a minimalist throbbing soundtrack and brief phrases superimposed over the images: "Fight Fear, Fight Distress, and Fight Chaos," closing with the slogan "Fight with the Canadian Forces." ("Fight Terror" was reportedly dropped after test-audience screenings didn't approve.)

Hillier, who was much loved by the grunts in all branches of the military for speaking up clearly, bluntly, and frequently, seems to have no police counterpart. An anecdotal survey of varying ranks in several police forces cite him and Major General (ret'd) Lewis Mackenzie as true examples of leadership. Calling terrorists "scumbags" was a refreshing break from the politically correct diplomacy of our times, no doubt resonating with street cops who have their own "shit rats" to contend with. But they have more in common than that. In fact, the Mounties signed on with the Canadian Forces to help bolster their recruiting efforts.

On March 3, 2007, correspondent Jeff Esau filed an article with the *Globe and Mail*, headlined, "Military, Mounties teaming up to attract new recruits."

"Under pressure to step up recruiting in the face of Canada's declining birth rate and aging workforce, the RCMP and the Canadian Forces have begun working together to achieve their enrollment targets," wrote Esau, who had obtained the five-page memorandum of understanding through an Access to Information request. The memo created the first-ever Strategic Recruiting Partnership between the Mounties and the military. Until March 2009, the two groups were to share resources, staff, multimedia-production capabilities, demographic information, survey results, best practices, and facilities. They also planned to team up for recruiting tours and events, which raised intriguing possibilities as everyone was free to set up shop at a forum like the International Hockey Federation's World Junior Championships in Ottawa right after Christmas 2008. Efforts to promote the forces on some college and university campuses were thwarted by a ban on military recruiters by those who denounced Canada's presence in Afghanistan. It was unclear if the Mounties would ride into town alone in such situations.

Generally, however, it seemed a logical partnership to help both become more competitive in what internal military documents termed an "intense and relentless" battle for young minds and bodies with other public- and private-sector employers. Both groups claimed their operational mandates would not blur or overlap as each offered very different opportunities to a similar pool of candidates.

And that might have been the key to police recruiting. Instead of identifying specific groups, then making those wishing to compete as equals, on merit, to earn their way as remedial students who needed extra help to compete, the police might do better to target the wider generation. The military benefits from being less visible, soldiering, sailing, and flying far from home, as opposed to the police, who we see everywhere and who may ticket us. Given that disadvantage, why not, like the military, challenge young people—at a time when several departments were openly recruiting older candidates with military or at least life experience—to follow in the footsteps of those who had gone before them. If they didn't have the long history of inclusion enjoyed by the military, they could at least appeal to their pride in their ancestry and in being Canadian. Native recruits would seem to be a no-brainer. The simple fact is that without their tribal alliances in the War of 1812, Canada might not exist today as a sovereign state, but as the Americans' fifty-first state. Freed blacks and escaped slaves left Canada and returned to the United States to fight for the Union army and navy in their Civil War from 1861 to 1865, including service with the fifty-fourth Massachusetts Volunteer Infantry Regiment immortalized in the Hollywood movie *Glory*.

Hillier certainly thought outside the box, raising the possibility of fast-tracking landed immigrants to citizenship if they served in the Canadian military, a variation on the U.S. policy that has historically attracted recruits from distant lands, including Canada, dating to the American Civil War. Otherwise, Canadian citizenship is one of the few requirements to serve in the armed forces, which offers opportunities and challenges to any and all who step up.

"If you want to sail the seven seas in the most high tech ships in the world, fly high performance aircraft, or get a physical and mental challenge with the satisfaction of dealing directly with people when they desperately need help the most, you come see us," Hillier told the media, explaining the new military philosophy toward recruitment. "We're moving from a passive approach to a more active and aggressive one. We've got to make recruiting every service man and woman's business. Most people don't know about us."

This young generation has a chance to step up and repay their ancestors who sacrificed so much, and help preserve the freedoms sought by their parents and grandparents who came here hoping to find a new and better life. Should this not prompt the police, those who oversee them and those contemplating joining them, to rethink their strategies and motivations? How, in all good conscience, can anyone come to a country they value for its health and safety and equal opportunity and not step up to help preserve those same virtues? That's not a question of race or gender, but a desire to serve and protect and reflect the values of the community. It may not lead young police to policing, but no one should join the police without wanting to be a police officer who will keep the peace and enforce the law. That core value is not the sole domain of either gender or any nationality, religion, or culture.

While the special attention paid by recruiters may flatter target police candidates, most of them doubtlessly apply wishing to be judged on their own merits. Lamenting that policing still views itself as a "white man's club" is in no way a concession that anyone not in that specific club, real or imagined, is in any way inferior. Whatever tensions exist in the ranks, and all workplaces have tensions, surely no one accepted into the front lines believes they need special attention, extra help, or even the hint of a free ride to compete. Levelling the playing field does not mean tipping it the other way. Surely women and visible minorities are every bit as proud as white men. Surely they seek role models and mentors, not patronizing managers more interested in perception rather than actual performance or achievement and equal opportunity. Perhaps appealing to those higher, nobler qualities might better the odds of recruiting the best and brightest, not just the least dangerous, as evidenced by officer comments that they hesitate to call for backup if they don't trust the responders. Surely that would seem to send a more believable message to everyone of the conviction that competency is not at question, and certainly not a question of race or gender—that given a chance, they can compete on their own merit with anyone. That sentiment, conveyed to the media, would then be shared with those who demand diversity for the police, but not for their own callings.

The police have already done much more than any others on this front, resulting in far greater diversity than would be found in any newsroom, in Parliament, any provincial legislature or city or town hall, more than in the military, and far, far more than in the courts or amongst doctors, nurses, firefighters, and paramedics.

The reality is that female police officers are still newsworthy to the mainstream media. Ottawa deputy chief Sue O'Sullivan made headlines as a frontrunner for the chief's spot when Vince Bevan retired; Inspector Adua Porteous, of the Vancouver police tactical support section, found herself in the media spotlight as the highest-ranking female in the department, even when no woman was in the running to replace Chief Jamie Graham when he retired in 2007. (Caroline Daley had retired four years earlier as deputy chief.)

Sue O'Sullivan has been in the front ranks pushing for equality, diversity, and respect in the workplace, but she has never lost sight of the fact that in addition to changing times, the expectations of the people the police want to recruit have also evolved. She notes that the police now have at least three generations in their ranks, ranging from the last wave of baby boomers, who are set to retire en masse, to the younger Generations Xers (those born between 1965 and 1985) and Y (aka the Millennials, born between 1978 and 1994). At least one veteran and much-honoured police officer did his best to prepare police leaders for the generational shift in attitude that was sailing their way as early as 2003. And he advised the old guard that they might have to be the ones to change to get the most out of the new kids on the beat.

Inspector Gord Schumacher, of the Winnipeg police, addressed the looming demographic shift back when Generation X was the target. But even through Generation Y and the Millennials, their impact on policing remains as relevant today as when Schumacher penned his article in 2003: "Qualities of Police Leadership: A Snapshot on Leading Generation X." It was perhaps the most eloquent and relevant heads-up for police managers of how their ideas were about to be challenged and transformed by the new generation of recruits.

"Baby Boomers are now in charge with Generation X making up the majority of the police service complement. Do we still have individuals like Sgt. Webb and Officer Smith who value duty before pleasure, respect for authority and adherence to rules? Maybe, but for the most part the Xer's have a different agenda, one that seemingly places them before the organization. Commitment and loyalty, though still acknowledged, are defined differently to include terms like: balance, informality and self-reliance," he wrote.

Conceding that police leaders might balk at what they were seeing in this new wave of officers, he urged them not to fight it. While the new breed might not be like the departing generation, Schumacher insisted they were consistent with good policing, noting: "Values and ethics may be slightly different but the enthusiasm to do the right thing remains."

The key to success, he continued, would be to properly manage them to develop an effective, efficient, and stable workforce. How best to do that when "efficiencies, productivity, budget restraints, morale, and manpower shortages" were all weighing heavily on police managers who were now facing a generation that made demands in what seemed a "never ending" attempt to influence their workplace. Identifying motivation as a key ingredient, Schumacher specified the need to motivate by instilling "positive morale" and excitement for assignments.

"Morale at its foundation begins with feelings of self-worth and fulfillment," Schumacher wrote. "Generation X police officers need to feel that their views are seriously considered and that they as individuals mean something to the organization. Police leaders must be transparent and can't be subversive in how they approach their members; they must be able to clearly explain ideas and the thinking behind them from an organizational perspective. Absolute management behind closed doors can create an atmosphere of mistrust and discontent and, no surprise, is not conducive to harmonious leadership."

Schumacher, who as a superintendent (as well as a lawyer, university professor, and co-chair of the Manitoba Law Enforcement Torch Run for Special Olympics) in 2006 was honoured with the Excellence in Law Enforcement Award. After twenty-six years with the Winnipeg police, he headed the Criminal Investigation Bureau and was acknowledged for his substantial contributions to developing Canada's national security legislation and for the instrumental role he played in creating the national strategy on cross-border policing. He had the credentials and the message: that the new breed of peace officer wanted to know the plan and where they fit into it.

"The Generation X police officer wants to be informed," he stressed. "Gone are the days of blind obedience. The softer, gentler approach will build an understanding that police work in the new millennium is truly a team approach."

While honesty was deemed vital to fostering relationships and respect for a leader, Schumacher called for more open dialogue and better communication up and down the chain of command.

"The Generation X police officer thrives on being told the truth and will descend into an 'us and them' mentality when they feel honesty is being cloaked behind an ulterior motive," he cautioned. "Generation X is watching. As a police leader, every move you make is being observed and emulated. Lead by example ... The Generation X police officer respects your position; your job is to project a leader that will be respected as an individual—with that comes success. Remember that every generation has the same proportion of intelligence, ambition and desire, and it is a mistake to think that it is always the subordinate who needs to change behavior."

Schumacher described the "pillars of leadership" as "motivation, honesty, trustworthiness, transparency and leading by example" and termed them building blocks for building a strong, stable workforce.

"These qualities however cannot breed success in isolation," he cautioned. "They must be nurtured with the knowledge that Generation X police officers are different. Not recognizing or valuing the ways they differ means failing as a leader. Success will be defined by the ability to adopt the pillars of leadership and the desire to channel different approaches into meaningful results."[9]

Schumacher also addressed retention, his insights endorsed by a 2008 report by Linda Duxbury, as mentioned earlier, a professor with Sprott School of Business at Carleton University in Ottawa. She confirmed that contemporary employers "don't get" the new generation of employees who routinely rate "personal satisfaction" over "getting ahead" in the workplace. The days of a "captive workforce," which Duxbury said had spoiled employers for the past thirty years, were over, reported *Calgary Herald* journalist Susan

Hickman in January 2008. The new generation, she determined, wants "exciting work, free training and, most important, lives outside of their jobs. If they're not happy with their work, they'll quit."

Duxbury warned that employers who don't understand will be hit hard by employee turnover—a vital concern. In December 2006, Dr. John McFerran posted to his corporate website that a recent Accenture survey of 250 Canadian senior executives wrote online that "the inability to retain talent is the No. 1 challenge endangering leading companies' bottom lines" in the short-term future. "Fifty-one per cent of respondents ranked this as their top concern, up 11 per cent from results collected in a similar survey last fall."

McFerran termed the situation a "human-resources crisis," but said "trust and satisfaction" could help weather the storm. The similarities to policing seemed evident—a new breed of employee with new priorities in a time of stiff competition for their services. If the police recruiters had an edge, it was that they offered a great potential opportunity for personal satisfaction, with pretty good pay and retirement benefits. The trick would be to overcome the dark times in the job as Duxbury warned; "Suck it up and be grateful you have a job" was no longer an option for management.

Terming the private sector "Darwinian" and challenging the public-sector panacea of throwing money at all problems, Duxbury said "great pay and job security" are no longer enough to keep employees around. To retain staff, she recommended employers build credibility, focus on the positive, maintain a sense of humour, build on their employees' strengths, adapt to their needs and "run with the wind, not against it [because] if you don't change the work environment, someone else will."

Meanwhile, as the baby boomers retire, opening management spots to those from Generation X, the arrival of the next wave of police recruits, the so-called Millennials representing Generation Y, are needed to step into the front lines. As described in an earlier chapter, this new breed of police officer needs to feel their contributions are valued or they are apt to leave. Thus, retention becomes as great an issue for police forces everywhere as simply finding suitable candidates to employ. A larger attitude shift by all managers, not just the police, was required to reject the negative stereotypes associated with the Millennials identified by Barbara Moses in an article she wrote for the *Globe and Mail* in spring 2008, and reprinted by the Canadian Police Association in the summer edition of its members' magazine, *Express*. Arguing that every generation has its conceit that it is better than those that follow, she left no doubt that she was tired of hearing disparaging descriptors concerning Generation Y: "They're brash. They're pampered. They're self-absorbed. They're high-maintenance. They're obsessed with work-life balance. They have no loyalty."

Conceding that Generation Y is more likely to view a good job and good working conditions as a right rather than a privilege, and have "less tolerance for unpleasant work environments, including micromanagement by their bosses," their work ethic and contributions should not be lost because they are less likely to give in to demands on their time for no apparent good reason. And while they are far more adept with technology than older generations, she cautioned that flashy electronics did not define them. Rather than worrying about such minor issues, Moses concluded that managers should simply start paying closer attention to the "unique personality characteristics and motivators of each and every one of their workers, no matter what their age." In time, another generation would come along to replace the Millennials as the target for recruiters, as Moses reminded her readers that all "generational stuff is fleeting," noting that Generation Y would soon start families, buy houses, and become "debt slaves" like previous generations. And, she suggested, no doubt complain about the next generation.

While police recruiters everywhere competed with increasing intensity for the best candidates, the Ottawa police began to stand out as one of the more enlightened forces when it came to identifying, recruiting and retaining targeted candidates through their outreach program.

As the staff-sergeant in charge of recruiting, Gravel took his message to a larger audience, writing about the need to put all candidates on equal footing. Perhaps mindful of the allegations he had investigated in his own force that some recruits were being groomed for interviews, he was adamant that the police should not have to convince people to become police officers, because if they didn't want to do the job, they wouldn't do it well. He proposed that what was required was for the police to learn new ways to nurture recruits while making organizational change to support it. There was no sense recruiting someone who would leave if they felt unappreciated or unwelcomed. Support, once the candidate had been sworn as a peace officer, had to come from training centres, coach officers in the field, supervisors, and rank-and-file colleagues.

"It is up to us, as professionally prepared and well-trained members of well-established organizations with years of tradition, to reach out and figure out how to do things correctly," he wrote. "It is not up to individuals with no support, with conflicting traditions or with misconceptions to step up to the plate and figure things out for themselves and fix things for us."

Gravel concluded by arguing that the time for talking was long past: "The leadership required to support the ever-changing approaches to recruiting is also crucial to the future successes of police services, and that includes moving beyond the usual rhetoric about wanting to reflect the diversity of the community. It's time to bring such statements into reality."

Gravel had been featured earlier in the April 25, 2005 edition of the *Canadian HR Reporter* by Uyen Vu who had written about the Ottawa police diversity recruitment strategy. Recalling a time when he could simply pull two hundred files to cull when the chief said they needed to hire thirty constables, Gravel had lamented that those files no longer represented the growing diversity of the community. His goal was to attract enough outreach candidates that recruiters could once again simply consult those files, safe in the knowledge they would get an equitable cross-section of candidates.

Vu wrote a followup article in the August 14, 2006 edition of the same publication, praising Ottawa for again blazing a trail with their latest diversity survey, writing: "The survey reflects the thinking at Ottawa Police Services that there's more to diversity than the representation of four designated groups. The way the police service conceptualizes it, the diversity initiative is part and parcel of the strategy to be 'employer of choice for all.'"

Gravel was as interested in training as he was in recruitment and tried to air his concerns at the highest level of policing. Submitting an article entitled, "Developing our managers for the oncoming demographic shift," for publication by the *Canadian Association of Chiefs of Police Journal*, he wrote: "The solution to consider is to invest in developing the talent that already exists within your personnel and giving them the opportunity to discover where their strengths lay so that they can position themselves to do what can be of the best benefit to the organization and the communities they serve. What exists in most police organizations today is training, not development! Training is giving the staff the skills they need to keep them capable of meeting today's minimal requirements. It is what we call 'stand-still' training. It simply keeps the organization running smoothly. This is an expense.

"Development is about giving staff the innovative workshops and courses they need that tie departmental learning plans to the organization's overall objectives. Staff members are developed to recognize where their best talents and strengths exist and are developed accordingly to support organizational changes, strategic plans or business cases. It is generative and is very much about being creative. This is an investment. Simply put, training meets an immediate past need; development moves you forward into the future."

At a time when police everywhere are scrambling for innovative approaches for the future, the CACP rejected the article. Perhaps Gravel offered too much insight; he says he was told it was too long.

However, beyond the debate about recruitment and retention, we still have to somehow define exactly what we expect our police to be. Whatever that may be, we also have to accept that they will not be able to do it alone. We each have a role to play in preserving the peace and ensuring officer and public safety.

NINE

BREACH OF SOCIAL CONTRACT

The police are the community and the community are the police.
—Sir Robert Peel

When British parliamentarian Sir Robert Peel, who is generally considered to be the father of modern policing, defined his concept of the "new" police in 1829, it should have been clear to everyone that creating a new profession of arms to preserve the peace and enforce the laws of the land did not in any way absolve the public from their role and responsibility for looking after one another. What Peel envisioned, and what everyone seemed to accept, was a social contract by which the police would represent the society they were sworn to serve and protect, and the public would support the police's efforts. There are those among us who believe the contract was signed with invisible ink. The contract has been repeatedly broken—and rarely by the police. If you took every police abuse and excess in this country since Confederation and multiplied by whatever factor you choose, the number would still pale in comparison to the numbers of honest, hard-working, dedicated peace officers with whom we have been blessed.

But there is a caution that, like the governments we elect, we may get the police we deserve.

Many believe that policing entered a new, more empowered era in the world created after the terrorist attacks on September 11, 2001. Horrific as those events were, there was an ominous sign much, much earlier that society had unalterably changed for the worse—another terrifying event that stunned not only America but the world, and it involved only one death. At 3:20 a.m., March 13, 1964, a twenty-eight-year-old middle-class woman was returning home from her job as a bar manager in New York City when she was raped repeatedly, then stabbed to death, steps from her home while thirty-eight witnesses—all neighbours—ignored her screams for help for more than an hour. One did yell at her assailant to leave her alone; another eventually called the police after first phoning a friend to ask what he should do. The police arrived within minutes of the call, but it was too late. Catherine "Kitty" Genovese was dead.

An equally harrowing tragedy played out twenty-five years later in Montreal when Marc Lepine entered an engineering class at l'École Polytechnique on December 6, 1989, ordered the male students and professor out of the room, and began a shooting rampage that left fourteen female students dead before killing himself.

The accepted police strategy at the time was to create a security perimeter and wait for tactical teams to arrive before entering a building with an armed hostage taker. In the Montreal case, police did not enter the building until twenty-four seconds after learning that the unidentified gunman was dead. That policy has changed: today, the first police to respond to the call in many jurisdictions would enter the building with new, shorter assault rifles. The police already have more than they can handle, just trying to catch truly bad people, and a lot of times they don't try very hard even then. That's not the fault of the front lines, whose priorities are set by their superiors. And if the boss tells you to get the speeders and get the drunks and get the stats and get the photo ops, well, that's what you tend to do after a while. And so whatever idealism may have existed is beaten out of every constable who has joined any police force since Peel drafted his Nine Points outlining the role he perceived police playing:

1. The basic mission for which the police exist is to prevent crime and disorder.
2. The ability of the police to perform their duties is dependent upon public approval of police actions.
3. Police must secure the willing co-operation of the public in voluntary observance of the law to be able to secure and maintain the respect of the public.
4. The degree of co-operation of the public that can be secured diminishes proportionately to the necessity of the use of physical force.
5. Police seek and preserve public favour not by catering to public opinion but by constantly demonstrating absolute impartial service to the law.
6. Police use physical force to the extent necessary to secure observance of the law or to restore order only when the exercise of persuasion, advice and warning is found to be insufficient.
7. Police, at all times, should maintain a relationship with the public that gives reality to the historic tradition that the police are the public and the public are the police; the police being only members of the public who are paid to give full-time attention to duties which are incumbent on every citizen in the interests of community welfare and existence.
8. Police should always direct their action strictly towards their functions and never appear to usurp the powers of the judiciary.
9. The test of police efficiency is the absence of crime and disorder, not the visible evidence of police action in dealing with it.

Those guiding principles should still apply today. A tenth principle, which is never cited because it was presumably so evident to Peel that he didn't even bother to include it, is the one that may be causing us problems today. The police have always answered to politicians and the public, and are constantly under scrutiny by them, the press and, most recently, an increasing number of academics. That's as it should be. But they have always tried to reflect the community and its values and felt supported by the public. This raises the question of how do you get people too apathetic or too lazy to vote to take the time or make the effort to involve themselves in their individual and community well-being? Arming our police does not absolve the rest of us from our responsibility to be involved in preserving the peace and respect for the law. Community policing will not work without community/public/citizen involvement. What can we do to help the police and what must they do to resolve public apathy?

Quite simply, policing in Canada has always been based on that social contract of social interaction and mutual respect. The police execute their duties with the support and consent of the public. Both sides are guilty of dropping the ball and breaching that vital and honoured agreement between the citizenry and the police but there seems to be some solid common ground, given the routinely high approval and trust ratings the police receive in public-opinion polls. But without increased interaction, rasing mutual awareness, respect and support, the public perception of the police, public safety, and national security is usually determined by media reporting. And the media can't be everywhere. So we and the police must bridge the void, not, as President John F. Kennedy said about sending a man to the moon and returning him safely to earth in the 1960s because it is easy, but because it is hard. In this instance, that concern for the safety of three astronauts applies to our own safety and the safety of those standing in the front lines of the thin bruised line. The evidence suggests that one person can make a difference.

Consider this simple fact: for years, women and children in Ontario were safer from sexual predators than those in any other province and territory in Canada. Yet, despite every study that has confirmed that women and children are the most vulnerable prey for sexual predators, only Ontario legislated that all police officers file their solved and unsolved sexual assaults and homicides on the RCMP computerized database the Violent Crime Linkage Analysis System (ViCLAS). Ron MacKay, then a Mountie inspector, was the first non-American trained as a behavioural criminal profiler at the FBI Academy in Quantico, Virginia. He oversaw the development of the system that was hailed after its launch in 1993 as a major break-through for public safety by Ontario justice Archie Campbell in his 1995 judicial review of the Green Ribbon Task Force, created in 1991 to investigate the Paul Bernardo and Karla Homolka schoolgirl murders. Although it was not fully operational until after Bernardo and his ex-wife, Karla Homolka, were in custody, it was widely believed that had ViCLAS been available, and had it been used, it would have helped solve those abductions and murders much sooner.

Fred Maile, the Mountie investigator who broke Clifford Olson in the interrogation room in 1982, was adamant that ViCLAS would have helped him link the first-known Canadian serial killer to his earlier crimes, and possibly saving lives, had it been operational back then. A prototype, the Major Crime Organizational System (MACROS) had been designed by Keith Davidson, a former Mountie sex-crimes investigator in E Division, which had blazed trails with CLEU and the OCA. MACROS's defining moment was to link the brutal 1992 rape of a Surrey schoolgirl to identical "indicators" in attacks that had taken place earlier in nearby Richmond, Burnaby, and distant Prince Rupert. In less than a half hour after the data was input, MACROS had got the first hit in a case that had defied overwhelmed investigators chasing down 700 leads, with no real suspects for months. Phone calls to investigators helped identify a common suspect who was identified from a photo lineup by the Surrey victim. The man confessed and was sentenced to eight years in prison.

The Bernardo case marked the first time that all other aspects of "behavioural" policing—criminal and geographic profiling and forensic psychiatry—coalesced behind the scenes at the same time on the same case. None of those expertises were ever going to solve a crime nor replace the need for police investigators, but all of them were powerful tools to help them determine where to look and what kind of person to look for in horrific stranger murders where the police have literally thousands of suspects and no leads. ViCLAS was the final piece to the puzzle. The system that links violent serial crimes to a single predator by his "signature" at the crime scene is used across Canada and has been adopted by several American states (which find it superior to the FBI's Violence Criminal Apprehension Program [FBI-VICAP] that only tracks homicides), and exported worldwide. While compliance rates are high in Canada, Ontario, and later Quebec, was the only province to legislate its use. That lack of support and political will among senior police, politicians, and bureaucrats may not be surprising, based on an information session presented in 1994 to the Canadian Association of Chiefs of Police. Hardly anyone showed up as it apparently conflicted with golf. At the end of the presentation, MacKay's mentor, Assistant Commissioner Joop Plomp, who had navigated ViCLAS through the red tape at Mountie headquarters, thanked the few police chiefs in attendance for showing up, then let loose a stream of vitriol that left no one in the room with any doubt of his low opinion of those who had risen to the top ranks of their profession but would opt for the golf links rather than learn about a revolutionary system to link crimes by their behaviours.

ViCLAS had been a tough sell for MacKay, who had to travel across Canada with an idea that would generate hours more paperwork to front-line investigators who were already buried under mountains of paper. But he persevered, refusing promotion and sacrificing his career to ensure the project stayed on track.

He retired as an inspector; his hand-picked replacement started at the higher rank of superintendent. In retirement, MacKay envisioned how best to adapt ViCLAS to a private-sector application. He came up with Arson Crime Linkage Analysis System (ACLAS) to profile and link suspected serial arsons. It should have been an easy sell to government and the insurance industry. It wasn't. He seemed to be making progress with the Ontario Fire Marshal's Office and the National Research Centre's (NRC) Canadian Police Research Centre. People listened politely, but no one ever seemed to do anything. And then the project died. MacKay never knew exactly why.

"ACLAS is intended to save time, save money and save lives," he told anyone who would listen, explaining that only one in five arson cases is likely to be solved using traditional investigative techniques, at least partly because there is so little evidence: whatever survives the inferno is usually destroyed by the efforts to extinguish the fire.[1] There seemed to be a real need for this system. In 1997, when MacKay was trying to drum up interest, the 12,799 fires believed to have been set deliberately killed 55 people, injured up to 300 firefighters, and destroyed property valued at $181,819,292. Only one in five was solved—1,395 resulted in criminal charges; 1,152 were "otherwise" cleared. That 20 per cent success rate was only marginally better than the 18 per cent reported in the United States by the FBI Uniform Crime Reports for the same year. The U.S. Federal Emergency Management Agency (FEMA) had ranked arson as the second leading cause of death in residential fires; and the International Association of Arson Investigators (IAAI) listed it as the third leading cause of home deaths, while commercial arson topped all causes for death, injury, and financial loss.[2]

"Clearly, early detection and intervention in serial arson cases are critical,"[3] MacKay said. No one argued. But no one stepped up with the money to support the project either. The NRC office was a one-man shop, which had, ironically, earlier helped broker Kim Rossmo's Rigel geographical profiling system that could locate a predator's likely home or workplace using complex mathematical algorithms. It wouldn't find a needle in a haystack, but it could point investigators to the right stack in a hayfield. Rossmo had done his early work while working for the Vancouver police. He was dismissed in 2000 for saying a serial killer was roaming the city's East Side and preying on prostitutes. By the time he was vindicated with the arrest and conviction of pig farmer Willie Pickton, Rossmo had moved to Texas where he flourished and is generally acknowledged as the inspiration for the popular TV crime drama *NUMB3RS*.

As a Mountie, MacKay had believed no one ever succeeded unless someone else wanted you to. Plomp had been his guardian angel on the Force but once retired and working in the private sector, he was on his own and still found himself being strangled in red tape. There was a brief glimmer of hope that things might improve, that the process might be more streamlined by a "Red Tape Review" (RTR) implemented in 2003 by the Mike Harris Conservative Ontario government. Once again, having a talented person working on a worthwhile, and much needed, project wasn't enough.

Ron Bain, a former deputy chief for Peel Regional Police and the lead investigator for Justice Archie Campbell on his high-profile reviews of the Green Ribbon Task Force and the SARS epidemic that crippled Toronto in 2003, got the nod to head the RTR, succeeding Roger Hollingworth who had left to be police chief in Amherstburg, near Windsor, Ontario, in 2003. Appointed by the Progressive Conservatives, Bain enjoyed the autonomy and ministerial latitude for quite a broad and extensive scope. He conducted "a ton" of interviews and reviewed adequacy issues and police policies, looking closely at ways to improve the areas of criminal investigations and court-related issues—vital areas he believed would benefit most from streamlining. However, his anticipated fourteen-chapter report never really got past the skeleton stage, and was put aside when he was asked to join the SARS Commission for the first time. When the Liberals were swept to power, the report was allowed to die on the vine for whatever reason, and nothing was ever done with Bain's partial findings. The government later purged the file. Nothing remains.

If Bain was disappointed, it wouldn't have been the first time. Before joining Peel in 1979, he was working for a small-town force in Parry Sound, the heart of Bobby Orr country, when he found himself in charge of a toxic-waste cleanup following a train derailment on November 10, 1979. He put out an emergency request for heavy equipment, but was advised there would be none coming for some time. Everything was racing toward another toxic derailment west of Toronto where Peel Regional Police were in the process of evacuating about 226,000 residents of Mississauga with others being relocated from Etobicoke and Oakville to escape the railcar explosions that were seen 100 kilometres away and tossed one 90-ton tanker more than 675 metres. There was virtually no panic in the orderly evacuation, no injuries or deaths, and no looting. This

"Mississauga Miracle" remained the largest peacetime evacuation in North American history until the 2005 evacuation of New Orleans when it was ravaged by Hurricane Katrina.

Making do with what he had, Bain used booms to stop the leaking oil from polluting the pristine waters of Georgian Bay at Parry Sound. He knew his limitations and acted accordingly. The next time that happened, he would be a catalyst for incredible change, first in Ontario, then Canada as a whole.

In June 1988, Christopher Stephenson, eleven, was abducted at closing time from the Shopper's World mall in Brampton, Ontario. He had been shopping with his mother and sister and had had a haircut. While waiting for his mother and younger sister browsing in a sewing shop, he was approached by Joseph Fredericks who had been stalking the family for the past five minutes. Later, the Stephensons learned that the convicted pedophile, recently released from prison, pulled a knife from under his jacket, jabbed it into the boy's neck, ordered him to pick up the bags and start walking. When his mother couldn't find him, she darted from corridor to corridor looking for Christopher. An employee at the hair salon they had visited said she saw Christopher walking out with a man. The alarm was sounded to mall security and Peel Police. The mall doors were locked within minutes, but Christopher had vanished.

Jim Stephenson learned at a stag party for his brother-in-law that his son was missing. He headed to the police station where he quickly realized from the tone and nature of the questions that he was a suspect. Experience had taught the police that missing and abducted children are most often taken by a family member. But that was not the case this time.

Dozens of investigators scoured the mall, the roof, and nearby fields, but there was no trace of Christopher. Less than forty-eight hours later, his stabbed body was found within clear view of police headquarters.

At the preliminary hearing, the judge ordered the trial to proceed and granted a change of venue to distant Stratford, meaning lost days at work and additional travel and accommodation costs for the grieving parents living at the west end of Toronto. A sympathetic Crown attorney helped their cause by putting them on his witness list. Now the province would at least pay their hotel bills.

At trial, the Stephensons learned through medical testimony that Fredericks was rated highly likely to re-offend and that his record of prior escalating violence almost assured he would eventually kill someone. Sitting with Bain and another Peel investigator at the break, Jim Stephenson asked them how the system could foul up so badly to turn a predator like Fredericks loose on an unsuspecting public. Bain was sympathetic. He agreed it was wrong, but added the police couldn't do anything about it and asked the father what he was prepared to do about it. Stephenson was livid. How dare this cop ask such a question of a father who just lost his son to a pedophiliac sadist who should never have been set free?

Fredericks was convicted of murder and sentenced to life in prison, but the family wanted more and pushed for a coroner's inquest to get answers to explain who and what failed to protect their son from a released felon who was at high risk to re-offend. But Fredericks appealed his conviction, effectively delaying an inquest until it was heard, possibly three or four years. When Fredericks was murdered in Kingston Penitentiary by fellow inmate Daniel Pouline on January 3, 1992, the inquest was scheduled.

Shopping for a lawyer to ask the tough questions they wanted answered, the Stephensons were first referred to an office high in the TD Centre overlooking Toronto Harbour. At the short meeting, the attorney told them their wardrobe suggested they couldn't afford him. Their second referral was to a young lawyer who referred them to a senior partner at his firm who agreed to represent them. What they expected would be a ten-day inquest stretched to seven months. Legal fees would exceed $300,000 and not even mortgaging their home would come close to paying them. Borrowing money from family, the Stephensons went public, selling buttons with Christopher's picture on them. Money poured in from across Canada and the United States. The federal government agreed to pay any shortfall. (Fredericks had been released from a federal institution before he killed Christopher.)

Among the jury's seventy-one recommendations was a call for

new legislation to keep violent high-risk offenders who were not designated "Dangerous Offenders" in prison indefinitely, or until they are no longer deemed a risk to the public. Another recommendation called on Ottawa to establish a national Sex Offender Registry (SOR) to include the names, addresses, and employers of released predators and pedophiles. The final recommendation was unprecedented—that progress on implementing the other recommendations be reviewed annually to ensure they were not shelved to gather dust.

Ottawa refused to create a national registry, arguing it already had the Canadian Police Information Centre (CPIC) to log all charges laid and stayed, convictions and acquittals. But CPIC provides only historic, not current, information and operated on such outdated technology as to be virtually useless. The federal government's response was to pump millions of dollars into updating and upgrading CPIC, which made it compatible with its FBI counterpart. But it still would not do the job of a registry.

Meanwhile, Bain, who had managed the investigation into Christopher's abduction and murder, invited Stephenson to talk to police about his experiences and dealings with police as a victim of violent crime. His honest portrayal of what was done well and poorly led to changed police methods and attitudes.

Stephenson understood now why Bain had told him the only way things would change was for people like him to speak out, to push government to enhance public safety. It was too late to save his own son, but if he wanted to spare other parents from enduring the emotional agony he and his family had endured, he had to do something.

The first step was to get involved with the Ontario branch of Victims of Violence, a support group co-founded by Gary Rosenfeldt whose sixteen-year-old son Daryn was murdered by child killer Clifford Olson in 1981. With Ottawa still refusing to create a registry, the Stephensons were delighted to get a phone call from the Ontario Attorney General's Office to advise them of their plan to create a provincial Sex Offender Registry—the first in Canada. They jumped at the chance to be involved, but were slower to accept the offer to call it "Christopher's Law"—the first law in Canada to bear a person's name. Jim Stephenson finally accepted it as a fitting tribute to his murdered son, and the legislation took effect in April 2001. The SOR is housed at OPP headquarters in Orillia.

In the summer of 2001, provincial premiers from across Canada, impressed with what Ontario had created, and worried that they now lagged dangerously behind, unanimously agreed to lobby Ottawa for a national registry. When Ottawa continued to balk, Ontario offered to help set up provincial registries across the land by providing its software, training. and expertise.

In September 2001, Jim and Anna Stephenson were granted a meeting with the Solicitor General of Canada and were granted permission to bring along an associate from Victims of Violence, John Muis, who, unknown to their hosts, was a Toronto detective sergeant with twenty years' experience. In less than a half-hour, he countered every argument that CPIC could do the job of a registry. After fifteen years, the Stephensons have shown the need for a national registry. Introduced as Bill C-23, the *Sex Offender Information Registration Act* (SOIRA) was tabled in the House of Commons on December 11, 2002, and debated at second reading on February 21, 2003. It died on the table when Parliament prorogued in November. Parliament reconvened on February 2, 2004, and Bill C-16 (formerly Bill C-23) was re-introduced to the Senate ten days later. It received royal assent on April 1, 2005, and came into force on December 15 that year, mandating offenders to comply with a court order to register.

And women and children across Canada were just a little bit safer, thanks to the Stephensons and their few allies like Bain and Muis. But their efforts require ongoing vigilance from the rest of us. On January 9, 2008, *Maclean's* magazine reported that the federal SOR had become "a national embrarrassment." Writing about the tragic case of notorious child molester Peter Whitmore, journalist Michael Friscolanti recalled the chilling details of the predator's sexual rampage before police finally tracked him down to a farm in Saskatchewan on August 1, 2006. Whitmore had been jailed earlier, but released despite warnings from parole officers that he was "one hundred percent" guaranteed to re-offend. Yet he was not listed in the national Sex Offender Registry. Whitmore was just the tip of an iceberg.

"The registry can barely keep track of sex offenders who are ordered to comply," Friscolanti wrote. "At last count, 16,295 names appear on the system; 1,270 are considered non-compliant. Some of those people never registered at all. Others have failed to check in as required—317 in Ontario, 201 in Alberta, 134 in British Columbia. Quebec is the worst, by far. The province is home to 2,554 registered sex offenders. One in five (480) are missing."

Warnings and pleas from the RCMP to fix the registry fell on deaf ears through successive Liberal and Conservative governments, their efforts crippled, according to internal government documents obtained by *Maclean's* under the *Access to Information Act*, by "Ottawa's obsession with privacy and the federal powers' resolve to protect the rights of convicted sex offenders."

"I'm not sure that public access is the answer, but I'm bloody sure this isn't the answer," Paul Gillespie, former head of the Toronto police child exploitation unit, told Friscolanti. "This is a national embarrassment."

It's all clear evidence that having finally been pushed into action by the provinces who threatened to simply adopt and tie into the Ontario registry—still far superior to the federal copy—the feds still have no idea of what it is for or how it is used. As *Maclean's* noted: "Every aspect of the registry benefits the sex offender, not the public or the police…. The database can only be used to help solve a crime, not prevent one."

Not everyone may have that stamina and staying power; indeed, even the Stephensons didn't realize they possessed those traits. They quite simply had no idea what to expect and what price they would pay—not just financial—to find justice and vindication for their son. The grim reality is that while everyone seems to have an opinion about the police—and the courts—few know much about them.

Think about it. How often do we actually encounter police officers up close and personal? If we see them on the road, we tend to slow down and wait for them to leave. If they stop us, it is usually an unfailingly polite conversation ending with a ticket. Then we are wished "a nice day" and go our separate ways. Anyone who has truly, desperately needed help from the police cannot adequately explain the sense of relief, the sudden sense of calm that the officers will make the problem better or even make it go away. They feel safe, protected and, perhaps only for a short while, grateful. Resentment against the police is easier to understand in a way because all they had to do was show up when you didn't want them to. Those limited encounters, however, give us little insight into policing or the police. So what does? What shapes our views of them? Lawyer Maureen McTeer spelled it out fairly succinctly when she told a roomful of policewomen at the Canadian Police College in Ottawa: "Canadian police forces should not underestimate the impact of American movies and TV shows on our view of police work and police officers."

Speaking at the 1997 Canadian Police College workshop "Women in policing in Canada: The year 2000 and beyond—its challenges," McTeer was there to remind her audience that women have never enjoyed a free ride throughout history—and that Canada was no exception. In her preamble to her presentation, "The Evolution of Women in the Justice Field," the attorney recalled her own experiences when she entered law school in 1973 as one of a few women in a male-dominated profession. The dean at that time had fought to have no more than eight women admitted and resigned when more than that registered. Law schools and the legal profession in the 1970s, she recalled, "were very hostile places for women." Her ensuing success and the policewomen in the audience were proof that women in policing, the law, and the judiciary were not the mere novelties and fads as they had once been dismissed. Their generation's accomplishments had advanced the struggles of those who had crusaded for acceptance in earlier times. And the price they had paid would make it easier for the next generation to be accepted into their rightful place in the thin blue line, regardless of gender, sexual orientation, or ethnicity. The hard times faced by the first generation of Canadian policewomen were merely a symptom of worse times for women in general. McTeer reminded her audience of the role they had played—and continued to play—in the larger context of women's "ongoing struggle for rights and equality of opportunity."[4]

While once upon a time female officers were viewed and judged by many in the public by such glamorous seventies television standards as *Police Woman* and *Charlie's Angels*, male officers were also pigeonholed with *Dragnet* and *Dirty Harry*. While contemporary depictions have improved (*Law & Order* and *The Closer*), the cumulative effect has been that many people mistake pop culture for cop culture.

Hollywood has not always been kind to the police. Nor have novelists. Borrowing from author Joseph Wambaugh's string of police-fiction hits, many of them made into movies, it became fashionable to show the police as overindulging, overdrinking borderline burnouts, some suffering from post-traumatic stress disorder long before that diagnosis was widely accepted. Then we had a rash of southern, redneck sheriffs and deputies, many of them closet Klansmen, fuelled by racial bigotry and abuses ranging up to murder. Criminals often fared better on the big screen than the police, as anti-heroes ranging from the love-them-and-shoot-them Barrows in *Bonnie and Clyde*, to Arlo Guthrie, who's arrested for littering in *Alice's Restaurant*. Even the back-alley tactics of the supposed good guys like Gene Hackman's Popeye Doyle in *The French Connection* cracking suspects' skulls in back alleys while cracking the heroin pipeline back in the accepted policing style of the 1960s and '70s can cause some sense of unease today when street thugs are likely more violent than ever.

Interestingly, the Canadian police, especially the Mounties, have always fared better on the silver screen than the Wild West American shoot-'em-ups. While the argument can be easily made that American filmmakers have never let the facts get in the way of a good story, they are equally adept at distorting their own history through literary licence.

In their books *Hollywood's Canada* and *The Mountie: From*

Dime Novel to Disney, authors Pierre Berton and Michael Dawson paint vast panoramas of Mountie movies that have graced the big screen, often so Americanized as to be unrecognizable, but giving U.S. audiences a love for their gun prowess in *North West Mounted Police* (1940) and their vocal cords in *Rose Marie* (1954) as well as a host of other films. Then they seemed to fall from grace and out of sight until Paul Gross revived their popularity as a by-the-book Mountie paired with a tough no-holds-barred Chicago cop in the TV series *Due South* (1994–96).

Not only has television, more than Hollywood, determined our image of policing and the police, it has also influenced our expectations. *CSI* and its Miami and New York City forensics spinoffs have altered jury expectations forever as they patiently endure eyewitnesses, expert testimony, and other physical and circumstantial evidence, all the time anxiously awaiting the DNA and forensics evidence.

Cops don't seem to watch a lot of cop shows, although many praised *Barney Miller* (1975–82) as the most honest police show on television, forgoing the grit of the streets to focus on the antics in the extremely diversified (and possibly dysfunctional) squad room, the character-driven show clearly conveyed the drama and despair of policing. What held the unit together in the face of adversity, and incompetent upper managers, was the remarkable Captain Barney Miller, played by Hal Linden. And what sustained the officers was their loyalty and faith in one another—still trademarks of the police today. More sitcom than drama, *Barney Miller* also revealed their gallows humour. A good contemporary example of that may be the following online satire purporting to be a police answering machine:

> RING.
> Hello. You've reached [your local] Police Service Voice Mail. Please pay close attention as we update your choices almost daily as unusual circumstances arise.
> Please select one of the following options.
> To whine about us not doing anything to solve a problem you've created, press 1.

To inquire as to whether someone has to die before we do something about a problem, press 2.

To report an officer for bad manners, when in reality that officer is trying to keep your neighbourhood safe, press 3.

If you'd like us to raise your children, press 4.

If you'd like us to take control of your life due to your chemical dependency, press 5.

If you'd like us to instantly restore order to a situation that took years to deteriorate, please press 6

To provide a list of officers you personally know so we will not take enforcement action against you, press 7.

To sue us or tell us you pay our salary and you'll have our badge or to claim an officer's career is over, press 8.

To whine about a traffic ticket or to complain about the wasteful use of police officers rather than keep your dumb ass in line, press 9.

Please note your call may be monitored and recorded to assure proper citizen support.

And remember, we're here to save your butts, not kiss them.

Thanks for calling [your local] Police Service and have a nice day.

The irony may be that, for its time, this piece of audio fiction may be a more honest portrayal of policing as seen by the police who overwhelmingly resist the urge to say "Fuck It, Drive On" (FIDO) because some days they believe they are damned if they do and damned if they don't. Meanwhile, the public forms its views of policing from such reality TV shows as *Cops*, which bear little if any semblance to the realities of policing in Canada.

In March 2009, the *Edmonton Journal* ran two articles days apart about a topic almost never mentioned in the mainstream media: extreme police discontent. Softening the acronym to "Forget It, Drive On," the lead item cites association unhappiness with what it views as "a 'dysfunctional' disciplinary process that puts officers under harsh and unfair scrutiny, the city's police union charges."

Edmonton Police Association president Tony Simioni pulled no punches, telling the *Journal*: "Officers would rather just drive past an incident and avoid the disciplinary measures that might result from them intervening, than do honest, aggressive, assertive policing that the citizens of Edmonton expect and have a right to expect. Our members are running scared because of the unrealistic level of disciplinary accountability here in Edmonton, as opposed to the rest of the province, and the country, for that matter."

The association has reportedly allied itself with criminal lawyers among others to ask the province to establish a civilian body to investigate police for allegations of misconduct. Deputy Chief David Korol replied that the police are expected to act professionally and the Solicitor General doesn't seem to have any plan to review the disciplinary process, believing that the process the police feel works against them actually benefits them.

Edmonton police do appear to have some issues. The March 24, 2009, article reports that the force held twenty-one disciplinary hearings in 2008 while Calgary held only one. No one else in Alberta had any.

"The level of scrutiny and accountability is out of proportion to the rest of the province, and the rest of the country," said Simioni. "The only way to restore public confidence in the police disciplinary process is to hand the whole thing over to the public ... The system is broken and it needs to be fixed."

Days later, Simioni said, in another interview, that he could understand why a few officers were adopting the FIDO mentality, but added that he does not condone it. He assured Edmontonians that they need not fear that crimes would go unsolved or criminals unpunished, presumably in the courts. He said officers might hesitate to run licence plates, fearing they'd be asked months later why they did it and concluded: "We have to have some kind of show of reasonableness and support for our troops from leadership rather than immediate prosecution or unfettered referral to the disciplinary process."

But for all their angst and anxiety, the police keep coming back, knocking on doors or knocking them down as the situation requires.

Then there are the few who stand up and speak out, risking and too often sabotaging their careers to expose exactly what's happening behind the Blue Wall and why it matters to the rest of us. These whistle-blowers tend to be shot down by their superiors for their efforts. They don't consider themselves heroes, nor are they treated as such. Despite recommendations, legislation, and invitations to step forward, few do for fear of retribution. It's never easy to do the right thing, and those who act in the public interest seem guided by higher moral standards and Edmund Burke's maxim "All it takes for evil to flourish is for good [people] to do nothing."

Among those listed on the Federal Accountability Initiative for Reform (FAIR) website who have stepped up and paid the price are:

- The "RCMP Five" who exposed the RCMP pension fund scandal: civilian Denise Revine and Mounties chief superintendent Fraser Macaulay, Staff Sergeant (ret'd) Ron Lewis, Staff Sergeant Steve Walker, and Staff Sergeant Mike Frizzell. All were reprimanded at the time, but later awarded the coveted Commissioner's Commendation for outstanding service, and a Commons committee unanimously passed a motion that the five be publicly commended and that a commendation be tabled in Parliament. Prior to this, no Canadian whistle-blower had ever received formal thanks or recognition from the authorities.
- Alan Cutler was transferred after complaining about improper procurement practices in Public Works, leading to the Gomery Inquiry.
- Brian McAdams's thirty-year career in the foreign service ended suddenly in 1993 after he exposed corruption at the Canadian consulate in Hong Kong and the infiltration of Chinese organized crime members and spies into Canada. His work saved the Canadian government an estimated $50 million, prevented the entry of more than 1,000 organized crime figures such as Triad, Yakuza, and Mafia members into Canada, and revealed

China's extensive espionage activities in Canada, which have now been confirmed by CSIS, Chinese defectors, and others.

- Corporal Robert Read, a twenty-six-year veteran of the RCMP was fired after investigating government corruption, beginning in 1996 in the aftermath of McAdams's 1993 allegations involving the Canadian High Commission in Hong Kong. In the course of his investigation, he discovered evidence of the corruption and what appeared to him to be a massive cover-up of that evidence. Read's investigation involved very rich and powerful members of the business community in Hong Kong, political connections in the People's Republic of China and the Liberal government of Jean Chrétien. He was vindicated by an RCMP external review committee, which accused the Mounties of seriously mishandling the investigations into complaints that Asian Triads had infiltrated the embassy. The committee also found that the national police force was reluctant to investigate foreign affairs employees who were suspected of taking bribes from China's rich and powerful, many of whom are widely known to be part of a communist spy network. In its ruling, the committee said that Read was justified in taking his concerns to the media and ordered him reinstated. The RCMP refused. Read lost his appeal in Federal Court. The Supreme Court refused to hear his case.

- Bob Stenhouse, a highly decorated eighteen-year veteran with extensive undercover experience, was ordered to resign for disclosing RCMP media strategies for outlaw biker gangs, believing them to be a mere public-relations exercise. He was reinstated in 2004, but later resigned.

- Constable Perry Dunlop, a police officer in Cornwall, Ontario, uncovered evidence of an alleged pedophile ring. When Cornwall police did not act, he alerted the Children's Aid Society and was charged under the *Police Act*. He was subsequently cleared of any wrongdoing, as judges ruled that his duties to Children's Aid superseded his responsibilities as a police officer, but he was later jailed for contempt of court for refusing to testify at the inquiry, claiming he had lost all faith in the process.

- Bruce Brine, who had twenty-two years of policing experience and a 1994 Governor General's Award for Exemplary Service, was fired from his job as chief of the Halifax ports police in 1995 after he alleged that senior officials within that department were getting kickbacks from the Hells Angels. The ports police were disbanded in 1998 and the ongoing investigations were abandoned. Much of the material from the files of those investigations was listed as missing when Mounties began to pursue his obstruction complaint. The Nova Scotia Human Rights Commission awarded him a cash settlement, an apology, and a letter of reference from the port authority.
- Ron Robertson's dismissal is the latest in a series of events that began in 1998, when he came forward with concerns that the Edmonton police had been infiltrated by organized crime.

There have, of course, been internationally recognized instances of whistle-blowing. Daniel Ellsberg made the cover of *Time* magazine and the front pages in newspapers around the world when, in 1971, he leaked the Pentagon Papers, exposing the extent of American involvement in Southeast Asia. FBI agent Colleen Rowley, WorldCom internal auditor Cynthia Cooper, and Enron accountant Sherron Watkins were jointly named *Time's* 2002 Persons of the Year, going public with their concerns about their respective employers. Officially, they were deemed "whistle-blowers," but in reality, each was doing her job as her conscience dictated.

Such are the coping skills—everything from dark humour to whistle-blowing—for peace officers who seem unsure just where they stand with anyone any more. As the violence in the streets escalates and even the traditionally welcoming rural countryside becomes home to more organized crime and meth labs, the police are questioning how much support they can expect from politicians, the press, the public, and the courts. Worst of all, they distrust many above them in management where careerism and "dysfunctional discipline" seem to flourish. That's changing. Front-line officers are beginning to question and push back. Where once the Mounties coined the slogan "Mess Up, Dress Up, Fess Up" to describe the plight of the hapless officer paraded before a disciplinary hearing, today they are more apt to speak up for their rights aided by the court ruling that they cannot be denied an association for collective bargaining.

Similarily, in Edmonton, where disciplinary hearings quadrupled when Mike Boyd became chief with a mandate to clean up the force, the association would like to see alternative dispute resolutions besides conventional disciplinary hearings.

The best cops can't *not* be cops—it is who they are, and policing, which translates for them into helping others, is what they do. Nothing will prevent that, not even the changing face and new challenges confronting them in the future, just around the corner and further down the road.

And everyone should start thinking through the potential consequences of what those changes will mean to officer and public safety.

THE TIMES THEY ARE A-CHANGIN'

Am I safe? Are you competent? Can I trust you?
—Beverley Busson, first female commissioner of the Royal Canadian
Mounted Police

While it remains unclear what we expect from our police, Busson, the twenty-first commissioner of the RCMP who declined to be considered as a permanent replacement for Giuliano Zaccardelli after his abrupt resignation, has consistently listed the above three questions as those the public has every right to ask. But she stresses that the public, in return, has to understand what the police do within the larger context of public security.

"Police, prosecutors and the judiciary are integrated partners in the criminal justice system but the reality is that it is the police whose actions and judgments are often scrutinized the greatest through the luxury of 20/20 hindsight," she wrote to local media in 2000 in response to allegations of a botched investigation after the acquittal of the man accused of murdering eight-year-old Cindy Tran, of Kelowna, British Columbia, in 1994.

"The reason for this is the simple fact that police actions and investigations are the only component in the justice system where decisions must sometimes be made in a split second due to immediate public safety needs, where conclusions must sometimes be drawn from incomplete or best-available facts, and where public and news media expectations for quick results are at its peak."

But she was equally insistent that the police must be held to account.

"Indeed there are very few professions in society with the level of scrutiny applied to police officers. In the case of the RCMP there are multiple levels of internal checks and balances including the stringent Code of Conduct which holds all RCMP officers to an exemplary standard of behaviour; there is an independent national public complaints commissioner assigned to be the watchdog over RCMP conduct; and there is the ongoing transparency of being accountable to national laws pertaining to access to information … when the entire case is heard, the courts themselves will test the credibility of police testimony."

But, like the media, the police can't be everywhere. And they can't always predict what's going to happen next. When tens of thousand of Tamils protesting in Toronto descended on Ottawa in mid-April 2009, no one apparently knew they were coming. This suggests that our intelligence agencies aren't as on top of things as they might be. True, the demonstrators were never identified as terrorists—many were Canadian citizens—but they were protesting in support of the Liberation Tigers of Tamil Eelam, a group on Canada's list of terrorist organizations as well many terror watch lists around the world. The demonstrators were demanding that Canada, and later the United States, intervene to stop the bloodshed in the civil war between the Tigers and government troops in Sri Lanka, seemingly oblivious to the Canadian government's previous lobbying to halt that violence.

Lawyer David B. Harris, a former CSIS chief of strategic planning who also served as counsel to an intervenor organization at the Air India and Iacobucci terror inquiries,[1] in an op-ed piece for the *Ottawa Citizen,* wrote that "they [the protesters] should have been stopped.… This is a question for counterterrorism authorities or whoever is left to run Ottawa when the Tigers, doubtless tiring of police outreaching, liaising and dialoguing, eventually toss the city back to its leaderless residents. The enforcement of our laws is doubly important at a time when near-boundless immigration, related demographic shifts and radicalizing communities mean that officials could increasingly be tempted to profit politically from appeasing dangerous, but influential, groups. Canadians must hold their politicians and bureaucrats accountable for acting in the national interest. In the meantime, we must remember that our behaviour in such matters is studied carefully by Hamas, Hezbollah, al-Qaeda and other extremist groups that target Canada and the West. They take a professional interest in knowing which cities conduct themselves like soft targets."

Harris made credible points, but the police on the ground had more immediate concerns. Policing and related costs were projected to top $900,000 as single-day throngs hit an estimated 25,000 in Ottawa in the days before and into the Easter long weekend. Many officers' long-weekend plans and leaves were cancelled as the overtime meter started ticking. This was after they had filled the streets of Toronto and Montreal, also apparently with no advance awareness. And they returned to Toronto on May 10, closing the Gardiner Expressway and choking other major traffic arteries. While everyone agreed that people have a right to protest, it was less clear what obligation they had to confine their masses to public spaces like the lawns of provincial legislatures or Parliament Hill.

The Tamil protest was unlike any protest the police had encountered before. Overall, the Tamils were orderly, and there were few arrests, at least in the early protests. But whereas most protesters arrive, make their point, cause some noise, then get back on the bus, these groups never left, holding their ground 24/7. Neither they nor the cities ever seemed to sleep. The Ottawa Police Services Board told the media they were asking the federal government to pony up and pay the costs, which seemed logical considering the Tamils weren't protesting city bylaws.

The same argument could be made in Toronto for funding from the provincial government who were the apparent target on this occasion. Terming their occupation of the Gardiner Expressway as "a very dangerous situation," Police Chief Bill Blair did not seem impressed that the protesters had used their children to block that normally busy, and often clogged, thoroughfare. Recalling the earlier blockade staged outside the U.S. embassy on University Avenue, Blair said the situation had escalated "well beyond merely a democratic process into an unlawful assembly." He tempered his response to the situation and to the media hoard, however, confirming the protesters were breaking the law, and that "we will have to move them out of there, but our response in doing that has to be proportional to the threat they have created." The chief also confirmed that he called on nearby police forces, the RCMP, the OPP, and kept the Toronto police day shift on duty to ensure "sufficient resources" in the hope of negotiating a peaceful resolution.[2]

If anyone has ever wondered why policing costs sometimes go through the roof in very abrupt and unexpected ways, they need only have walked along the Gardiner in Toronto or Wellington Street in Ottawa on those frantic days.

That's how vulnerable the police are when it comes to consuming their dollars. As noted earlier, a single homicide investigation, which can generate hundreds, even thousands, of leads, and no real suspects, can drain millions from the budget. Even with reserves set aside in anticipation of such human tragedies, how do you budget for thousands of people who arrive, blockade, camp out, and won't leave? You don't. How do you budget for fuel for your fleets of cruisers, SUVs, and vans, when speculators cost you tens of thousands of dollars every time they drive up the cost of gasoline at the pumps a fraction of a cent? You can't. And if that doesn't seem like much to contend with, consider that OPP commissioner Fantino told the Hamilton Canadian Club on January 16, 2008, that every penny increase at the pumps meant another $250,000 a year to fuel the OPP's 1,200 cruisers and other vehicles used by 7,500 officers and support staff who patrol about 122 million kilometres a year responding to some 800,000 calls for service.

Just prior to the Tamils descending on Ottawa, *Citizen* columnist Randell Denley wrote about rising police costs, which was headlined "Ontario hikes cost of police bonuses, pensions," complete with an anonymous quote that this was going to cost taxpayers a lot of money.

You can't write off the opinion piece to simple police, or even government, bashing. (On December 20, 2007, Denley had written that the police were worth every penny.) But you can challenge a fact or two. Citing the raises as a "misguided act of generosity" by the Ontario government, he predicted that municipalities across the province could be "on the hook for millions of dollars in additional policing costs." He supported that by pointing out that once one police force gets a raise, they all seem to get that raise, which translates into higher property taxes for everyone. Noting that the province did not draw a line with the OPP by refusing to pay the retention bonuses negotiated in city departments to keep veterans on staff (there were too few recruits to replace them if they all retired when they could have), their recent agreement with the Ontario Provincial Police threatened to drive up the $3.3 million that Ottawa taxpayers were already doling out for their local "experience bonus" by, according to his police sources, $630,000.

"It's difficult to see a compelling case for substantially enriching the OPP contract, especially when the province is deep in deficit," Denley wrote. "A rookie OPP officer starts at $44,492. In four to five years, he typically becomes a first-class constable with pay that will reach $81,000 by the end of this contract. Jobs like that are hard to find."

Not so. Those wages, by Denley's own accounting, were due largely to the perceived need for all levels of government to pay their peace officers well because they could not find enough recruits to fill the gaps in the thin bruised line with thousands set to retire in waves. His ensuing comparison to their contracted salary being rolled back to a 1.5 per cent increase made no mention of the fact the Mounties were fighting that in court, which had also ruled in their favour to associate for collective bargaining—ending their tradition as the only police force to lack that right and who, until fairly recently, had not even been paid overtime for additional hours worked. No matter, Denley concluded: "This OPP settlement is simply irresponsible. No wonder the provincial government doesn't want to talk about it."

As luck would have it, Commissioner Fantino was not shy to respond. His reply, printed in the *Citizen* within days, claimed the new contract was not a bonus but "fair compensation" to recognize an officer's years of service and the fact that he or she can be "deployed anywhere in the province on short notice." In fact, the OPP were quick to respond to pleas for help from Ottawa when the Tamils descended. Fantino dismissed Denley's claims as "nonsense" and insisted the money earned by the professionals "who put their lives on the line each day" to police the province.

Fantino wasn't the only chief to demonstrate he knew how to get out in front of a story to defuse potential damage to the image of their organization. Ottawa chief Vern White wrote regular submissions to the Ottawa media to state his case, explaining why something had or had not been done, and why they might need more money. Just as he rushed to the airport to calm cab drivers after an alleged assault on one of them by one of his officers, he's equally quick to reassure his constables and commissioned officers that he will back them when they take legitimate and legal risks in their daily duties and that he will support them, even if their efforts fail.

The Ottawa police chief defends his good officers and charges his bad ones under the *Police Act*. Interestingly, while he does not hesitate to seek dismissal for any officer he deems should not be on the force, he is a great believer in restorative justice for criminals as a way for a perpetrator to accept responsibility for their wrongdoing in lesser crimes. He would rather see someone own up to their actions and make amends than have them sit mutely in court and let their lawyer do all the talking.

In 2009, the media first reported that Ottawa had one of the lowest violent-crime rates among Canadian cities, then later revealed that the city police had the worst clearance rate for crimes in the country.[3] In other words, they were solving fewer crimes than other major police forces. White responded quickly both times. He offered no excuses, conceding that Ottawa residents deserved better, and promised to do what he could to fix it. The story died right there because the media had nothing more to write about. Readers might have been reminded of Denley's column on September 11,

2007. Entitled "No guff from this chief," it began by praising Ottawa's new chief as "the real deal."

"In his first three months on the job, the chief has gotten into controversies over crack pipes, surveillance cameras and support-our-troops ribbons," Denley wrote. "None of them has made a dent in his image as a blunt-speaking straight shooter. He's asking for a budget increase of nearly 10 per cent, and he's going to get it. He's gaining ground in his campaign to get a youth drug treatment centre and he's won over the president of the police association. Not a bad start."

White told the Ottawa police board when they hired him away as chief of Durham Region, east of Toronto, that he would serve for five years, not one day more. He is not like most chiefs you meet, mincing few words in his opposition to a needle-exchange program for addicts, his frustration with the lack of a youth treatment facility, and his blunt attack on a system that allows two or three days' consideration against a prison sentence for every day the accused was held in custody. Taken to task in the media for that last stand, he fired back, vowing not to be silenced on issues that risked bringing justice into disrepute. In fact, the only people who seem capable of ignoring White are the federal bureaucrats he wrote to, asking for $900,000 toward the cost of policing the Tamil protest, which was clearly aimed at the federal government. As of late October 2009, he had heard nothing.

Asked for a list of others who seem to share his philosophy, he immediately names Ian Davidson, who resigned as chief in Sudbury to become Ontario's new public-safety czar in May 2009, where he will wield more power than any of his predecessors. Other police chiefs who have demonstrated their ability to transform troubled forces are Mike Boyd, in Edmonton, and Saskatoon chief Clive Weighill, a twenty-eight-year veteran with a "what-you-see-is-what-you-get" candour that seems to cut to the heart of any issue. Weighill has, according to one local columnist, so far avoided the "ticking time bombs" he inherited when he was named chief in 2005. Weighill gives a lot of credit to former chief Russ Sabo, a native Calgarian who, the May 8, 2009 *Saskatoon StarPhoenix* reported, had allegedly walked into a "hostile environment" after then mayor Jim Maddin "ousted" former chief Dave Scott.

"From the onset," the paper reported, "Sabo's was a difficult task, given Scott's relative popularity with the rank and file. He was handed the Stonechild inquiry, the convictions of two officers for unlawfully confining Darrell Night, and the David Milgaard inquiry, among other scandals."

Weighill credits Sabo with beginning the healing process for the wounded police service by focusing on outreach to First Nations and Metis groups, which had become so bad that the media reported members of those groups would think very carefully before calling police for assistance. As David Hutton wrote in the *StarPhoenix*: "For decades, Saskatoon had a police service compris[ing] officers hired for their toughness and expected to keep the peace." But in 2000, Darrell Night accused police of dumping him on the edge of town before dawn when he was drunk on a cold January morning. That set off a series of other accusations, and an inquiry into the 1990 freezing death of seventeen-year-old Neil Stonechild after officers dropped him roadside wearing only a light jacket in frigid weather. Even today, patrol officers report they deal with the after-effects of what became known as the "starlight tours," with the question often raised after handcuffs are applied: "Where are you taking me?"

Weighill is widely credited with turning that around. But Saskatoon—in fact, others in Saskatchewan—still take their lumps in annual crime surveys. On March 5, 2005, the *StarPhoenix* reported that the city had topped the list as Canada's most dangerous in the annual *Maclean's* poll. Based on per-capita crime stats from 2007, the worst five cities for crime were all in western Canada: Winnipeg, Regina, Prince George, B.C., and Edmonton. Saskatoon mayor Don Atchison denounced the stats as outdated and misleading, insisting the crime rate appeared higher because people still reported crimes there and the police are more zealous about pursuing probation breaches.

"What's happened here is *Maclean's* magazine has done a wonderful job of misinterpreting all the facts," Atchison told the

StarPhoenix. "It's [the coverage] an oxymoron. Because we're doing such a good job it gets reported in a negative fashion."

Caledon, Ontario, which is subcontracted by Peel Region to the OPP, was again named the safest city in Canada.

Using 2007 rates per 100,000 population for six crimes—homicide, sexual assault, aggravated assault, vehicle theft, robbery plus breaking and entering—*Maclean's* calculated the percentage difference from the national rate for each of the six crimes. Saskatoon was ranked first in aggravated assault and robbery, fourth in homicide and sexual assault, twentieth in breaking and entering, and twenty-first in vehicle theft.

However, a month later, using its new Crime Severity Index, Statistics Canada's Canadian Centre for Justice Studies showed Regina having the worst crime numbers for 2007. "We're not saying there's any more crime," a spokesperson explained. "It's nothing new. It's just a way of telling us the proportions of those more serious crimes."

So who do you trust? If you live in those cities, possibly no one, but certainly not the compilers of numbers. That's not terribly new. While public-opinion polls continue to rate trust and confidence in the police highly, Jeff Latimer, as the Canadian Justice Department's principal statistician, concluded in the 2007 National Justice Survey (NJS), "Tackling Crime and Public Confidence": "Confidence in the criminal justice system is generally low compared to other public systems, such as health and education. The central concern appears to be around sentencing practices and the need for reparation, accountability and ultimately rehabilitation to prevent future criminal behaviour. A large segment of Canadians also believe that criminal justice policies should be proportional to the seriousness of the crime. In other words, proportionality, which is the fundamental principle of sentencing in Canada, is highly supported.

"Some of the strongest predictors of confidence in the criminal justice system appear to be amenable to influence. For example, increasing public trust in the accuracy of official justice system statistics (e.g., parole-granting rates, crime rates) may result in an increase in public confidence. Moreover, focusing sentencing reform not only on the quantum of the sentence, but also on the nature of the sentence, may result in increases in confidence.

"Finally, as with any research project, the 2007 NJS has identified a number of future research questions. Why do Canadians generally have a lack of trust in the accuracy of official criminal justice statistics? How do Canadians perceive the concepts of reparation, accountability, and rehabilitation in terms of their harshness? And is it possible to increase public confidence by addressing these two specific issues?"

So, statistics and the courts, not the police, appear to be on the public hit list. The police also view the courts as an arena for gamesmanship between lawyers. The longer defence counsel can string out the early proceedings, the more chance the investigating officer will move, retire, get sick or hurt, witness memories may fade, details blur, accidents or illnesses may strike and, until very recently, in Ontario at least, even if their client was convicted, they could be freed on the spot for time served, factored at two or three to one per day incarcerated. No one ever seems to do hard time and police officers say they sometimes feel that former family court judges hearing criminal cases sometimes seem anxious to strike deals that would accommodate everyone, treating an assault like it was a custody hearing. And while the courts ruled that the Mounties had the right to organize, they also made it easier for the police to be sued by the public. That would be fine—the police right down to the constable level are generally the first to agree they should be held accountable and held to a higher standard—but given the legal sleight of hand that seems to play out in the courtrooms and the penchant for some to launch false complaints with no risk of even a reprimand for trashing a cop's name and career or wasting the court's time, well, they are admittedly a little leery about their prospects in court.

Their frail legal status was underlined by a letter from Robert Marshall to the *Winnipeg Free Press* on November 17, 2008. Headlined "Stripping police of their rights," he commented on Manitoba justice minister Dave Chomiak's promise to revamp the provincial *Police Act*, noting that the biggest change would be "courtesy of his made-in-Manitoba solution to the hot-button issue of police oversight." Identifying himself as one of several former police officers who at some time investigated police-related shootings, he agreed that change was overdue. Citing the Ontario Special Investigations Unit (SIU), which investigates the police in cases involving the discharge of a weapon or injury or death in any incident involving the police, Marshall asked what Manitoba could learn from Ontario in the wake of several "critical inquiries" over the SIU's eighteen-year history. Noting that André Marin, the Ontario ombudsman and a former SIU director, had recently slammed his old department and "pummelled the much-hyped vanguard of truth and justice to 'toothless tiger' status," Marshall said it raised three red flags:

1. Suggesting that investigative staff halt the practice of wearing ties, watches, and rings or carrying paraphernalia that might identify a former policing status or affiliation with a police organization. That quick fix to the perception of police bias was immediately implemented.
2. Trying to make it an offence, punishable by imprisonment, if officers failed to co-operate and comply with the SIU. For some, such optics may be OK but in a fluid system the devil really is in the details. Good evidence is voluntary evidence. Danger accompanies evidence that is a product of coercion and our legal system, quite properly, takes a dim view of information gained courtesy of any threat, including imprisonment.
3. And the mother of all slippery slopes—that "the director of the Special Investigations Unit should exercise the authority to suspend an officer's entitlement to legal representation at an interview, if the interview would otherwise be unreasonably delayed beyond 24 hours."[4]

"Marin has to be kidding," Robert Marshall wrote. "The Supreme Court's archives are jammed with precedent on this issue. The SIU investigates criminal cases, not just bad apples in the workplace. So the law matters and the high court is quite clear; the subject of a criminal investigation has a right not just to a lawyer, but to one of his choosing. Suspend the fundamental right to counsel? Canada is a signatory to the United Nations' International Covenant on Civil and Political Rights, which contains provisions guaranteeing the right to legal assistance in criminal matters. The right to legal representation is sacrosanct, basic, essential, and something that can only be waived by the individual. Charter rights are not something to be surrendered at the behest of a provincial bureaucrat trying to compensate for his agency's inability to put a case together."

Marshall challenged readers to imagine being a cop, routinely thrust into extraordinary circumstances: "Forced to take a life in a world governed by legal hocus-pocus. Then imagine having your central, lawful rights suspended by an agent of the state who is conducting that investigation." This touched on the apparent irony unique to policing, that while officers wield great power to keep the peace, preserve law and order, and protect public safety, they sometimes seemed to forfeit their rights for exercising that power. In a split second, making possibly a life-and-death decision, their actions would be condemned by those who weren't there, claiming to apply cold logic to an incendiary moment with the luxury of distance and time separating them from the reality and peril of that moment. All they asked for was a fair hearing and Marshall agreed that the foremost hallmarks of Manitoba's new oversight agency must be honesty, competence, and credibility.

"It must be a body that inspires confidence," he concluded. "And it must be one that respects the rights of all parties."

If the thin bruised line was battered and stretched to the breaking point already, police managers continue to find new ways of thinning it further. The most popular seems to be seconding staff, rarely front-line constables, to distant locales on someone else's nickel, most often, but not exclusively, the United Nations or the Canadian government. The arrangement would be explained in the media as an excellent way for local officers to gain first-hand experience in distant lands or even remote areas of Canada, to better understand, and more productively "interact" with, new Canadians from those areas. It was less clear that those who went had been, or would ever be, involved in policing the ethnic communities whose homeland they were to visit. Nor was it clear that there was any trickle-down effect to the front-line constables who would in fact be patrolling those communities. The same was true for commissioned officers who were lucky enough to get their ticket punched by attending the Rotman program at the University of Toronto, equivalent to an MBA in police leadership, or sit in on a lecture or panel discussion with the brilliant minds at the Nathanson Centre for the Study of Organized Crime and Corruption. How did what they learn and gain, beyond advancing their own careers, benefit their force or their subordinates who were the boots on the ground in the areas where the crimes were happening?

Some things will likely never change. Canadians will continue to argue the French-English dynamic. Male officers will be split on their thoughts on the efficiency of having female officers or diversity targets, while the good officers, representing both genders and all ethnic origins and sexual orientations, will look at others and at their own and be happy to work with the good cops and saddened to find there are bad cops upon whom they must rely, no matter who or what else they may be.

Senior managers see the world differently, as they must. They have policies to enact, regulations to enforce, desks to fill, and presentations to make, without which their force ceases to function. Ask any of them to identify the top issues in policing and almost all will promptly identify recruitment and possibly retention. Many police managers will also cite what they consider to be the disturbing and rising encroachment of private policing, most of them insist should be called private security. By whatever name, this new breed of enforcement is answerable to their employer, not the state or the public. The studies abound on the rise of private security that presumably will complement, not compete with, the public police.

It had better work that way. The police as we know them answer to us and the law as much as to their immediate supervisors: the sergeants and staff sergeants who make all the difference in the world to a unit—good and bad. The sergeants are the conduit between top and bottom. The sergeants, along with some front-line supervisors and tactical teams, are generally those in most departments who are issued and authorized to carry Tasers. With the outcry, the hand-wringing, and the tragic deaths involving conducted electronic weapons, we need to know if the people wielding them are competent to do so responsibly. If we are going to issue such weapons to our police, we must do so expecting them to use them. And if they are being abused by people who should never have been given them, they should be taken away.

In study after study about the rise of private policing and private security, and the prevalence of paid-duty and "Gypsy" cops, almost all stress that only the *public* police are accountable to the law and oversight. The others answer to whoever signs their paycheque. That's not a healthy basis for broad powers.

Those who know little about the police beyond what we see in the movies, on TV, or read in books or in the media, need to know that you cannot isolate them into a one-dimensional entity. They are different than most, if only because they go to work armed. But they rely on us as much as we count on them to show up when we need them and to be accountable for what they do at all times. It's not an easy demand to meet, but it's not an easy life to live. It is, or at least can be, to steal a line from the "gritty" new police TV drama *Southland*, "a front-row seat to the greatest show on earth." And they're hiring. Everywhere.

The police do not and cannot operate in isolation. If their Blue Wall separates the thin bruised line into a unique place, our worlds occasionally intersect and often overlap. The police, like the rest of us, are affected by politicians, public servants, judges and juries, lawyers, reporters, broadcasters, and public opinion, which translate into public support. On January 1, 2009, *Globe and Mail* reporter André Picard related a story that showed the police at their most human. Writing about a forty-seven-year-old homeless woman, Tracey, who burned to death in downtown Vancouver a few days before Christmas when the candle heating her makeshift shelter set her meagre possessions ablaze, Picard discovered the "crucial but largely invisible role" police play in public health. Reporting that the police had visited her three times that night, each time pleading with her to let them take her to a shelter, they had hung around to chat when she refused, offering her food and cigarettes. Concerned for her welfare, they had no legal power to move her, so they kept checking back.

"When her body was discovered," Picard wrote, "veteran police officers wept. They returned later to the site with flowers; a silent tribute to a woman who died horribly and horribly alone."

Picard noted that police usually get media coverage when they "appear to have screwed up"—when someone is killed by Taser or when a suspect dies in custody or a riot erupts or someone wrongfully convicted is exonerated.

"Rarely does the banal reality and everyday importance of policing get recognized," Picard continued. "Police have the often thankless task of dealing with every imaginable challenge thrown their way, from helping children cross the street to ensuring that homeless people do not freeze to death on any given night, not to mention dealing with emergency evacuations during natural disasters, picking up the pieces (sometimes literally) after motor-vehicle collisions and getting drunken teenagers home safely after breaking up a party."

Picard seemed surprised to realize the police are front-line "warriors" in the field of public health around the clock, every day of the year.

"The most difficult and thankless work that police do is with those on the margins of society, those whose only crime is being sick—usually with a severe mental illness or addiction," he noted, adding, "Occasionally, these interactions go sideways, with much media coverage and second-guessing of decisions made in a split second. Yet these highly publicized 'police failures' are the exception. For the most part, police do a remarkable job of dealing with mental, physical and emotional traumas and the social woes they cause. For all our criticism, officers mete out far more compassion and caring than they do bullets and baton blows. They deploy it every day as they deal with the tempest-tossed that the rest of society is so quick to turn a blind eye to. And yet we never seem to find a way to say, "Thank you."

Well, almost never.

On April 8, 2009, eight-year-old Victoria "Tori" Stafford disappeared while walking home from school in Woodstock, Ontario, a city of about 35,000 people 125 kilometres southwest of Toronto. Media across Canada carried the story for weeks. On July 20, an observant OPP constable recognized terrain near Mount Forest, northeast of Woodstock, as matching a description given by one of two people suspected in Tori's disappearance and possible murder. Human remains were subsequently found. Fearing the worst, OPP officers at the scene snapped to attention and saluted the hearse as it transported the remains away for forensic examination. The moment was captured by the press and the photo appeared across Canada.

On July 21, the police called a press conference to announce that forensics had confirmed their suspicions. The announcement was meant to comfort the grieving family as best as it could, offering solace and closure even as the last spark of hope for their daughter's safe return was extinguished. The sense of loss not only permeated the Woodstock community who had followed the media coverage of the police efforts, but also the police force who had searched and hoped for a happier ending. At least one member of the public realized what they had done, what they had hoped to do, and the price they paid for doing their job.

On July 29, a letter from Trish Triebner, the mother of an eight-year-old girl who also lives in Woodstock, appeared in local community newspapers across Wellington County where the police had focused an intensive search for Tori since May 20. Admitting that she did not know Tori or her family, Triebner had nevertheless been touched by their suffering, but also by the extent to which the police proved themselves willing to go to find the missing girl, "leaving no stone unturned," as had become their motto. Thanking the police for "bringing this little angel home to her family," Triebner wrote:

> To the officers who have been working on this case—I thank you so much.

To the officers who haven't worked on this case but had to fill in for those who were—I thank you so much ...

For sacrificing your own family time for another's family. For feeling so deeply about his particular assignment when you didn't have to. For never ignoring any angle of this investigation even though it may have led you down roads you didn't want to go down. For many of you investigating on your time off. For never forgetting that your job is to protect our children. For showing up to work every day knowing it was going to be a hard or difficult day. For going above and beyond your job description. For publicly showing support for all of the functions held in Tori's honour. For taking the time to chat with our children to let them know you were their friend who was making the world a better place—one assignment at a time. For staying steadfast in your quest to being Tori home. For making any sacrifice unknown to the public. For making a difference—in our lives and in our world.

So many times, in investigations such as these—our officers and the investigators get overlooked and under-thanked. I want you to know that you haven't been. We appreciate your hard work. You are making a difference.

There was to be no happy ending to this story, only closure, which is intended to be something positive when in reality it extinguishes the last spark of hope that a missing loved one will be found alive and unharmed. Nor would others be spared the anguish and torment suffered by Tori's family. Media reports of falling crime rates and arguments that such tragedies are isolated do little to calm the fears of parents everywhere who suddenly fear for the safety of their own children. Brigadier-General Jonathan Vance could have been speaking about Woodstock, Ontario, or any other centre in Canada, when he explained to the CBC the fear that gripped the population in Afghanistan: "Whether they feel there's a threat because there's actually a threat or simply a perception is immaterial. What they perceive is real to them."[5]

Like Lewis Mackenzie who wrote about his life in the military and chose a police story to illustrate the true qualities of leadership, there seems little difference between OPP commissioner Fantino insisting the police "can't arrest their way out" of the Native land claim protest, the bad will and occasional violence at Caledonia or to Brigadier-General Jonathan Vance predicting that victory cannot be won solely at the point of a gun without honest politicians and a functioning infrastructure in Afghanistan.

Vance, the head of Canadian troops on that mission, leads from the front, joining night patrols with his soldiers, what he termed a basic tenet of leadership, to see first-hand what his troops are up against and to hopefully encourage them with his presence.

"It's very good for me to get a really close look at what's going on," he told the CBC. "I can read the reports ... but that's nothing like actually being there. And these patrols are often a great opportunity to engage the local population directly."

Police leaders, and their political overseers, could learn from his example, if only to ride along with front-line officers to experience their reality on busy city streets and endless rural roads. That's why Chief Vern White has tried to take every member of Ottawa city council on a tour of their city to view it as his constables do. If nothing else, it would be good for them to see for themselves what effect their policies and priorities have on their constables. As Vance suggests, what looks good on paper doesn't always translate well into reality. It seems a logical step as the police inevitably transform themselves from their traditional paramilitary command-and-control system that simply does not resonate with the new generation of recruit. As Eli Sopow asked Canadian policewomen in 2008, if the United States Marine Corps, revered for its combat tenacity and paying any price to accomplish an objective, can evolve to a more enlightened and inclusive structure of consultation, why can't the police?

Vance, discussing a distant war without any intention of touching on police issues, nevertheless described a host of similarities between his profession of arms and the minimal-force police response, escalating only with the immediacy of a threat to the public or themselves. But the similarities were evident when he was asked to comment on the perceived lack of progress in Afghanistan.

"It is an intensely complex environment," he told CBC Radio. "Just imagine the kind of project it would take to turn around a community at risk in Canada. All of the things that would need to happen. Imagine that same community at risk and all the social ills that could beset it at the same time … and then try to get that done quickly. These things take time. And there's a lot of things to do, lining it up so that you get the effect you want or what they need when they need it is a huge challenge. So it is slow."

At home, given the broad expectations we have for our police, they will be front and centre in any situation that threatens an at-risk or healthy community.

But good intentions are not enough. Despite the happy news that the RCMP has recruited an all-time high of 1,783 cadets in 2008–09, we still have fewer officers across Canada today than in 1975 when James Ahern first sounded the alarm that policing was in crisis in the United States. And while the recruitment news is encouraging, what of retention? Despite the tough economic times, the Mounties have begun paying recruits $12,000 when they sign up. What happens when times get better? Will those who sought job security remain in policing or follow the money back to safer careers?

As Ahern noted in 1973, cops want to be cops, and if they have to be frustrated, they want to be frustrated cops, not frustrated social workers or lawyers or whatever else society and government throws their way. But fixing the police is like tackling organized crime: it's most effective when you aim high. Strong leadership is vital to effective policing. Perhaps our top cops need to take a page from the unofficial military manual crafted by former chief of defence staff Rick Hillier and reach out to the public.

Hillier became the most visible leader in Canada, not because he was elected to his position, but because he commanded a national institution, had a national audience, tried to recruit an entire nation to his cause, and spoke out loudly, clearly and often on issues that had to be addressed. He also learned to have front-line grunts attend events with him because they are the face and spirit of the military. The same could be true for the police, whose leaders tend to surround themselves with senior ranks at public events.

Hillier learned from watching politicians publicly humiliate previous military leadership following the Somalia debacle and insisted, when offered the job as CDS, that he have the full backing of the prime minister, the entire Cabinet and the funds to make the changes that needed to be made. Hillier knew he would fail without that total commitment if he was to succeed in a bureaucratic arena dominated by process over production, where, as he notes in his memoir, everybody can say "no" and nobody can say "yes."

When he launched his Hillier Inspiration series, a leadership tour across Canada through 2010, he invited Ottawa police chief Vern White to share his stage at the debut presentation at the National Arts Centre in Ottawa, on November 16, 2009. Both plain-speaking men tackle problems directly as they arise, guided by a strong moral compass and clear sense of what is right and wrong, justice versus the law. Only White lacks a national forum, but give him a stage and he certainly doesn't mince his words.

"My belief is that we have too many senior police leaders, using that term loosely, afraid to lose their job," he told the crowd of about 200 at the NAC. "So afraid of losing their job that they have stopped doing it, allowing their fear to stop their creativity and therefore excellence in everything they do."

When Hillier and White were interviewed by Steve Madley on CFRA radio in Ottawa prior to their speaking engagement, it was evident that the two officers are kindred spirits, each respecting what the other does and has accomplished. Having praised the military, White then observed that his officers are also on the front lines at home and "go to war every day." Insisting that he has the safest job in his police department, White believes that the least he can do is risk his career for those who risk their lives daily. He wants his officers to be leaders, not followers, because that is what the public expects when they call for help at four o'clock in the morning. To accomplish that, he tries to encourage and reward those who seek alternative solutions to old problems, support them when they fail and encourage them to try again. He risks his job to influence public policy to ensure the best solutions are brought forward and he encourages creativity by offering opportunities.

As a leader, he must offer a clear vision to see the need for change, try to inject the adrenaline to conquer the fear of change and encourage the passion to create sustainable change.

"The challenge I see in policing, and in the public sector, is that many want the safe road," he said, noting that it is better to forge ahead and forge new relationships—exactly as Hillier had done in his bid to "Recruit Canada."

White accepted a five-year contract in Ottawa and warned the police board that he would not stay beyond that. It's obvious he has made a powerful and positive impact on the police, the politicians, the media, and the community. Time will tell if his legacy will survive his departure and if his changes will be sustained.

Regardless of how that plays out, the front-line officers will continue to do their jobs, no matter who's in charge. But they can't do it alone.

Arrayed in a thin bruised line to shield us from the perfect storm that threatens to engulf us, the Blue Wall is at risk of cracking under the strain. Make no mistake, if the police falter, undermined by absent leadership, intrusive oversight, injudicious courts, or simple failure to engender the public support they need, we are all at risk. The threat is real; the peril imminent. Yet all is not lost. There is hope … but the clock is ticking!

ACKNOWLEDGEMENTS

Writing any book is a lonely venture, but no author does it alone. In this instance, I was overwhelmed by those who generously agreed to share their time, their experiences, and their insights to help me "get it right" and to better understand the daily realities—good and bad—in their professions, spanning the ranks, serving and retired, from constable to chief and commissioner, in management and police associations. Civilian contacts provided fresh eyes and new experiences to the larger themes of leadership, legal issues and the inescapable impact of the media, which can be brought to bear on anyone in any field at any time.

Attempting to name them all would be to risk missing someone. You know who you are, so please take credit or embrace deniability as it best serves you. My thanks to Jane Hall, Ron Lewis, Michael Eastham, and Andy Maksymchuk for writing their memoirs that shed refreshing new light on policing by those who lived and breathed the job; humanizing a little understood profession with wit and wisdom that prompt laughter and tears. I hope more follow their leads.

I want to thank my agent, Hilary McMahon at Westwood Creative Artists, who brought me back to Key Porter Books, publisher Jordan Fenn and editor Carol Harrison, who massaged my writing into more polished prose and suffered with me through computer glitches and health issues to meet deadlines. I also want to thank cover designer Alison Carr, copy editor Liba Berry, lawyer Peter Jacobsen for his deft observations and suggestions, publicist Jennifer Fox, vice-president of marketing Tom Best, marketing manager Daniel Rondeau, and the many reps who did so much to get this book into your hands. Thank you all.

As always, I want to thank my wife Irene for her enduring support on so many levels as this book slowly came together (yes,

I shall now clean my office, dear.) and our children, John and Jodi, who still care after having flown the nest and started new lives and families.

Most important, my heartfelt appreciation goes out to the devoted men and women in the thin bruised line. We all sleep a little safer at night because of you. Thank you all.

NOTES

PROLOGUE

1. James Ahern, *Police in Trouble: Our Frightening Crisis in Law Enforcement* (New York: Hawthorn Books, 1972).

CHAPTER I: STORM WARNINGS

1. Online transcript of the testimony by former RCMP commissioner Giuliano Zaccardelli, OPP commissioner Julian Fantino and Edmonton police chief Mike Boyd, "Proceedings of the Standing Senate Committee on National Security and Defence Issue 5—Evidence—Meeting," February 25, 2008. http://www.parl.gc.ca/39/2/parlbus/commbus/ senate/Com-e/defe-e/05evb-e.htm?Language=E&Parl=39&Ses=2&co mm_id=76).
2. Ibid.
3. Ibid.

CHAPTER 2: CRISIS IN COMMAND

1. Richard A. Gabriel and Paul L. Savage, *Crisis in Command: Mismanagement in the Army* (New York: Hill and Wang, 1978) 167–8.
2. Ibid., 177–8.
3. Anthony Reinhart, "Bring RCMP into Caledonia, Poll says," *Globe and Mail*, October 20, 2006. See also uncredited, "Caledonia Violence Feared at Non-aboriginal March," *Globe and Mail*, October 14, 2006, as well as anonymous online post to the website for CD 98.9 FM, http:// cd989.com/modules/news/article.php?storyid=6531.
4. Eli Sopow, "The RCMP as an Emotional Organization," *British Columbia Organizational Development Network* newsletter, June 2007, www.bcodn.org. See also Sopow's "Communications Climate Change at the RCMP" at http://www.allbusiness.com/ crime-law-enforcement-corrections/law-police-forces/8889230-1. html as well as his PowerPoint presentation at http://74.125.95.132/ search?q=cache:I2QDd9jTfrgJ:www.cprsvancouver.com/professional_ development/ppt/strategic_connectivity.ppt+Sopow+AND+RCMP+as+ an+emotional+organization&cd=1&hl=en&ct=clnk&gl=ca .
5. Ibid.

6. Jane Hall, "Changing the Face of Leadership from Within: Gender Differences in Leadership Styles," presented to the International Consortium for Public Safety Leadership, in Tallahassee, Florida, July 15, 2008.

CHAPTER 3: WOMEN

1. "Ottawa Police Say They Face Workplace Harassment, Bias," www.cbc. ca, April 24, 2007.
2. Native Women's Association of Canada workshop, "Policing and Aboriginal Women," at the twenty-second annual NWAC general assembly held in Winnipeg, 1996. http://www.nwac-hq.org/documents/ PolicingAboriginalWomen.pdf.
3. Ibid.

CHAPTER 4: INTRUDER ALERT

1. Hon. Sidney B. Linden, "Commissioner's Statement Public Release of Report", May 31, 2007, http://crpr.icaap.org/index.php/crpr/article/ view/30/27.
2. ———, The Ipperwash Inquiry, inquiry testimony at http://www. attorneygeneral.jus.gov.on.ca/inquiries/ipperwash/report/index.html.
3. Margaret Beare and Tonita Murray, "The Ipperwash Inquiry: Research on Police Governance, Independence and Accountability," *The Canadian Review of Policing Research*, 1 (2005), http://crpr.icaap.org/ index.php/crpr/article/view/30/27.
4. Linden, "Commissioner's Statement Public Release of Report."
5. Shannon Kari, "Ontario Ombudsman in Conflict, Critics Say," *Vancouver Sun*, June 11, 2007.
6. Vern White address to the Salvation Army in Ottawa provided to author.
7. Gary Dimmock, "Mounties Admit: 'We're Outgunned'," *Ottawa Citizen*, July 28, 2006.
8. Ibid.
9. "Montreal May Ban Insults to Police," CBC News, http://www.cbc.ca/ canada/montreal/story/2009/01/26/mtl-policeinsults0126.html.
10. Melissa Dominelli, "Survey Reveals Many Police Officers Unhappy at Work," http://edmonton.ctv.ca/servlet/an/local/CTVNews/20090106/ edm_morale_090106/20090106?hub=EdmontonHome.
11. Ibid.
12. Robert Head, "The Politicization of the RCMP," http://www. garrybreitkreuz.com/publications/2007_new/155.pdf.
13. Ibid.
14. Ibid.

CHAPTER 5: COURTING DISASTER

1. Hon. Justice Michael Moldaver, "The State of the Criminal Justice System in 2006: An Appellate Judge's Perspective", Court of Appeal website, http://www.ontariocourts.on.ca/coa/en/ps/speeches/state.htm.

CHAPTER 6: TAKING CARE OF BUSINESS

1. Doug Clark and Peter Appleton, *Billion Dollar High: The Drug Invasion of Canada*. (Toronto: McGraw-Hill Ryerson, 1990).
2. Motorola, Inc. press release, September 30, 1997. Motorola and the IACP are joint sponsors of the award.
3. Chad Skelton, "Out of Control: Criminal Justice System 'on the Brink of Imploding'," *Vancouver Sun*, March 11, 2005, http://www.canadianjusticereviewboard.ca/article-justice%20system%20imploding.htm.
4. Ibid.
5. Ibid.
6. "I'm Not Going to Die Here Tonight,' Survivor of Fatal RCMP Shooting Recalls Thinking," CBC News, http://www.cbc.ca/canada/saskatchewan/story/2009/02/27/dagenais-knopp.html.
7. Judy Monchuk, "How Safe Are Police Officers in Rural Canada?," *Regina Leader-Post*, July 18, 2006.
8. Ian Bailey, "Are the Police Spread Too Thin?," *Globe and Mail*, March 14, 2009.
9. Ibid.

CHAPTER 7: LIES, DAMN LIES, AND STATISTICS

1. Heather Polischuk, "Less Crime or Fewer Crimes Reported?," *Regina Leader-Post,* September 12, 2008.
2. Department of Canadian Heritage, "Redesigning Federal Programs for the Periodical Industry," http://www.pch.gc.ca/pc-ch/conslttn/fcm-cmf/106-eng.cfm#a2.
3. Scot Wortley and Julian Tanner, "Data, Denials, and Confusion: The Racial Profiling Debate in Toronto," *Canadian Journal of Criminology and Criminal Justice* 45, no. 3 (2003).
4. Alan D. Gold, "Racial Profiling and Good Science," *Canadian Journal of Criminology and Criminal Justice* 45 no.3 (2003).

CHAPTER 8: RECRUITMENT

1. Ottawa Police Service, "A Process Review of the Outreach Recruitment Process with the Outreach Recruiting Team," November 2007.
2. Andrew Seymour, "Quota of White Male Recruits 'Never Intended,' Officer Says," *Ottawa Citizen*, November 14, 2007.

3. ———, "Police Diversity Plan Under Attack," *Ottawa Citizen*, December 21, 2007.
4. ———"Quota of White Male Recruits 'Never Intended,' Officer Says."
5. Syd Gravel, "Diversity Recruiting Is about Getting Candidates on Equal Footing," *Canadian HR Reporter*, October 10, 2005.
6. Common approximation from multiple sources. See also, Jane Hall, "Changing the Face of Leadership from Within: Gender Differences in Leadership Styles," presented to the International Consortium for Public Safety Leadership, Tallahassee, Florida, July 15, 2008.
7. Canadian Association of Chiefs of Police Annual Report 2004, http://www.cbupub.com/cacp/cacp2004/cacp2004.pdf.
8. Transcript of the speech delivered by General Rick Hillier, Chief of the Defence Staff, at the Conference of Defence Association Annual General Meeting, in Ottawa, February 24, 2006.
9. Gord Schumacher, "Qualities of Police Leadership: A Snapshot on Leading Generation X," *Canadian Police Chief Magazine*, Winter (2003), 25–26.

CHAPTER 9: BREACH IN SOCIAL CONTRACT

1. Ron MacKay, interview with author.
2. Ibid.
3. Ibid.
4. Maureen McTeer, Canadian Police College workshop "Women in Policing in Canada: The Year 2000 and Beyond—Its Challenges," 1997.

EPILOGUE

1. David B. Harris, "They Should Have Been Stopped," *Ottawa Citizen*, April 15, 2009.
2. Melissa Leong, "Gardiner Occupation 'Unlawful' and 'Dangerous,' Says Police Chief," *National Post*, May 10, 2009.
3. "National Crime Rate Drops for Third Year in a Row: Report," *Ottawa Citizen*, July 18, 2008.
4. Robert Marshall, "Stripping Police of Their Rights," *Winnipeg Free Press*, November 17, 2008.
5. Brigadier-General Jonathan Vance with Anna Maria Tremonti, *The Current*, CBC Radio, October 13, 2009.

INDEX